COMPOUNDS AND COMPOUNDING

Are compounds words or phrases – or are they neither, or both? How should we classify compounds? How can we deal with the fact that the relationship between the elements of *sugar pill* ('pill made of sugar') is different from that in *sea-sickness pill* ('pill to prevent sea-sickness')? Are compounds a linguistic universal? How much do languages vary in the way their compounds work? Why do we need compounds, when there are other ways of creating the same meanings? Are so-called neoclassical compounds like *photograph* really compounds? Based on more than forty years' research, this controversial new book sets out to answer these and many other questions.

LAURIE BAUER is Emeritus Professor at the School of Linguistics and Applied Language Studies at the University of Wellington, Victoria. He has published many works on morphology including *English Word-formation* (Cambridge, 1983), *Introducing Linguistic Morphology* (2003) and *Morphological Productivity* (Cambridge, 2001).

T0384584

CAMBRIDGE STUDIES IN LINGUISTICS

General Editors: P. AUSTIN, B. COMRIE,
S. CRAIN, W. DRESSLER, C. J. EWEN, R. LASS,
D. LIGHTFOOT, K. RICE, I. ROBERTS, S. ROMAINE,
N. V. SMITH

Compounds and Compounding

In this series

COMPOUNDS AND COMPOUNDING

LAURIE BAUER

Victoria University of Wellington

CAMBRIDGE
UNIVERSITY PRESS

CAMBRIDGE
UNIVERSITY PRESS

University Printing House, Cambridge CB2 8BS, United Kingdom

One Liberty Plaza, 20th Floor, New York, NY 10006, USA

477 Williamstown Road, Port Melbourne, VIC 3207, Australia

4843/24, 2nd Floor, Ansari Road, Daryaganj, Delhi – 110002, India

79 Anson Road, #06–04/06, Singapore 079906

Cambridge University Press is part of the University of Cambridge.

It furthers the University's mission by disseminating knowledge in the pursuit of education, learning, and research at the highest international levels of excellence.

www.cambridge.org
Information on this title: www.cambridge.org/9781108416030
DOI: 10.1017/9781108235679

First published 2017

Printed in the United Kingdom by Clays, St Ives plc

A catalogue record for this publication is available from the British Library.

Library of Congress Cataloging-in-Publication Data
Names: Bauer, Laurie, 1949- author.
Title: Compounds and compounding / Laurie Bauer.
Description: Cambridge ; New York, NY : Cambridge University Press, [2017] |
Series: Cambridge Studies in Linguistics | Includes bibliographical references and indexes.
Identifiers: LCCN 2017016349 | ISBN 9781108416030 (Hardback : alk. paper) |
ISBN 9781108402552 (pbk. : alk. paper)
Subjects: LCSH: English language–Compound words. | English language–Word formation. |
English language–Morphology. | Construction grammar. | Cognitive grammar. |
Linguistic universals.
Classification: LCC PE1175 .B28 2017 | DDC 425/.92–dc23
LC record available at https://lccn.loc.gov/2017016349

ISBN 978-1-108-41603-0 Hardback
ISBN 978-1-108-40255-2 Paperback

Contents

Figures

Tables

Preface and Acknowledgements

There are three direct motivations for this work. The first is that early in 2015 I was asked to write a chapter on compounds in English (Bauer *in press*). In writing that chapter it quickly became clear to me that I had much more to say than would fit into a chapter, and that many of the issues that deserved consideration in the study of compounds were worthy of a least a chapter each. Several of them have had books written about them. The second motivation is from a comment I made at the Universals and Typology in Word-Formation II conference held at Šafárik University, Košice, Slovakia, in August 2012. The organisers asked me to provide a summary of that conference at its end, pulling out common threads. One of the things I noted, in an attempt to be provocative, was that we had seen a number of papers where the classification of compounds had been raised as an issue. I suggested that if we had not got a classification of compounds after 4,000 years of work, we might be asking the wrong questions. I may still be asking the wrong questions, but I have tried to change the ground a little here. The third motivation is that I realised in the course of this project that I first started to take the study of compounds seriously at the beginning of 1973, when I narrowed the topic of my PhD down to compounding. So I have been working on and with compounds for more than forty years, and developing my own view of compounds gradually over that period. Some of my ideas remain unchanged from my thesis (completed in 1975 but published as Bauer 1978), many others have changed radically since then, under the influence of my own and other people's research on compounds specifically and my own evolving ideas about language and linguistics. Those ideas have evolved as the linguistic landscape has evolved. When I started my thesis, Chomsky's Extended Standard Theory was a recent innovation and cognitive grammar had not been developed at all. These days, though I would hesitate to call myself a cognitive linguist, I have been strongly influenced by many of the ideas of cognitive grammar and, within that overall framework, by construction grammar and exemplar theory. These trends in linguistic thought have changed my ideas about compounds considerably, and this book is an attempt to formulate my own personal view of what is going on in compounding in the light of such influences. This means that even where I reprise matters that I have covered in earlier publications, my conclusions are not necessarily the same and are not necessarily viewed in the same context. At the same time, I have to recognise that because my viewpoint is unashamedly personal, it is only one viewpoint among many, and that my ideas and conclusions are necessarily controversial. While I try to build my conclusions into a coherent view of what is going on in this area of language, readers may accept some of my conclusions but reject others, and I cannot necessarily assume that everything I conclude will be accepted with equal alacrity by my readers. This accounts for my sometimes appearing to leave my options open.

I should like to thank Winifred Bauer, Natalia Beliaeva, Andrew Chesterman and Liza Tarasova for providing examples, and Natalia Beliaeva, Pavol Štekauer, Liza Tarasova and Peter Whiteford for comments on an earlier version of the typescript. I should like to thank Paul Warren for the data referred to in Section 3.2.3, and my ELT colleagues at Victoria University for responding to the questionnaire discussed in the Appendix. Finally, I should like to thank the team at Cambridge University Press, including the anonymous readers who commented most helpfully on the first draft. Versions of parts of Section 2.7.6 and the Appendix have previously been the subject of presentations at conferences of the New Zealand Linguistics Society. While thanking all these people, I must point out that they do not necessarily agree with me, and they are not responsible for the way in which I have interpreted their comments.

Abbreviations and Notational Conventions

A	adjective
ABE	abessive
ABL	ablative
ABSL	absolutive
ADJLZ	adjectivaliser
ADV	adverb
AORII	aorist of class II
CONT	continuous
DEF	definite
DERIV	derivational marker
DO	direct object
GEN	genitive
ILL	illative
INE	inessive
INF	infinitive
INST	instrumental
LE	linking element
M	masculine
N	noun
NEUT	neuter
NMLZ	nominalization
NON-NEUT	non-neuter
NP	noun phrase
NUM	number
P	preposition
PASS	passive
PAST	past tense
PERS	person-marker
PL	plural
PP	prepositional phrase
PRES	present tense
Q	quantifier

SG	singular
SUBJV	subjunctive
V	verb
3	third person
♦	is morphologically related to
•	break between morphs not indicated in the orthography/ transcription
*	unacceptable
?	of questionable acceptability
italics	cited examples; words; word-forms, morphs; titles
SMALL CAPITALS	lexemes; glosses of grammatical items
/ /	enclosing phonological representations
< >	enclosing orthographic representations
[ ]	enclosing constituents; enclosing editorial comment or addition
' '	enclosing meanings or glosses; enclosing terms; enclosing dialogue; enclosing quotations
" "	enclosing quotations within quotations; as "scare quotes"

1 *Introduction*

Most linguists would agree that the following items are compounds: *football, grey-green, people mover, research professor, stir-fry.* Although these items differ in a number of ways (whether they are written as one or two ortho-graphic words, whether they function as nouns, verbs or adjectives, how the relations between their elements need to be specified), they share the fact that they are made up of two elements each of which is used elsewhere in the language as a word in its own right. The precise borderline of what counts as a compound may be fuzzy, as we shall see, but central to the notion is that it is possible to make lexical entities out of words, which are themselves lexical entities. The process by which these compounds are formed is termed 'com-pounding' (sometimes 'composition').

Compounding is often thought of as the simplest kind of word-formation: it does not require special obligatorily bound items, but uses elements which are already part of the language. In many languages the (morpho)phonology of compounding is simpler than the (morpho)phonology of derivation. Com-pounding does not necessarily involve shortening or subtraction, it does not necessarily involve specialised markers of compound status, it does not involve discontinuous morphology or any of the problems that cast doubt on the notion of a morpheme. In languages that have frequent compounds, compounding is often acquired earlier than other kinds of word-formation (Berman 2009). Only the semantics of compounding remains difficult to deal with, since the superficial formal simplicity of compounds appears to mask a great deal of semantic complexity.

Against this background, it might appear that compounds would be the best understood of all methods of word-formation, the most fully described, pos-sibly even the one about which there is most agreement. Nothing could be further from the truth. Compounding remains a controversial area of linguistic description, both in terms of cross-linguistic typology and in terms of the description of a language like English. There is no overall agreement on such basic issues as the definition of a compound. Accordingly, there can be no agreement on whether compounding is a linguistic universal or not. Even the question of whether compounding is a morphological process or a syntactic one is not settled, though I have implied above that it is morphological by using the terms 'word' and 'word-formation'. There is huge disagreement about the classification of compounds, though often this arises from lack of proper consideration of the subject rather than from deeply held convictions. And there is certainly disagreement on where the boundaries of compounding are to be found and about the terminology of compounding.

This work will not solve these problems, but its aim is to clarify the issues, and to suggest solutions to at least some of the problems that face workers in this area of linguistics.

So the aim of this book is to explore the area of compounding, in English, but also in other languages, in order to determine whether a coherent position on compounding which answers some of the main problems that compounds provide can be found. Having said that, my own expertise is in Romance and in Germanic (the first by training, the latter by exposure), and my experience of the other languages I shall cite is very much second-hand. I recognise this as a problem: I am inevitably biased by my own experience. My hope is that while there are clearly languages which have "compounds" which are rather different from those we are used to in, say, English, or more generally in Standard Average European, it is nevertheless the case that compounds cross-linguistically share a great deal, so that this book has a common core which it can address.

I am also aware that there is very little, if anything, that is uncontroversial in the study of compounding. It follows that the proposals I shall make here will be controversial. Hence my statement just above that my aim is not to solve the problems; rather I hope to encourage discussion and provoke alternative analyses which can explain more than the solutions I propose here.

At various points in this book it will be clear that I have been influenced by Construction Grammar (e.g. Booij 2010). I have also been influenced by cognitively based approaches to grammar, largely as introduced to me by my students (Tarasova 2013, Beliaeva 2014; see also Ryder 1994). These influences have changed my perspective from that which will have been obvious in my earlier works. At the same time, I believe that the points I am making here are valid whether we wish to approach compounding from one of these points of view, or whether we wish to use a more formalist approach to the study of grammar. The theoretical framework of the analyst will certainly influence the relative importance given to the various points raised in this book, but the questions raised here have to be answered by anyone who wishes to understand or work with compounding as a linguistic phenomenon.

2 Compounds and Words

2.1 Introduction

Perhaps the basic assumption underlying compounds is that they are words – they even are called 'compound words' on some occasions and are often defined as being words whose elements are words. There are two major problems with this insight. The first is that sequences of words are usually syntactic structures, not morphological ones, so we need to justify this conclusion, not merely accept it as an assumption. The second is that we have no generally accepted definition of a word. Not only is there no definition of word, we have a number of distinct elements which are viewed as being words of different kinds, and definitions of words of any of these kinds prove to be difficult or controversial.

In this chapter the notion of word will be considered, and criteria which might seem to distinguish single words (which may be morphological structures) from sequences of words (which are syntactic structures) will be analysed. It should be borne in mind that the canonical word, at least in English, is morphologically simple: *car*, for instance. In other languages the canonical word may involve inflectional morphology as of necessity: it is impossible to cite the Latin word *carrus* 'cart' without providing a case, gender, number marker for it. While inflection will prove important in some respects later, we are not primarily concerned with inflection here except as a guide to something else. And what we are primarily concerned with is words which, if we ignore inflectional marking, are not morphologically simple but are constructions.

2.2 Words, Words, Words

The distinction between a lexeme such as ARRIVE and a word-form such as *arrived* is well-established in the literature, as is the Lyonsian (Lyons 1968) notation employed here. The only point to underscore is that *arrive* is also one of the word-forms which can realised the lexeme ARRIVE: the full set being, on most accounts, *arrive, arrives, arrived, arriving*. Where the distinction between lexeme and word-form is not crucial, the typographical distinction will not be maintained, and italics will be used.

The notion of word-form is partly (perhaps largely) derived from the notion of inflection. The word-form represents not only the relevant lexeme but also all the relevant inflectional categories. For Lyons this implies that items that do not mark inflectional categories cannot be lexemes. Following Bauer et al. (2013: 8) this view is not accepted here: there can be a lexeme FROM or a lexeme LIKEWISE, but these lexemes are only ever represented by a single word-form.

Another way of viewing the word-form is that it is the realisation or representation of the morphosyntactic word (for the terminology see Bauer et al. 2013: 10), that is, including all relevant inflectional material. On this basis, the word-forms *arrive* and *arrived* in the list given just above are each interpretable as more than one morphosyntactic word: *arrive* could be the infinitive, the imperative or a non-3SG present tense; *arrived* could be a past tense or a past participle. Again, the morphosyntactic word will not be the primary focus in what follows. What is important here is that the word-form may not always be a simple concept.

When we are dealing with compounds, the general assumption is that we are dealing with items which are words in the sense that they are lexemes (see Bauer 2004a, sv *compound*). This does not imply that the citation form of the constituent "words" must be included in the form of the compound. While an English compound like *carpark* contains two elements each of which could be used as the citation form of a lexeme, the Latin form *agri·col·a* 'field·cultivate·er = farmer' does not contain the citation form of *ager* 'field' or *colere* 'to cultivate' (Oniga 2014: 167). It is for this reason that compounds are sometimes said to be made up of elements which are stems or roots: not because the implications are fundamentally different, but because stems and roots are required minima for lexemes, and some representation of a lexeme is required in each element of a compound. It would be true to say that *carpark* contains two roots or two stems as well as to say that it contains two lexemes. In some languages, calling the realisation of the lexeme in a compound a root or a stem may be more precise than saying that it is a lexeme: a stem is a distinct form of a lexeme to which affixes are added, the root is the smallest part of the word that realizes the lexeme. In English, the distinction rarely matters.

2.3   Orthographic Words

There is a general assumption that orthography reflects native-speaker intuition about wordhood, and that orthographic unity is a sign of being a word.

Correspondingly, lack of orthographic unity is taken to indicate that a construction is syntactic. There is plenty of evidence to support such a viewpoint, but also evidence against it. In any case, the evidence from unity and the evidence from lack of unity are not equivalent.

A word like *altogether* began life as a phrasal expression *all together* (*OED*); the two may now be distinguished from each other. The phrase *in so far as* is thus spelt in the *OED*, though it is now frequently found as <insofar as>. The prepositions *into, onto* also started out as two orthographic words (*OED*). In all such cases it seems that frequent co-occurrence leads to univerbation. It is tempting to include things like *before-tax* (as in *before-tax profits*) in the same category, but the hyphen here may simply indicate that *before-tax* is to be read as a constituent acting as an attributive (in which use the hyphen is standardly employed: see Bauer et al. 2013: 56), rather than as an indication of wordhood. Be that as it may, there is evidence of a diachronic shift from multiple orthographic words to single orthographic word. Similar cases of vacillation in usage between one and two orthographic words can be found in Danish (Bauer 2000: 253, Dansk Sprognævn 2015), under similar circumstances.

The orthographic question can also affect items which contain obligatorily bound morphs. There is some evidence that prefixes are sometimes viewed as independent orthographic words. COCA (Davies 2008) provides examples such as those in (1).

(1)   hyper activity, hyper efficient, maxi systems, mega success, micro engines, neo Nazi, pre diabetes, pre pregnancy BMI, super glue, super loud

What we may be seeing here is change in the system: *insofar* is in the process of becoming a word in English, as is *hyper*, although one shows a tendency towards larger words, the other a tendency towards smaller words. Such periods of instability in change can be long-lasting, though, so that the system as a whole is never stable and never quite allows a match between orthographic criteria and other criteria for wordhood.

We might also interpret the use of hyphens with some very productive suffixes as evidence of a similar feature. COCA provides examples such as those in (2).

(2)   an almost **Christmas-y** lumination and loveliness
        The very **design-y** backgrounds
        The honey brings out the **perfume-y** herbs in the mix
        vintage-y leopard-print
        'What time is it?' # '**Dawn-ish**.' # 'Dawn-ish?' # 'Not quite dawn, no longer night.'

Ridley Scott's **noir-ish** *Blade Runner*
the **Warhol-ish** gig Jon Voight walked into in *Midnight Cowboy*.

In the case of *-ish*, the suffix can also be used in isolation: the example in (3) is again from COCA.

(3)   It's 68, 68-ish. GIFFORD: Yeah. **Ish**. It – you know what, it's warmed up.

It is difficult to know how to interpret such examples, but one possibility is that orthographic wordhood is not quite as much a yes-no question as we tend to suppose: there are degrees of wordhood, and some prefixes, for example, are very near the boundary of being independent words.

Given that prefixes and suffixes may not be securely non-words, it is very difficult to know how to interpret the orthography of compounds. It is well-known that the orthography of N + N sequences is variable in English: we can write *coffeepot, coffee-pot* or *coffee pot, wordformation, word-formation* or *word formation*. Nevertheless, the orthography is not infinitely flexible: <universityadministration> or <rail way> would both be odd. But hyphenation, in particular, seems to be so subject to fashion, house-style and individual preference (not to mention such factors as line-ends and typographical exigencies) that it is hard to draw firm conclusions from it. That is not to say that hyphenation is entirely free, either. Where a hyphen connects two elements in a three-element constituent, it is virtually invariably the case that the hyphenated items are a constituent in the longer constituent. These comments are, of course, restricted to English. Hyphenation in other languages may behave differently. But wherever it is used, it has to be asked whether its function is joining two elements (cf. the German name of the hyphen, *Bin-de·strich* 'binding dash') or keeping them separate, as it might be argued to do in <co-ordination>).

If we look away from hyphenation, this dual nature of the representation is not relevant. But the fact we regularly write <schoolboy> but never write *<universitystudent>, or that <textbook> is found but not *<librarybook>, tells us that some of the spelling conventions derive from word length (possibly associated with etymology or morphology) rather than with grammatical or semantic factors. That is, writing some construction as two words may not indicate that it is – in any but an orthographic sense – two words, though writing things together does seem to imply that they are seen in some sense as a single word.

Precisely what that sense is may require some consideration. It is, or was until recently, normal practice when reading a web address such as www.airnewzealand.co.nz out loud to say 'Air New Zealand, all one word'. The "one word" in such cases is purely orthographic and has no other implications. To the extent that this is true, it may suggest that orthography is the prime determinant of what is considered to be a word in English – something which brings an unhealthy circularity into the question of definitions, since the normal expectation among linguists would be that orthography should reflect linguistic intuitions, orthography always being dependent upon speech.

In short, the relationship between orthography and word-status is rather more fraught than is generally recognised. Clearly, if we look across a language like English as a whole, there is a tendency for orthographic unity to coincide with wordhood as defined by other means; but there are sufficient mis-matches for it to be difficult to take orthography as criterial in defining a word in any other sense. If we look beyond Standard Average European, the mismatches, while different, become even more threatening to the idea of an equivalence between the orthographic word and the word in other senses.

2.4   Phonological Words

The whole reason that we have a notion of phonological word is that phonological words do not necessarily match other kinds of words. There is an added problem here, namely that there does not seem to be agreement on what constitutes a phonological word. In this section we will consider some potential segmental criteria and some potential prosodic criteria whose function, in general terms, is to delimit the word rather than to define a particular phonological sequence as being a word.

2.4.1   Segmental Criteria

We can divide segmental criteria for wordhood into two major kinds: those that show where a word begins or ends, and those that show whether a break between significant elements is or is not a word-break (the alternative being that it is a break between morphemes or formatives which are word-internal). Suomi (1985) calls these positive and negative word boundary signals, respectively.

As an example of segmental boundary marking, consider terminal devoicing (*Auslautverhärtung*) in German. No monosyllabic stem acting as a word-form in German can end in a voiced obstruent: *Rad* 'bicycle' is homophonous with *Rat* 'council', even though the genitive forms, *Rades* /ʁɑːdəs/ and *Rates* /ʁɑːtəs/ respectively, are not homophonous. However, the devoicing also

affects obstruents with following voiceless obstruents within the word-form
(e.g. *gib·st* 'you$_{SG}$ give' is /gɪpst/) or with a following morpheme boundary
within the word-form (*lieb·lich* 'adorable, lovely' is /liːplɪç/) (Hall 1992:
28–29). Wiese (1996: 200–205) shows that this is better described as a
syllable-structure constraint rather than a matter of morphological structure
at all, but finds some instances which are awkward for that analysis. So,
whatever this process is marking, it is not – or is not only – the word. The
roughly comparable phenomenon in Russian (Cubberley 2002: 73–77), while
it differs in details from the German, also fails to mark the word uniquely.

As an example of a segmental phenomenon showing that two elements
belong together, consider Japanese rendaku. Rendaku is the voicing of an
initial voiceless obstruent when that obstruent is the second element of a
compound. Some examples are given in (4) from Itô and Mester (2005:
40–41).

(4)   *Japanese rendaku*

1st element	gloss	2nd element	gloss	Compound	gloss
iro	'colour'	kami	'paper'	irogami	'coloured paper'
asa	'morning'	kiri	'mist'	asagiri	'morning mist'
maki	'rolled'	sushi	'sushi'	makizushi	'rolled sushi'
hana	'nose'	chi	'blood'	hanaji	'nosebleed'
ike	'arrange'	hana	'flower'	ikebana	'ikebana'

Note that although the voicing rule is mostly regular, the voiced equivalent
of /h/ is /b/, as in *ikebana*. Rendaku does not apply (a) if there is a voiced
obstruent in the second element (*kami* 'divine' + *kaze* 'wind' > *kamikaze*
'kamikaze' because of the /z/), or (b) if the compound is a coordinative
compound (*me* 'eye' + *hana* 'nose' > *mehana* 'eyes and nose' – see Section
4.6 for more detail on coordinative compounds), or (c) when non-native
elements are involved (Itô & Mester 2005: 42–43). Despite these generalisa-
tions, and the productivity of rendaku, many authorities see the process as in
principle unpredictable.

Here we see that, even if we look away from the cases which are totally
unpredictable, rendaku marks only a subset of compounds, because only a
subset have phonologically appropriate form to allow the marking.

Many languages have a feature of vowel harmony. Vowel harmony is the
agreement of vowels for some phonetic/phonological feature within (typically)
the word. Thus vowels within the word may agree as to frontness/backness, as
to tenseness, as to roundedness and so on. Although there are languages in
which compound words show such agreement (Chukchee is one such;

see Bogoras 1922: 892–894), in most (including Finnish, Turkish and Turkana) the elements of a compound but not the compound as a whole are the domain of vowel harmony.

2.4.2 Suprasegmental Criteria

In many languages, stress is cited as a feature which defines the word. This is perhaps particularly so in those languages in which stress plays a demarcative function, and stress falls regularly on the first (Czech, Finnish), last (Hebrew, Turkish) or penultimate (Polish, Swahili) syllable of the word. Even in such languages, the phonological word defined by stress tends to differ from the word in other senses because unstressed function words and clitics have to be included within the stress-defined unit, but not within the word viewed as related to the lexeme.

In some tone languages, compounds may be marked tonally, either by patterns of tone sandhi or by other means. For example, Chao (1968, cited in Dixon & Aikhenvald 2002: 11) notes that in Wu dialects of Chinese, tone sandhi within a compound is different from tone sandhi between non-compounded words. In Bambara N-N compounds only the first syllable may be either high or low, all subsequent syllables being high tone, independent of the tone of the element in isolation (Creissels 2004), which is also the pattern shown in non-complex words.

2.4.3 Discussion

What all these determinants of phonological words have in common is that they fail to match any lexico-grammatical sense in which a compound might be "a word". In some cases it is difficult to see how they could: if terminal devoicing systematically marked the ending of every word, every word would have to end in a voiced obstruent. Under such a scenario, many final obstruents would appear devoiced so often that it would not be obvious that they had any voiced correlate (consider the history of the German directional adverb *weg* 'away' which is only ever pronounced with a final /k/, although it has an orthographic – and etymological – link to the noun *Weg* 'way' in which alternation between /g/ and /k/ can be heard).

It may be that there are cases where the phonological word and the word in other senses match much better. If that is the case, however, there is no need for both constructs. Discussion of a phonological word separate from a word implies a mismatch or a non-exhaustive analysis.

The discussion in this section has been oversimplified in that it has assumed that one phonetic or phonological factor might act as a defining criterion for the word. It is much more likely that some cluster of phonetic or phonological criteria would have this effect. In a language like English, such factors might include degree of aspiration, stress, vowel and consonant length, various phonotactic constraints (e.g. that /zf/ cannot occur within a monomorphemic word or that /ŋ/ cannot appear at the beginning of a word). It is not clear that such factors as a set can actually define the set of words in a way that matches other notions of word any better than the individual factors can. Suomi (1985) argues that even with vowel harmony and first-syllable stress, various phonological criteria do not uniquely identify non-phonological words in Finnish.

2.5   Listedness and Wordhood

Scrabble players will be very familiar with the challenge that something is not a "real" word, but something that has just been made up. "Real" words, in common parlance, are listed in dictionaries. Words like *patriation* (which is not listed in the *OED* with this meaning) in (5) are correspondingly not "real" words.

(5)   '"Selective patriation"? What in God's name does that mean?' the prime
        minister looked from one to the other until his gaze settled on Derek Farmer.
        'Is it even a word?'
        'If it wasn't before, it is now, Geoff,' said Farmer. (McNab, Andy. 2015.
        State of emergency. London: Bantam, p. 68)

To phrase this differently, there is an expectation that words should be listed, while there is no expectation that phrases or clauses should be listed. The concept of listedness is not a simple one: listedness for the individual speaker may not be the same as listedness for the community; it is not clear to what extent listedness is a psychological matter (in which case *comes* may well be listed as a function of its high frequency) and to what extent it is a derived from unpredictability (in which case *cat* is listed, because its form cannot be predicted from its meaning, but *comes* is not listed, because its form can be predicted from the form of *come* and the meaning).

Di Sciullo and Williams (1987) spend some time in showing that there is no necessary link between wordhood and listedness. Not only are there words which are not listed (as illustrated by (5)), there are non-words which are listed. On the one hand, morphemes are presumably listed, especially if they can be used productively, since the meaning of *-ise* is as unpredictable as the meaning of *cat*. But there are also items which are larger than words which are listed. These include the types listed in (6).

(6)   a. *Idioms*: kick the bucket, shoot the breeze, sour grapes, take the biscuit
        b. *Phrasal verbs*: fall in (as a soldier), put down (a dog), screw up (a
           driving test)
        c. *Proverbs*: many hands make light work, too many cooks spoil the broth
        d. *Quotations*: to be or not to be, that is the question, What therefore God
           hath joined together, let not man put asunder, Ignorance, Madam, pure
           ignorance
        e. *Other syntactic objects*: How do you do?, Point of order!, Way to go!,
           I have partaken of an elegant sufficiency of the delicacies of the table.

Because these chunks do not inflect as units, they cannot be lexemes, so that, *pace* Lyons (1977: 23), the term 'phrasal lexeme' is misleading. They are made up of lexemes, inflected as necessary, but are syntactic units whose meaning or use is not entirely derivable from the meanings of the individual items within them.

Di Sciullo and Williams (1987) term such items 'listemes'. Because the relationship between *list* and *listeme* is not parallel to that between *phone* and *phoneme* or *morph* and *morpheme*, I prefer the term 'lexical item' (Carstairs-McCarthy 2002: 15). 'Lexical unit' is also found (Cruse 1986).

There is another way in which listedness is sometimes taken to define compounds. Brugmann (1900: 359ff, cited in Jespersen 1942: 134) claims that for something to be a compound it must have a different meaning from the meaning of the elements when they are freely combined. Brugmann terms this 'isolation', though the term has since been used to cover rather more than just semantic specialisation.

It is difficult to know just how this should be applied. Given *toy shop* (stressed on *toy*, 'a shop in which toys are sold') and *toy shop* (stressed on *shop*, 'a shop which is itself a toy') or *headstone* 'a keystone; a tombstone', is one of the relevant meanings isolated and the other not, and if so, how do we tell which is which? (Incidentally, Jespersen 1942: 136 says the two meanings of *headstone* have different stress, but this is not supported by the *OED* or by Wells 2008; there may have been a change here.) Do *iron bar* and *gold medal* illustrate 'free combination' or compounds, and how can we tell? To put this in another context, it can be difficult to know just when we have a compositional meaning for a particular construction and when we do not. Is the meaning of *gold medal* simply the result of combining the meanings of *gold* and *medal* in an appropriate construction, or is the fact that *gold medal* has implications of 'overall winner', which does not seem to be implicit in either *gold* or in *medal*, mean that this is a case of isolation? There is a huge literature on compositionality, but most of it shies away from such questions, and Wisniewski and Wu

(2012) show how complex it can be to view such constructions as compositional. Even the use of 'constructed meaning' (*sens construit*) (Corbin 1991) to distinguish the meaning provided by the morphology from the lexical meaning of the word in usage does not seem particularly helpful. If the constructed meaning of *headstone* is 'stone related in some way to a notion of head', all that does is suggest that no compound is compositional in its meaning, even a nonce formation. This removes compounds from all discussion of compositionality, but still leaves problems of differences in transparency (if that is not the same thing).

It seems likely that there are degrees of isolation in this sense. Consider, for example, the following collocations with *iron*: *iron age, iron deficiency, iron gum* (AusE), *iron hair, iron maiden, iron road* (or the German equivalent *Eisenbahn*, since the English is no longer current usage), *iron roof, iron shot.* The *iron age* is the period during which working with iron was first introduced, rather than something parallel to the golden age (though see *OED* for this sense). *Iron deficiency* is specifically dietary or agricultural, rather than the lack of ore for making steel, for instance. An *iron gum* is a gum tree that has wood considered to be as hard as iron, while *iron hair* is grey in colour, rather than hard. The *iron maiden* was not a maiden in any literal sense (and the figurative sense is not easy to discern) but was presumably made of iron. The *iron way*, on the other hand, is made of steel not iron (as is the related *iron horse*). An *iron roof* is made specifically of corrugated iron, not just any iron. An *iron shot* is a shot made with a golfing iron, which today is not made of iron. It may be the case that none of these is entirely compositional, but some require rather more explanation than others, even with respect to a literal sense of *iron*. Various attempts have been made to explain why this should be. For instance, Libben (2010) argues in such cases that there is a compound element *iron* which may be distinct from, and semantically less specific than, the free lexeme *iron* (and see further the general discussion in Körtvélyessy et al. 2015). The observation of varying degrees of transparency is, however, not in question.

It is tempting to put isolation down to frequency (the number of times the particular construction is experienced by a speaker): the longer a collocation exists, the more specific connotations (or, indeed, denotations) can become attached to it. But this is not always the case. Consider, for example, *cow belt*, listed by Ayto (1990) as first occurring in English in 1989, which means 'the conservative area of heartland Hinduism in India, where cows are sacred' (compare the American *Bible belt*), which has an extremely specific meaning right from first use, a meaning which is not necessarily deducible from the meanings of the elements. At another extreme, *gold ring*, though a well-established collocation, seems to be pretty well compositional.

We have already seen in (6) that idioms are listed, and lack of compositionality is a sign of idiomaticity. Saying that compounds must be idiomatic (and therefore must be listed) seems simply to say that a compound is, by definition, a subset of idioms. Clearly, to the extent that the term 'compound' is ill-defined, it can be defined in any way, but it is not clear to me what is gained by this definition. Since any construction can be idiomatic, having a special label for one particular idiomatic construction seems odd. The notion that a compound is just a type of idiom seems to have at least three implications:

- There is a construction type which has no name when it is productively and compositionally produced, but which gains a name when it becomes idiomatic.
- No compound is unspecified in terms of the relationship that holds between its elements. *Basketball* cannot mean 'a ball woven out of cane' because *basketball* means a sport. *Basket shoes*, because it has no established meaning and is therefore not a compound, could mean 'shoes woven out of cane'.
- While strings of two nouns, for instance, are likely to be compounds, strings of three or more are less likely to be compounds, because the construction as a whole is less likely to be non-compositional. Consider, for instance, the attested example *university student research centre report* (BNC; Davies 2004). *Research centre* might be a compound, *student research centre* is probably a compound in the institution involved, but the whole construction is not a compound, because *university* and *report* are both compositional when added to the rest. So while such a definition does not rule out recursion in compounds, it reduces it considerably.

None of these implications seems to me to be obviously valuable, and certainly not without further argumentation. Correspondingly, the definition of a compound as a subtype of idiom seems poorly founded.

2.6   The Typology of Words

When it comes to the typology of words, we are rather stuck in the nineteenth century, with nobody having produced a generally-accepted typology to replace the division of languages or word-types into isolating, agglutinating, fusional and polysynthetic. This is unfortunate, since there is general agreement that this typology, although it may have some minor benefits, is not particularly helpful.

Firstly, it is not particularly helpful as a classification of languages, since many (most? all?) languages have words of more than one type. In the English sentence *The babysitter waits for the grandparents to return*, we can argue that *babysitter* is polysynthetic, *grandparents* is agglutinating, *waits* is fusional and the other items are isolating. But even if individual analyses are disputed, it is not clear that it makes any difference to anything beyond the analysis of that particular word.

Secondly, it is not helpful in that the definition of polysynthetic is too broad. Fortescue (1994) provides a list of ten distinct factors which might be considered to be part of polysynthesis and a mini-typology of five types of polysynthetic languages. His factors include noun-incorporation into verbal stems (this is dealt with further below, see Section 3.6), large inventories of obligatorily bound morphemes, integration of locative, instrumental and other non-arguments into the verbal stem, and productive morphophonemics leading to a multiplicity of allomorphs. In his typology, Fortescue distinguishes between two distinct kinds of affixation: recursive systems and the use of what he terms 'field' affixes which mark precise location or instrument. Equally the papers collected in Evans and Sasse (2002) indicate that polysynthesis is not a unitary category, even if it provides a useful cover-term.

It is clear that the distinction between fusional and agglutinating does have some import for inflectional systems: fusional languages have shorter word-forms and have declension/conjugation classes, while agglutinating languages have longer word-forms and have no such inflectional classes, for instance. It is equally clear that languages can have features of agglutination and fusion (see Karlsson 2006 on Finnish), so that the types are not pure, but canonical. But it is not clear that this helps in the definition of a word or the recognition of a word in a particular language. Dixon and Aikhenvald (2002: 8) cite the case of Bantu languages where items that are viewed as prefixes in the orthographic system of one language are viewed as separate words in the orthography of a neighbouring and closely related language. Julien (2006: 619) points out that the aspectual morpheme *le* is sometimes written as an affix and sometimes as a separate word when Mandarin is presented in Roman script. It would seem that there is a certain degree of arbitrariness in determining words.

Indeed, typologically, we have to question whether all languages must have a word at all (Dixon & Aikhenvald 2002). Many languages have no lexeme to denote what we might think of as a word, and many linguists have suggested that the notion of word is not helpful in the analysis of a variety of languages, from isolating to polysynthetic ones. If individual languages do not have words and compounds are words, then those languages cannot have compounds. But it may be that a better analogy is with the phonological units of mora, syllable and foot. Any spoken language can be analysed as having all three, but in Japanese the mora is clearly of the utmost importance for the structure of the language, the syllable far less so, in French the syllable is important, but the mora less so, and in English the foot is crucial in, for example, the analysis of verse structure, but the boundaries of the syllable are hard to determine and the mora, while valuable to linguists, is not a unit which has a common-language term to denote it. If the same is true of words, then morpheme, word, compound and phrase may be items of varying significance in individual languages, not all of them meriting common-language terms in every language, though all of potential interest for the linguist.

2.7   Grammatically-Related Criteria for Wordhood

Although there is a long history of discussion of grammatical criteria for wordhood, it has been revived in recent years specifically in respect of compounds, and then specifically with reference to English. These criteria may work for other languages better than they work for English, but there is little evidence to suggest that to be true. Accordingly, exemplification and discussion here will be largely in terms of English: further discussion of these criteria in other languages would be welcome.

2.7.1   'Minimal Free Form'
Bloomfield's (1935: 178) celebrated definition of a word as a minimal free form is perhaps the best-known of these approaches. A minimal free form is an element which can stand as an utterance in its own right and contains no smaller items which fulfil the same criterion. Bloomfield says that it must not be composed entirely of smaller items which fulfil the same criterion, but this may be overly restrictive on the term 'minimal'. The criterion immediately creates a problem for compounds. *Blackmail* may well be able to stand as a free form, but so can both *black* and *mail*, so it is not a minimal free form. But it is not only compounds which cause the problem. *Cakes* could stand alone as an utterance, perhaps in answer to the question *Do you prefer cookies or cakes?*, but *cake* could equally well stand alone, though in answer to a different question. So *cakes* contains a minimal free form (though it is still one itself in Bloomfield's version). The example does raise a number of questions about what precisely we mean by a 'free form', since *cakes* is countable and *cake* (in isolation) is not, yet few linguists seem to be happy in seeing two different

lexical items here (see Bauer et al. 2013: 557–558). In French, where there are many clitics, an utterance like *je ne le sais pas* 'I NEG it know NEG' is traditionally presented as a sequence of orthographic words, as shown here, but may well be a minimal free form. In contrast, English *I'll*, which also contains a clitic, is probably not a minimal free form, since *I* occurs as a free form at least in the speech of language purists.

We also have to consider the problem of use versus mention. *Cat* could stand alone as the answer to questions like *Did you say cat or hat?* or *What is a three letter word denoting a domestic animal that chases mice?*, but where use rather than mention is required, it is hard to make *cat* stand alone, unless as a vocative (and there are many count nouns which it is hard to imagine being used as vocatives). More normally, it would co-occur with some kind of determiner: *a cat, the cat, my cat*. Determiners such as these rarely occur in isolation, and if they are words are words for other reasons, namely that they can be separated from their nouns: *a (famous) cat, my (old) cat*, and so on. Many past tense verbs are rare in English as stand-alone elements (as opposed, say, to Italian, where such usage is common): *I wandered lonely as a cloud* is perfectly normal, but *Wandered* sounds distinctly odd and at best would need a lot of context to make it work. On the other hand, given a question like *Are you cold?*, it seems perfectly normal in English to answer with the form *Ish*, although we would probably otherwise deny that it is a word.

All in all, the notion of a minimal free form isolates some things that we think of as words but fails to isolate some others.

2.7.2   *Criteria Involving Structural Integrity*

In general terms the word is seen as a structurally cohesive unit. This means two things: the first is that if it is moved, it is moved as a unit; the second is that it cannot be freely interrupted by extraneous material.

The movement criterion is not as simple as it appears. Certainly it is true in highly fusional languages that the order of words need not be fixed, but that the elements within the word tend to be fixed. So we find examples like that in (7), cited in Bauer (2003: 63) from Classical Greek (Herodotos I, 30, 3):

(7)   nun oːn   himeros   epeiresthai   moi   epeːlthe   se
       now therefore a.desire   to.ask   to me   has come   you

       ei tina   eːdeː   pantoːn   eides   olbiioːtatton
       if someone   already   of.all   you.have.seen   most.fortunate

'Now therefore a desire has come over me to ask you whether you have already seen someone who is most fortunate of all'.

Note that while all the individual words remain units, the form glossed as 'you', for instance, is displaced from the rest of its syntactic constituent. In other languages, though, such criteria are more difficult. Certainly it is possible to have a sentence like (8), with a displaced direct object noun (and in principle, we might do the same thing with morphologically more complex items), but in English (as opposed to other languages like Greek) it is not the word which has been moved but the syntactic constituent of direct object, although that constituent is minimally composed of a single word. Compare (9).

(8)   Plums, I love.

(9)   a. ?Plums, I love yellow.
        b. Yellow plums, I love

The uninterruptability of the word is, in general terms, a much stronger criterion. Given *I consolidated my position* one cannot get *I con-position-solidated my or *I con-as-best-I-could-solidated my position or any other random interruption. There are two major classes of exception, though: insertion and intermediate structure building. I shall illustrate insertion with expletive insertion in English and clitic insertion in Udi.

In English it is possible to insert an expletive into words of an appropriate prosodic structure to make a more forceful or emphatic version of that word: *abso-bloody-lutely, kanga-bloody-roo, Tala-fucking-hassee*, and so on. Many authorities call the process 'infixation', but infixation implies the presence of infixes, and affixes are by definition bound morphs, which is clearly not the case with these expletives, so 'insertion' seems a more defensible terminology. The process of insertion is reasonably well-known: any disyllabic expletive can be inserted immediately before a syllable which carries (primary or secondary) stress, with a preference for two syllables before the insertion. But it is frequently the case that this canonical structure is contravened in some way. *Ala-damn-bama, Portu-sodding-gal* and *ur-fucking-bane* show different kinds of contravention. It is also the case that where the insertion point can come between a prefix and the base, despite not fitting the stress criterion, the morphologically defined insertion point is preferred, as in *un-fucking-believable* and *over-fucking-excited* (Bauer 2015a). In all these cases, there is another possible form in which the expletive precedes the relevant word: *fucking absolutely, bloody kangaroo* and so on. So expletive insertion looks like a morphological rule that reorders a word from elsewhere in the sentence into the middle of the word and breaks the uninterruptability criterion. This kind of exception is not widely reported from other languages, but the fact that it exists at all is worrying for this criterion.

Harris (2000) argues that person-marking clitics in Udi can interrupt a verb word, and that this breaches the uninterruptability criterion. Udi is a Caucasian language, closely related to Lezgian. In this language, subject agreement markers on the verb are clitics, closely related in form to independent personal pronouns. In some instances, these markers are found suffixed to the verb form, as in (10).

(10)   ägär   un   bezi   bak·a·y·n
        If   you_SG mine   be·SUBJV·PAST·2SG
        'if you will be mine'

In other instances, however, the clitic is found inside the verb-word, either dividing an incorporated element from the verb to which it is incorporated (11a), or before the present-tense marker in intransitive verbs (11b) or interrupting the base (11c).

(11)   a. äyel   kala·ne·bak·e
            child.ABSL   big-3SG-become-AORII
            'The child grew up'.
        b. box·ne·sa
            boils·3SG·PRES
            'it boils (intr.)'
        c. kaγuz-ax   a·z·q'·e
            letter-DAT   receive-·1SG-receive·AORII
            'I received the letter'.

Because the relevant entities are clitics the criterion that they are moved from elsewhere in the sentence is met, and because some of the landing sites result in discontinuous morphs, the criterion of insertion is met. Endoclitics (clitics which can be attached inside the word) like this are rare, but are found in a number of other languages. They are problematic for the notion that the word is uninterruptable in general terms, though uninterruptability may nevertheless be a feature of the word in some languages.

Intermediate structure building is a problem for compounds in particular, though in principle it also affects other structures. Given an expression like *hospital board* (nearly half a million hits on Google), is *hospital health board* (over 12,000 hits on Google) an interruption or not? If we bracket *hospital health board* as [hospital [health board]], we see that rather than *health* interrupting *hospital board, hospital* has been added to the front of *health board*. This is not an interruption, though it looks like one. Rather, a new intermediate structure has been built. Similar examples can also be built with inflectional systems, such as the French *donnait* '[he/she/it] used to give' and *donnerait* '[he/she/it] would give' where the *-er* is not an interruption (and so not an infix), but a suffix added to the stem to make a new conditional stem.

Something similar applies in the case of reordering of morphs within a word. For some authorities this is another aspect of structural integrity. But the difference between *houseboat* and *boathouse* or *guesthouse* and *house guest* must not be understood as reordering of morphs, but as the construction of a different unit according to the rules of the grammar. Most of the instances of words with alternative orderings of morphs in languages like Turkish or Japanese (Bauer 2003: 65) come under the same rubric: just because two orders are possible, it does not mean that reordering is possible. If the difference in ordering is meaningful, then it is not random reordering.

In all of this there is a vital fact about words, namely that they tend to stand out from other potential elements by their structural integrity. Unfortunately, the criteria are difficult to apply across language types, and other units may also show some degree of structural integrity. If this criterion is to be used, it needs to be made clear precisely how it works. Since it is often a crucial criterion in attempting to distinguish between compounds as words and similar constructions as phrases, such clarification is vital.

2.7.3 Accessibility of Elements

In general terms it is assumed that elements inside words are not accessible to syntactic processes or to reference. This implies that elements inside words cannot have pronouns refer to them, cannot be replaced by *one* and cannot be referred to by other processes. Thus the examples in (12) (which are not attested) are assumed by such criteria to be impossible.

(12)   a. He is a lift attend$_i$ant, but he does so$_i$ reluctantly. [*Contrast*: He attends to people's needs, but he does so reluctantly.]
        b. It's a bit fish$_i$y that she didn't catch one$_i$. [*Contrast*: I smell a rat, but I didn't catch one – *which may be zeugmatic, but where the reference works*]
        c. He$_i$ once said that he$_i$ wasn't a Marx$_i$ist. [i.e., that Marx once made this claim about himself. *Contrast*: He once claimed that he wasn't the bishop. Note that this example is perfectly acceptable if we imagine it embedded in a discussion about Marx – e.g. 'I learnt something interesting about Karl Marx the other day: did you know that ...'. Under such circumstances the subscripted *he*-pronouns can refer anaphorically to Karl Marx. But when the only source of the reference to Marx is cataphoric and within the word *Marxist*, problems of interpretation arise.]

Unfortunately, there is plenty of evidence that such things are perfectly possible, if rather rare. Some attested examples are provided in (13).

(13)   a. It'll be showery at first but then they'll clear away (Radio New Zealand, 7 am news, 1 Nov. 2001)
        b. The Chomskyan answer is obvious: that a 'Universal Grammar' exists as he says it exists (Matthews, Peter. 2001. *A short history of structural linguistics*. Cambridge: Cambridge University Press, p. 151)
        c. The air was spiced and he spotted a pot of it brewing on a burner (Sullivan, Mark. 2014. *Thief*. New York: Minotaur, p. 6)
        d. Murderers generally like to commit them when no one is watching (Rosenfelt, David. 2014. *Hounded*. New York: Minotaur, p. 89)
        e. Lego fan loves its infinite possibilities. (Headline in *The Dominion Post*, Wellington, 6 May 2014, p. A11)
        f. 'Not long ago some foxes got into the penguin enclosure,' she said. 'They killed about a dozen of them.' (French, Nicci. 2012. *Tuesday's gone*. London: Michael Joseph, p. 35)
        g. Here he found that the Greatest Story Ever Told had stopped for a tea-break. Dorothy Horncastle was dispensing mugs of the stuff from a large copper urn . . . (Hill, Reginald. 1990. *Bones and silence*. London: Collins, p. 275)

The examples in (13) show that reference can be both to elements in derivatives and elements in compounds, that reference can be made both to proper names and to common nouns and that the reference can be by pronoun or by other means.

Not only is it the case that reference into a word is possible, it is also the case that reference into a syntactic construction can be odd. Consider the example in (14), which I find odder than some of those in (13).

(14)   First proposed during Roman$_i$ times, a canal across the narrow isthmus was beyond their$_i$ capabilities. (Cussler, Clive with Jack du Brul. 2008. *Plague ship*. London: Michael Joseph, p. 208)

In the light of the evidence in (13) and (14), it must be concluded that whatever this criterion is measuring, it is not wordhood in any obvious sense. There are syntactic islands, and there are words which are not islands. More importantly, for present purposes, is that if reference can be made to elements within derivatives, we cannot use the fact that reference can be made to certain two-element (potentially compound) constructions to show that they are not words. That does not mean that the reference criterion is necessarily completely useless. To my mind, the invented example in (15a) seems worse that then invented example in (15b), for instance, and examples like those in (13) are rare. But if this criterion is to be developed to be a measure of wordhood, then it requires a much more subtle formulation than it has so far received.

(15)   a. He$_i$ is a Marx$_i$ist.
         b. A Marx$_i$ist is a person who admires him$_i$.

People who have studied this problem in detail (Douloureux 1971, Ward et al. 1991, Schäfer 2015) see the conditions for allowing reference into a word as being pragmatic rather than morphosyntactic. Harris (2006) even provides evidence that such a constraint is language-specific. They agree that this does not allow a good definition of a word, but are unable to provide a solid set of criteria to determine when such reference is and is not possible.

The other kind of pronominal reference is provided by *one*. *One*-replacement is often cited as being purely syntactic, so that if (16) is acceptable, it proves that the construction *Oxford College* is syntactic, whereas if (17) is unacceptable, it shows that *railway* is not syntactic but lexical.

(16)   Is King's an Oxford College or a Cambridge one?

(17)   Does that line of trees mark the railway or the motor one? [i.e., the motorway]

The trouble with this criterion is that, at least for many speakers, it seems that it is perfectly possible to allow *one* to refer back inside a word, even where the word concerned is not a candidate for a compound. Examples of relevant sentences are provided in (18), all accepted by more than half of the speakers polled in a small survey (see Appendix).

(18)   A miniskirt displays a lot more leg than a full-length one.
         A meta-rule can tell you more than a basic-level one.
         A pseudoscorpion is not as dangerous as a real one.

If *one* can be used to refer within words, then it cannot be used as a test to distinguish syntactic and lexical constructions. But even for speakers who do not find the examples in (18) acceptable, Giegerich (2015: 38, 106) argues that the impossibility of some *one* uses is determined by zeugmatic effects rather than be lexical versus syntactic status. It does not, he claims, indicate lexical cohesion.

2.7.4   Coordination

There is a claim (Payne & Huddleston 2002: 449) that lexical structures do not allow coordination of their elements, while syntactic structures do. This means that in (19a), where there is coordination, we must be dealing with a syntactic structure, while in (19b), where it is claimed that coordination is not possible, we must be dealing with a lexical structure. Compounds, it is claimed are lexical structures and not syntactic structures.

(19)   a. various London schools and colleges [i.e. London schools and London colleges]
          b. *ice lollies and creams [i.e. ice lollies and ice-creams]

The major difficulty with this criterion is that is demonstrably false that coordination is limited to syntactic constructs. COCA and the BNC provide examples like the following: *pre- and post-test methodology* (COCA), *pro- or anti-feminist* (COCA), *inter and intraobserver variation* (BNC), *over and underconstrained problems* (BNC). Again it is true that such examples are rare, and that is at least partly because there seems to be some semantic constraint on what prefixes can be coordinated as well as whatever formal constraints there may be: all the examples cited above give prefixes which contrast directly with one another, so that we would not, on these grounds alone, expect to find something like *a- and be-muse*. Studies of other Germanic languages (see e.g. Booij 2002: 171–174 on Dutch, Wiese 1996 on German) suggest that there are prosodic restrictions as well, so that the restrictions here are best formulated in terms other than words.

There is another problem here, and that is that intuitions appear to be extremely unreliable about what is or is not possible. Despite the claim that (19b) is ungrammatical, Bauer (2014) cites the examples in (20) to show that the claim may be incorrect.

(20)   Far too many ice-lollies and creams had been consumed but we were all happy little campers.
          http://yacf.co.uk/forum/index.php?topic=33253.120 (accessed 16 Jan. 2011)
          These nine months were filled with dripping ice lollies and creams, spilt soft drinks and lost maltesers.
          http://keeptrackkyle.blogspot.com/2006/07/tidying-up.html (accessed 16 Jan. 2011)
          to play with their buckets and spades, to paddle in the water, and to suck lots of ice lollies and creams.
          www.governessx.com/Introduction/IntroductionLibrary/ GovernessXLibraryABSissCDictionaryS.htm (accessed 16 Jan. 2011)

The fact that a single example is wrong (or is wrong for some speakers) does not, of course, prove that the principle is wrong. But it does suggest that extreme care needs to be taken in making claims in this area.

Finally on this point, note that if coordination can only be syntactic and not lexical, we must presumably conclude that items like *producer-director* are syntactic and not lexical because the two nouns appear to be coordinated.

Overall, this criterion seems too fraught with problems to be reliable in distinguishing between lexical compounds and non-lexical phrases.

2.7.5 Independent Modification

Payne and Huddleston (2002: 449) also claim that where an element can be independently modified, the construction must be syntactic. Where there is a word, it can only be globally modified. So in (21a) *south* modifies only *London*, showing that *London college* is a syntactic construction, while in (21b), the impossibility of *crushed* modifying only *ice* (it cannot mean 'a cream of crushed ice'), and the fact that it must modify *ice-cream* as a whole, indicates that *ice-cream* is a lexical unit.

(21)   a. two south London colleges
        b. crushed ice-cream

This topic has been considered in most depth by Bell (2014). She points out that [[AN]N] constructions occur approximately once in every 1,000 words of text on average, and that in 83 per cent of cases the AN is independently listed in the *OED* or found in Wikipedia. This suggests that such constructions are not freely formed. Bell cites examples such as *cold weather payments, Green Bay Packers*. An example of a residual type is *local office monitoring*. Even in these residual types the AN constituents are of higher frequencies than average AN collocations. In other words, an [[AN]N] construction indicates that the AN has some specific collocational status and is not randomly produced. That is why *big craft beer van* (attested on the side of such a van) has to mean that it is a big van: neither *big craft* nor *big craft beer* is an established collocation. This implies that any [[AN]N] sequence is lexical to some extent, which is supported to the extent that Bell failed to find an instance where the A in an AN construction of this type could be independently modified. Submodification was found where the AN was itself a compound adjective, as in *a very high speed backbone*. But *very cold weather payments* would only be possible if there were an official definition of something called *very cold weather*.

If that is the case, either *south London* or *south London college* in (21a) has to be seen as an established collocation, and *south London* seems to fit that criterion. Accordingly, the difference between (21a) and (21b) is not that one contains a phrase and the other a compound (as Payne and Huddleston propose) but that *south London* is an adjectival collocation which in turn allows a collocation with *college*, while *crushed ice*, although a collocation, is not one which collocates with *cream*. Seen from this point of view the whole question reduces to something to do with the vagaries of what happens to be a permissible collocation in English rather than a grammatical difference between two different construction types.

2.7.6   Global Inflection

Lexemes inflect, but elements within lexemes do not inflect for meaning or for their role in a sentence. A word like *cyclist* is perfectly normal, but we cannot contrast it with **cyclesist* to denote 'a person who habitually rides multiple bicycles'. Similarly, in English we do not find past tense forms used as bases in word-formation: dinosaurs cannot be called **plant-ate-ers*, even though they no longer eat anything.

When we look at compounds, this becomes rather more difficult to deal with. It is relatively common to find compounds whose modifying element is marked with some inflection. Some examples are provided in (22). However, that inflectional marker remains fixed independent of the inflection of the lexeme as a whole and is not influenced by the role the compound plays in the sentence.

(22) Danish: *børn·e·bog* 'children·LE·book'
      English: *arms-reduction, suggestions box*
      Finnish: *maa·lta·pako* 'country·ABL·flee.NMLZ = rural depopulation'
                  (Sulkala & Karjalainen 1992: 362),
                  praha·ssa·käy·mä·ttöm·yys·kompleksi 'Prague·INE·go·INF.
                  ABE·NMLZ·complex = complex about not having been to
                  Prague' (Karlsson 1983: 203)
      Hungarian: *bŭn·be·esés* 'sin·ILL·fall = fall into sin' (Kiefer 2009: 539)

Such instances are particularly problematic when the genitive case is involved. The genitive is, as much as anything, an adnominal case, so that when one noun submodifies another, we might expect to find the genitive used. Therefore $N_{GEN} + N$ (where the modifier precedes the head) looks superficially like a syntactic structure. If we make the claim that all such structures are syntactic, though, then we say, for English, that *the book's cover* is just the same as *the cat's-eye*, even though the first corresponds to *the cover of the book*, but the second corresponds *to the eye of a cat* (where the *eye* is metaphorical, due to its reflecting qualities in the dark, and *cat's-eye* means 'a stud marking lanes etc. in a road'; *cat's eye* can also be a semi-precious stone). Rosenbach (2006) argues in detail that there is a cline of what she calls determiner genitives (like *the book's cover*) through various kinds of descriptive genitives, at one end of which are things which behave indistinguishably from compounds. In other words, there is no hard line between $N_{GEN} + N$ and $N + N$ constructions, even if this crosses the border between syntax and morphology. This is an unexpected result, except possibly in Construction Grammar, where the morphological or syntactic nature of a given construction is not considered particularly relevant.

In the Germanic languages generally, what are today viewed as linking elements have largely derived from genitive markers. Some of them still retain a form which looks like a genitive marker. In some of the Germanic languages, there are arguments that these old genitive markers have lost their status as case markers and have become linking elements (which is how they are generally treated). For example, German *Universität·s·gebäude* 'university·LE·building' the linking -*s*- cannot be a genitive, because the -*s* genitive is not used on a feminine common noun like *Universität*. But if it is true that case markers can transition diachronically into things which are no longer case markers, then it would seem to follow that there are states which are on the borderline of case marking (genitive marking) and non-case marking, where there may be problems with either analysis. If the genitive is always syntactic, this would seem to imply a transition state between syntax and morphology. If the genitive can occur within a compound, there are two transition states, where the transition from case-marking to link-marking may be the result of the prior transition from syntax to morphology. The latter hypothesis seems more likely to me, but it is not clear what would indicate direct proof in either direction.

If the genitive is problematic, one alternative to genitive marking, the use of the construct state, is perhaps more so. In the construct state, nominals are placed side-by-side without any marking. The difference between grammatically adjacent nouns marking possession and lexically adjacent nouns marking a new lexeme could therefore be invisible. In Modern Hebrew, both types are single phonological words (Borer 1988, 2009). Borer (1988, 2009) points out, though, that despite these similarities, compounds and construct state nominal behave differently, in that the construct state nominals behave like syntactic units in terms of many of the factors that have already been discussed above. That is, the difference between compounds and possessive phrases may not be visible in the citation form but is determinable by the syntactic potential of the construct state form. On the other hand, Borer also concludes that construct state nominal may contain some features that otherwise are part of word-formation rather than syntax.

Overall, the situation here is clearly complex. There does seem to be an emerging consensus that adnominal marking, even if it has purely syntactic uses, does not necessarily always prevent the output construction from having features which appear to be morphological/lexical. The very complexity of the situation means that specific implications cannot be spelt out, but there is no contradiction between some internal inflection and morphological status.

2.8   Is There a Non-Word Solution?

In this section I want to consider what compounding might look like if compounding is a syntactic process and creates syntactic constructs rather than words. The point here is that it is important to know whether the notion of compound as word is something which is desperately important, or whether it is something which has become part of received wisdom without being particularly strongly supported.

The first sense in which compounds could be syntactic is the sense in which they are considered to be syntactic constructions in works such as Lees (1960) and Levi (1978). At the time these scholars were working, the lexicon was viewed as static and contained lists of known unpredictable items – the fact that *cat* means 'cat' and not 'fir tree', the fact that the past tense of STRIKE is *struck* and not *striked*. Anything which could be constructed by rule was constructed by rule, and the rules were syntactic. In other words, the syntactic component of the grammar was the only place in which productive processes could be dealt with. Compounds were viewed as items created by productive processes, even when such a derivation was semantically awkward. Thus, *hotrod*, like *madman* was derived from an underlying structure something like *the N is A*, even if *the rod is hot* does not help with the semantics of *hotrod* (Lees 1960: 129). It was also assumed to be axiomatic that synonymous surface structures with the same lexemes shared an underlying structure. So just as *Kim read the book* and *The book was read by Kim* had the same underlying structure, so did *The madman saw Lee* and *The man who was mad saw Lee*. Such an approach was dictated by the approach to formal grammar that was in vogue at the time, and was justified by the rhetoric of transformational generative grammar at that period. If we would probably now think that the grammar of the period was unsophisticated, or just plain wrong (e.g. in that *the madman* is not synonymous with *the man who was mad*), that does not negate the achievement of these scholars.

Because linguistic theorising has changed since then, and because the lexicon is now seen as much more dynamic than was considered possible at the period when Lees was undertaking his work, most people would not now wish to follow a model which resembles that of Lees or that of Levi in great detail. Such approaches showed that a syntactic approach to compounds was entirely possible, but also tended to show (inadvertently) that there were weaknesses in such approaches. So although we know that a syntactic approach is possible, on the basis of work like this we would probably not wish to adopt such an approach today.

A different approach is provided by Nielsen (1998), although it is presented only schematically. He claims that in a construction like *concrete floor, concrete* is not a noun but an adjective, created by conversion from the noun *concrete*. There is a certain amount of support for such a view from traditional lexicography. The *OED*, for example lists an adjective *iron* 'made of or resembling iron', as well as a noun *iron* which can occur in compounds such as *iron deposit, iron shears, iron trade*. Gove (1966) lists *alligator* in *alligator forceps* as an adjective, while the *OED* lists it as a noun. Gove (1966) does not specifically list *crocodile* as an adjective, however, even in *crocodile clip*, which is listed as an alternative to *alligator clip*. More generally, Nielsen (1998) suggests that it might be useful to recognise a new part of speech, which he calls the 'adstantive', when something that looks like a noun is used attributively with another noun. To some extent this is like the proposal in Nikolaeva and Spencer (2012) that it should be possible to view the attributive noun in N + N constructions as a syntactically modifying noun, which also implies a syntactic view of compounding.

There are many problems with Nielsen's analysis, quite beyond the increase in the amount of conversion that has to be recognised. First, as the example with *alligator* shows, it is not clear that the distinction (if there is one) between adjective and noun can be consistently maintained. Second, if they are all adjectives, as Nielsen seems to suggest, though his example is ambiguous in this regard, then we still have to distinguish between adjectives that carry the stress and adjectives that do not. This problem will be discussed in greater detail later (Sections 4.7 and 6.1) but is not necessarily helped by changing the allocation to word-classes of the attributive item. And third, if *concrete* and *alligator* are adjectives, what is *grass* in *grass-green*, *blue* in *blue-green*, *spin* in *spin-dry*, *baby* in *baby-sit*? By the same logic they should presumably be adverbs produced by conversion, but this is a new type of word-formation in English.

So there are various ways in which compounding can be viewed as a syntactic process. These have to be weighed against the factors which suggest that compounds are words, and consequently that any process which forms them must be morphological in nature. There is a real debate here, though in the current state of linguistic theorising, the solution with compounds as morphological constructs, words, seems to be preferred.

2.9   Discussion

It is well-known that the word is extremely difficult to define, even in a single language, let alone cross-linguistically (Dixon & Aikhenvald 2002, van Gijn & Zúñiga 2014, Hippisley 2015, Wray 2015). This is not a new observation. But to the extent that it is true, it makes defining a compound as a word difficult. This is not to deny that word may be a useful concept in some languages (possibly even most languages) or to say that there may not be some useful definition of word in terms of the intersection of canonical features. It is likely, though, that any such cluster of features will need to be defined differently in different languages, which makes any typology of compounding difficult since, if the compound is a word, and the words are not strictly comparable in terms of their defining criteria, the comparability of what is or is not a compound becomes dubious.

There are three questions which it might be hoped this chapter would have answered:

- Can we define a word independent of the language in which it occurs?
- If so, are compounds defined as words by this definition?
- Does what we know about words give us a good grounding for saying that some compound-like objects are words, while others are not?

The first of these we have, implicitly, answered negatively: there is more than one notion of a word, the criteria for wordhood of various kinds are not necessarily the same in all languages, the criteria for wordhood do not always agree and are often difficult to apply – indeed, in many cases seem to be practically and theoretically suspect. Consequently, we cannot answer the second question, and this is a problem for language typology. Even the third question is difficult to answer: it is not clear that we can use criteria for wordhood to define a set of compound words, but it might be possible to use syntactic criteria to define things which are not words, if we can agree on suitable syntactic criteria. Any such solution, though, will be likely to give rise to canonical categories (see e.g. Corbett 2007) rather than neat, well-circumscribed categories.

If that is the negative outcome of this chapter, there is also a positive one. That is that the majority of words seem to share some features which are relatively well-understood. The notion of structural integrity, in particular, seems to hold over a large number of cases, provided it is properly circumscribed. In languages with inflectional morphology, compounds generally take global inflection, and this may mark them as different from other structures where modifiers inflect independently of their heads. It may not be the case that we can cite criteria which will definitely determine whether something is or is not a compound (to some extent because scholars do not agree on what a compound is), but the notion that compounds are word-like, even if it does not prevent differences of opinion, holds a reasonable starting point for discussion.

3 *The Grammar of Compounds*

3.1 Introduction

This chapter is concerned with several factors involved in the grammar of compounds. These factors are not ways in which compounds are derived in individual languages, but general grammatical factors that are relevant for compounding in any language. The discussion is mostly illustrated with English, except where this is not relevant or not helpful, but is intended to have a wider scope.

The factors to be considered here are headedness, binarity, recursion, the interpenetration of syntax and morphology in compounding and the structures which compounding specifically permits.

3.2 Headedness

3.2.1 *Headedness in Syntax*

Where syntactic headedness is concerned, there is a set of criteria which seem to be well-established for determining headedness. The discussion here follows Zwicky (1985) and Hudson (1987). The criteria will be discussed one at a time.

1. SEMANTIC FUNCTOR. If we divide the elements in a construction into functors and their arguments, then it is the functors which are heads. In a VP construction of V + NP, this picks out the verb as head, in a PP construction of P + NP, this picks out the P as head and so on.

2. MORPHOSYNTACTIC LOCUS. The morphosyntactic locus is the word to which the inflection which situates a constituent in its wider context is attached (or the equivalent word which carries syntactic features if there is no overt inflection). In an Aux + VP construction, the morphosyntactic locus, where tense and person are marked, is the auxiliary. In a V + NP construction like *eats the vegetables*, the tense and person are marked on the verb, or if not, as in *eat the vegetables*, it is because of the morphosyntactic features on the verb

which make overt marking inappropriate. The status of this criterion would seem to be undermined by research by Nichols (1986) who shows that there are head-marked languages and dependent-marked languages, with inflection in many languages not on the head at all. Russian *s brat-om* 'with brother-INSTR' does not mark the prepositional head, but the dependent noun, while Tzutujil Mayan *ruu-majk jar aachi* '3SG-because.of the man' shows the inflectional 3SG marker on the head, the preposition (Nichols 1986: 60).

3. SUBCATEGORISAND. In a V + NP construction, it is the V which determines what the other items in the phrase may be. *Give*, for instance, can be subcategorised to accept *NP NP* (*give his mother a present*) or *NP to NP* (*give a present to her mother*). So the V is the head.

4. GOVERNOR. If one element in a construction determines the form of some other element in the construction, then it is the governor. So in many Indo-European languages a preposition governs the case of the accompanying NP. Thus, in Icelandic, the preposition *til* 'to' takes the genitive, and the verbs *gegna* 'obey' and *gleyma* 'forget' take objects in the dative (Einarsson 1949).

5. DISTRIBUTIONAL EQUIVALENT. If in a construction there is one element which has the same distribution as the construction as a whole, that element is the head of the construction. Since there are English sentences of the form NP [V NP] and English sentences of the form NP [V], V must have the same distribution as V + NP (giving rise to the distinction between transitive and intransitive verbs), and so the V is the head. Zwicky (1985) sees this as implying that the obligatory element characterizes the construction in the sense that it determines the word-class of the construction. That is, a noun phrase has a noun as its head because of this criterion (or, conversely, the phrase in which a noun is the head is called a noun phrase because of this criterion).

6. OBLIGATORY ELEMENT. This criterion overlaps to a large extent with the last, in that if V has the same distribution as V + NP, then NP must be optional and V remains as obligatory. Zwicky (1985) distinguishes between this and ellipsis, saying the ellipsis does not indicate optionality under this criterion.

7. RULER. Zwicky and Hudson's last criterion is that the head is the element that comes higher up a dependency tree than the other elements with which it collocates. Since this depends on other theorists (who are not all in agreement) it is difficult to apply and is probably already covered by the other criteria.

To these criteria we can add that the head is usually seen as being lexical rather than phrasal. Zwicky (1985) makes this point but does not use it as a formal criterion.

3.2.2   *Extending Headedness to Morphology*

The notion of headedness has also been extended to morphological constructions, but the criteria that are used in syntax are not all equally valuable in this
regard. Most linguists take only one or two criteria to be relevant in morphology. We will discuss this first and foremost with derivational morphology,
before considering compounds. In derivational morphology, the results for
words like *blacken, counter-attack, duckling* and *unhorse* are not always the
same.

1. SEMANTIC FUNCTOR. If we consider *blacken*, it seems appropriate that
we should see the suffix *-en* as the functor, since we can gloss *blacken* as
'make black', and the *-en* must have the same function as the verb in the gloss.
However, this could simply be because *blacken* is a verb and the suffix has
verb functions, something which is also true of the prefix in *unhorse*. If we
look beyond such instances, to examples like *calmness, parental, supersonic*
and even *outdo*, where the base is a verb, it seems that in every case we can
interpret the affix as a functor applying to the base and the base as the
argument of that function.

2. MORPHOSYNTACTIC LOCUS. The notion of the morphosyntactic locus
as marking the head is rather less solid in morphology than in syntax. There is
an alternative analysis whereby the location of inflectional morphology is an
edge-phenomenon, in English applying to the right-hand edge of the lexical
item. The case would need to be made language by language, but in English
we find evidence for this interpretation in forms of complex lexical items
which are not normatively accepted, forms like *mother-in-laws* (eight hits in
COCA) and *attorney generals* (92 hits in COCA). Evidence also arises from
things which we might consider to be errors, such as the examples in (1).

(1)   Then he called a week later and said never mind, so I never minded. (Parker,
      Barbara. 2000. *Suspicion of malice*. New York: Dutton, p. 65)
      If you ain't the fucked-uppest motherfucker I ever knew. (Constantine,
      K. C. 2002. *Saving room for dessert*. New York: Mysterious Press, p. 276)
      code of conducts (Radio New Zealand Morning Report, 24 Mar. 2015)
      make suring they work (Radio New Zealand National, 7 pm news, 20
      Mar. 2012)

Although the locus of inflectional marking may work well in some Indo-
European languages, we must also account for languages like Osage (a Siouan
language). In Osage (Quintero 2004: 8–9) agent and patient person-markers
precede the verbal root, while number and aspect follow the root, and the pre-
root markers may themselves be preceded and followed by derivational

markers. Choctaw (a Muskogean language; Davies 1986) and Tuscarora (an Iroquoian language; Williams 1974) both show apparently inflectional items on both sides of the root, but it is difficult to see in the sources cited just what happens with derivational morphology. In such languages, the morphosyntactic locus is apparently not unique, and so any criterion dependent upon it is impossible to apply.

It should also be noted that there are many types of affixation which, in themselves, provide problems for the notion that an affix is a head. These include circumfixation, or indeed any kind of parasynthesis, when formal elements are added to the base in more than one position simultaneously. A simple example of circumfixation is provided by the Dutch *ge·been·te* 'skeleton' from the base *been* 'bone', where neither *gebeen* nor *beente* exists independently. Although we might be able to say that there is a non-contiguous morpheme {ge...te} which is the head, when it comes to any criterion which depends on the placement of the affix, it will not apply.

There is also another implication in using the location of inflectional morphology as a criterion for headedness. That is, it prevents inflection (or at least, peripheral inflection) from being the head in the construction. While there is some evidence for this point of view (Bauer 1990), it is controversial (Di Sciullo & Williams 1987).

Because of these problems, and the apparent problems for this criterion in syntax, I am reluctant to use this criterion for headedness in morphology.

3. SUBCATEGORISAND. The deverbal nominal suffix *-al* in English is commonly said to require a base which has final stress (*arrival, removal*). The English adjectival suffix *-ly* is said to be productive with bases which denote people (*knightly, witchly*). So the suffix chooses an appropriate base. On the other hand, only bases which end in *-ise* or *-ify* can productively use the nominalisation suffix *-ation* (*collectivisation, calcification*). So the base chooses its suffixes. If these formulations are correct, we have a clash in determining the subcategorisand. Of course, it would be possible to formulate each of these constraints the other way round: stress-final verbs can take *-al*, human nouns can take *-ly* and *-ation* selects bases in *-ise* and *-ify*. But that might imply that there is no evidence here at all, that it is simply a matter of wording. That is not the case.

In general terms these constraints are worded as they are for economy and accuracy. It is not true that all final-stressed verbs can take *-al* (or at least, there are many which do not, like *condemn, pretend, subsume*, and because *-al* is of limited productivity, we can assume that they are unlikely all to gain such nominalisations), but all *-al* nouns are on stress-final verbs (except *burial*, which is etymologically distinct). Starting from the affix is more economical than starting with a list of possible bases. Not all human nouns have established corresponding *-ly* adjectives (*grocerly, lecturerly, pilotly, pupilly* are not in general use), but new forms in *-ly* tend to be on human nouns. Again, starting with the affix is an economical way of making the statement. On the other hand, it may be more economical to say that words ending in *-ness* can only have native suffixes following the *-ness* within the same word (e.g. *businesswise*) and not borrowed suffixes than to list for the relevant native suffixes that they can occur after *-ness*. In most cases the class of bases is less easily defined, so the most economical way to specify the selection is to start with the suffix, because this does not involve having an open class having to be marked piecemeal as taking a particular suffix. This implies that the suffix is the head. By the same argument, the prefix would be the head in appropriate constructions. Giegerich (1999) provides an extended argument in favour of the base being the subcategorisand, but despite that presentation the matter remains controversial.

4. GOVERNOR. The problem with this criterion in morphology is that it is not clear what it means to determine the form of some other element in the construction. In syntax, that form is inflectional form: 'form' in the sense that a word-form is a form. In morphology that is irrelevant. However, the base often determines the phonological form of the affix, as with the ordinal *-th* in English, which becomes /əθ/ when following a vowel (as in *twentieth*), or *en-*, which (usually) becomes *em-* before a bilabial (as in *emplane*). In other instances, though, the affix appears to affect the form of the base: *autu[m]* ◆ *autu[mn]al*, *China* ◆ *Chinese*, *electric* ◆ *electricity*, *erase* ◆ *erasure*, *feminine* ◆ *feminize*, *ser[iː]ne* ◆ *ser[e]nity*, *tolerate* ◆ *tolerable*, *transmit* ◆ *transmission* and so on (see Bauer et al. 2013: ch. 9). The most likely conclusion is that this criterion simply is not relevant in derivational morphology, but if examples like those above are relevant, then the criterion fails to give a consistent answer (at least in English).

5. DISTRIBUTIONAL EQUIVALENT. This criterion has been interpreted in morphological circles as meaning that the element which determines the word-class of the derivative is the head: *stupidity* is a noun because *-ity* is a noun (rather like *deep knowledge* is a noun phrase because *knowledge* is a noun). However, as phrased by Zwicky and Hudson, this is a matter of distributional equivalence, and *-ity* does not have the distribution of a noun because it is an obligatorily bound morph, while nouns are not. There are very few instances where we might have distributional equivalence. The main one is in an example like *duckling*, where the base has the same

distribution as the entire word, not the affix, and with prefixes like *counter-attack*, where again the base (whether noun or verb) has the distribution of the whole word. There are a few cases in English (and rather more in other languages) where an affix starts to take on the status of a word, but in such cases, like *nationalism* which might be described as an *ism*, the word ceases to be a clear derivative and becomes more compound-like. Because of the weight that has been given to the Right-Hand Head rule (Williams 1981), namely that the head of the word is the rightmost element in the word, examples like *counterattack* are not seen as problematic, while those like *duckling* tend to be ignored, and scholars are uneasy about examples like *unhorse*, where the prefix determines the word-class of the word as a whole (Nagano 2011). But the interpretation of this criterion is far more fraught than is generally allowed. There is another interpretation of this criterion which is sometimes applied (more usually with compounds than with derivatives), and that is hyponymy. Just as *deep knowledge* is a hyponym of *knowledge*, so, too, is *duckling* a hyponym of *duck* and *counterattack* a hyponym of *attack*. Again the criterion is difficult to apply, but even more so when we consider examples such as *untidy*, which is, by its very definition, not a hyponym of *tidy*. This alternative interpretation does not appear to make matters any easier.

6. OBLIGATORY ELEMENT. In syntax, it is often possible to find one lexical element which is all that is required from the relevant phrase to maintain the general sense (though not all the details) of the original. In an example like *He went in the French window*, we can have *He went in the window, He went in, He went*, and at each level something optional in the relevant phrase is deleted. In derivational morphology, this criterion and the last appear to merge. *Attack* can be the obligatory element in *counter-attack, duck* in *duckling*, but it is hard to go much further. If we take a more abstract approach, then the only obligatory element in a word is the root (often defined as what is left when all the affixes are removed, a definition which indicates that affixes are optional).

We can summarize this discussion as in Table 3.1.

A number of points arise from this discussion. The first is that although Hudson (1987) argues that the criteria align in determining headedness in syntax, that is not the case in derivational morphology. Insofar as the criteria are usable in derivational morphology, they do not appear to support a solution such as the Right-Hand Head rule, but something far more complex. Given all this, it seems very misleading to talk of headedness in derivational morphology

Table 3.1 *Summary of headedness criteria in derivation*

Semantic functor	Affix the head
Morphosyntactic locus	Criterion unusable
Subcategorisand	Affix probably the head, but controversial
Governor	Criterion irrelevant or inconsistent
Distributional equivalent	Criterion dubious
Obligatory element	Base probably the head

as equivalent in any way to headedness in syntax: if the notion is to be rescued, it would be better if it were to be rescued under another label (we have Bloomfield's 'centre' and Marchand's 'determinans' and 'determinatum' already available). The greatest irony is that the criterion which is generally used – to the exclusion of all others – is the interpretation of the distributional equivalence criterion that sees the element which determines the word-class of the new word as the head of the word. While much may be achieved with such a definition (as is shown by Lieber 1992), it demands a very different view of distributional equivalence than is used in syntax.

3.2.3   Headedness in Compounds

Discussion of headedness in compounds has tended to be restricted to the distinction between examples like *windmill* and examples like *egghead*. The first has been said to be headed, the second not to be. But this has been determined with reference to very few of the criteria we have been considering. We thus not only need to look at more criteria, we need to look at more compound-types. These must not only include types that are found in English, but types like Italian *portalettere* 'carry letters = postman', which is rare and unproductive in English, despite examples like *spoilsport* or Khmer *khɔh trɔw* 'wrong right = morality', which are non-existent in English.

1. SEMANTIC FUNCTOR. What the functor is in any given compound seems to depend on the word-classes involved in the compound. In Italian *portalettere*, the functor is *porta-*; in *blackbird* the functor is probably *black*, so that in *windmill* it is probably *wind*; in *downfall* the functor is *fall*; in Khmer *khɔh trɔw* it is not clear that there is a functor. In general, it seems that we need to look at the relationships between the word-classes in equivalent syntactic constructions to determine what the functor is in a compound. There does not seem to be any generalisation across compounds as such.

2. MORPHOSYNTACTIC LOCUS. It has already been argued that this criterion is of dubious value in either syntax or derivational morphology, and accordingly it must be ignored here.

3. SUBCATEGORISAND. It is not clear that there is a generalisation across compounds here, either. In synthetic compounds like *train driver* the verb *drive* has to be transitive to take part in the construction, and the first element must be the object of that verb (where it is not, as in *town crier*, we say that there is no synthetic compound; see below, Sections 3.6 and 5.4). But this implies that *drive*, which may not even be one of the elements of the compound, is the head of the compound, which is in itself a problematic conclusion. With A + N compounds like *blackbird*, it would normally be said that *bird* allows the presence of the adjective, as is the case in syntax. The same would be true if we allowed the adstantive analysis for compounds like *paintbox* (see above, Section 2.8). With examples like Khmer *khɔh trɔw* it is again not obvious that there is any subcategorisation. Basically, this criterion seems to work only sporadically.

4. GOVERNOR. There may be instances in some language where a particular element requires another element to be in a particular case, but I am not familiar with any such instance. In Germanic where there are linking elements, the form of the linking element is generally said to be determined by the first element (see Neef 2015, for instance). In languages where there is a fixed link, the link is determined by the construction rather than by the other element specifically (and the same is true where compounds have a specific stress or tonal pattern). This criterion does not seem to function.

5. DISTRIBUTIONAL EQUIVALENT. Distributional equivalence is the criterion which seems to be used most, and it is used in two different but overlapping ways. As in syntax, the head of the compound is usually said to be the element in the compound which determines the word-class of the whole compound. So in *blackbird, bird* is the head because *bird* and *blackbird* are both nouns. But in Khmer *khɔh trɔw* neither element can be said to be the head by this criterion, since neither determines the word-class of the whole. In *windmill* it might appear that either element of the compound could determine the fact that the compound is a noun, but on closer examination this is not true. If instead of a noun like *wind*, we consider a noun like *mouse* and think of the plural of a compound *house-mouse*, it is *house-mice*. So the compound as a whole is inflected as being in the same inflection class as *mouse*, so that must be the word which determines the word-class. In *windmill* we might not be able to tell definitively from the form, but it is consistent to see *mill* being the head by this criterion. Just what features percolate to the head in this manner is

not necessarily clear (Bauer 1990: 22–23), but they probably involve gender, number, tense, comparison – in other words, those connected with inflection class. Subcategorisation is not necessarily inherited: *go* is intransitive, but *undergo* is transitive, *dry* can be intransitive, but *blow-dry* cannot.

Words like *egghead* and *redcurrant* are headed by *head* and *currant* respectively according to this criterion. There are some apparently parallel words which are less obviously headed according to the same principle. The classic examples are the Toronto ice-hockey team the *Maple Leafs* (not the *Maple Leaves*) and *sabretooths* (not *sabreteeth*). But these examples are not typical (Bauer 2015b); variation in such forms is the order of the day, with regular inflection of forms which are names a better predictor than any other generalisation, but still far from perfect.

The alternative interpretation of this criterion, as was seen above in the case of derivatives, is the hyponymy criterion. Hudson (1987) terms this the 'kind of' criterion, and Allen (1978) calls it the 'ISA' criterion, but I will prefer the more technical 'hyponymy criterion'. According to this criterion, *mill* is the head of *windmill* (because *windmill* is a hyponym of *mill*), but *head* is not the head of *egghead*, because *egghead* is not a hyponym of *head*. This is the criterion that leads Bloomfield (1935) to distinguish between endocentric and exocentric compounds.

Although the distinction between endocentric and exocentric compound has been widely accepted in the literature, there have been a number of dissenting voices, including Coseriu (1977), Booij (2007), Barcelona (2008), Štekauer et al. (2012: 81) and Bauer (2016). The alternative view is that all those compounds which have been called exocentric are regular compounds which are interpreted according to some figure of speech, so that *egghead* is a case of synecdoche, *fire-dog* is a case of metaphor and *phone-neck* ('a pain caused by over-use of the phone') is a case of metonymy. I will retain the labels 'endocentric' and 'exocentric' for compounds defined by this hyponymy criterion, but note that saying that something has its centre by this definition in a particular position is not necessarily the same as saying that its head is in the same position. So in what follows a 'centre' is a semantic notion, while a 'head' is a grammatical one.

Part of the difficulty in any attempt to equate the centre and the head for compounds is what happens when there is no centre. This happens in a number of places with things which are classified as compounds, and the answer is not necessarily the same for all of these cases. We can consider a case like English *producer-director*, one like the Khmer *khɔh trɔw*, already cited (both these examples are coordinative, in that their meaning arises from a coordination of the two elements), cases like the English *egghead* and the English *blackhead* 'type of pimple', and a case like the Italian *portalettere*, also already cited, and a case like the English *downfall*, and finally, something which fails the hyponymy test for reasons of metaphor, such as *fire-dog*.

Fabb (1998: 67) comments on coordinative compounds that 'there is some reason to think of both words as equally sharing head-like characteristics'. This would include *producer-director* and *khɔh trɔw*. For other exocentrics, like *blackhead* and *egghead*, he says that these are 'without a head'. Katamba and Stonham (2006: 332) agree that exocentrics are headless (as do Adams 2001: 5, Carstairs-McCarthy 2002: 64 and Booij 2007: 78), but Katamba and Stonham say (2006: 333) that copulative compounds like *bitter-sweet* (and presumably *producer-director*, which is regularly put under this classification, a subtype of coordinative compound) are right-headed, because inflection is added to the righthand element. We have seen above that this criterion is not trustworthy and in this particular case would give a different result with Spanish examples like *niñas-prodigios* 'girls prodigies' (Scalise & Fábregas 2010: 114) where both elements are marked for plural. Semantically, Katamba and Stonham (2006: 334) say, such compounds have elements which are equivalent to each other. That is, that if you look away from the criterion of morphosyntactic locus, they do not appear to have any way of determining what is the head.

This is an astounding level of agreement from a rather superficial literature review. Unfortunately, it is not clear what it means for a construction to be headless, or for it to have two heads. If we look back to Jackendoff (1977: 29–30) we find the claim that 'each lexical category X defines a set of syntactic categories X′, X″...' which suggests that headedness is something that belongs to lexical categories as such (in which case both *black* and *head* in *blackhead* define syntactic categories which dominate them). An alternative interpretation might be that *black* and *head* in *blackhead* do not have lexical categories, only the compound *blackhead* has a lexical category, and only the compound can become part of the syntax. In effect, either of these seems to deny headedness a role below the level of the word. Note also that it is not clear from Jackendoff just how you can have two heads. Jackendoff (1977: 51) seems to allow for this in coordinate structures (which would correspond to coordinative compounds at levels below the word), but the two heads do not independently contribute to the greater syntactic construction.

Hudson (1993) states overtly that every phrase must have a head and that no phrase may have more than one head, but that is formulated within his own dependency theory, which is not accepted by all scholars. Other papers in the same volume suggest that at least noun phrases may have two heads (Radford 1993) or multiple heads (an idea which Payne 1993 sets out to argue against). An alternative view of this is that the notion of head should be split into several subsidiary notions (Zwicky 1993). This seems to resonate with the evidence from morphology. If we ignore the evidence from morphosyntactic locus as being too controversial (see above), then *producer-director* has two elements which might be the centre (as defined above in terms of hyponymy), *windmill* has one centre (*mill*), and *blackhead* and *egghead, portalettere* and *khɔh trɔw* have no centre. In terms of inheritance of word-class, *producer-director* has two potential sources of word-class (but *niñas-prodigios* has only one, because the compound has feminine gender, inherited from *niña*), *windmill, blackhead, egghead* have one each, and *portalettere* and *khɔh trɔw* have no such source. In terms of modificational structure (which element reduces the potential reference of the other), *producer-director* and *khɔh trɔw* have no head (though see just below for some discussion of *producer-director*), but *windmill, blackhead, egghead* and *portalettere* do have heads (*mill, head, head, porta-* respectively). There may be yet other senses of head which could be applied to these structures. While not all of the words have the same head according to each of these criteria, each of them has at least one head by at least one criterion, and the cases where there are two heads are cases of coordination (as is also the case in syntax).

In other words, we have two possibilities here. Either we deny the application of the notion of headedness to the internal structure of words (including compounds), or we realise that there may be multiple head-like notions applying within a word. If we accept the second of these, we have to be very careful with the term 'head'.

It is worth examining in rather more detail compounds like *producer-director* in English. Bauer (2010a: 206) cites the example in (2).

(2)   'I am a lawyer-musician, not a musician-lawyer', he says, 'My calling is the law'. (members.chello.nl/cvanderlely/pearls/articles/lawjournal.html Accessed 11 Mar. 2008)

This seems to imply that (at least some) speakers view the left-hand member of such constructions as being the more important part (and thus the head?). The example indicates that linguists must not be too hasty in assigning headedness (or in failing to assign headedness) on the basis of grammatical principles without considering usage.

On the other hand, a very small-scale pilot test on a class of psycholinguistics students found that when asked to place items like *red-orange, green-blue* on a colour chart, their answers did not differ significantly from those given in response to items like *orange-red* and *blue-green* (I should like to thank Paul Warren for running the experiment). This seems again to suggest an equivalence between the two members of such items and thus, perhaps, support dual-headedness. It might be that more sophisticated analysis including tracking the trajectory taken by the mouse in responding to such items, for example, would give different answers, but the superficial analysis does not pull out either element as the semantic centre.

6. OBLIGATORY ELEMENT. This criterion works best where the compound has a centre: *mill* is clearly the obligatory element in the compound *windmill* and can replace *windmill* on all occasions. At another level, any noun can replace anything in the head of a noun phrase, so that *blackhead* can be replaced by a noun, which shares its nominal quality with one of the elements in *blackhead*. An example like *khɔh trɔw*, on the other hand, has no obligatory element.

We can now summarize the discussion as in Table 3.2.

Overall, this is less than helpful. We can see why most discussions of headedness in compounds restrict themselves to the hyponymy criterion (and, to a lesser extent, the word-class inheritance criterion).

Given this result, the potential of saying that headedness does not apply to compounds (or more generally to morphological structures) must surely be a very strong one. The hyponymy criterion has some application to compounds but does not extend easily to derivational morphology (and the same is true with obligatoriness). The inheritance of word-class has some application to both derivational morphology and compounding.

Table 3.2 *Summary of headedness criteria in compounding*

Semantic functor	Criterion not helpful
Morphosyntactic locus	Criterion unusable
Subcategorisand	Criterion not helpful
Governor	Criterion not helpful
Distributional equivalent	Criterion splits into several subcriteria: semantic centre, word-class head (inheritance of word-class), and others. These do not agree and do not apply to all compounds.
Obligatory element	This seems to follow the criterion of distributional equivalence

If a form such as *portalettere* does not gain its nominal features from any element that occurs in the morphology, then we need to consider where those nominal features arise from. The obvious answer is that they arise from the construction. That is, in Italian there is a construction of the form $V + N_i > N_j$ such that the gender of N_j is largely predictable on the basis of information about the referent of N_j (von Heusinger & Schwarze 2013). Furthermore the semantics of the construction are approximately equivalent to 'someone or something that Vs N_is at some appropriate level of generalisation' (the 'level of generalisation' being read as 'professionally', 'regularly', 'by design' etc. – this is no different from most word-formation constructions; see below, Section 4.2). If we can do all of that with the construction, then it may also be possible to extend the notion of construction to cover so-called endocentric N + N compounds in English (like *windmill*) without specifically dealing with the notion of head at all. The construction would need to say $N_x + N_y > N_z$ such that N_z is a hyponym of N_y and of the same grammatical class as N_y. Booij (2009: 204) gives a more or less equivalent formulation but does not point out that it obviates the need for a notion of head. Constructions could also be formulated to account for the exocentric compounds, of various kinds.

If some notion of head is to be retained, on the other hand, it needs to be made clear that the derivational head is not the same as the head in a compound is not the same as a syntactic head. In that case we need to distinguish between a syntactic head, a semantic centre (defined by hyponymy), a grammatical centre (defined by word-class inheritance) and perhaps other kinds of head-features aligned with factors which might be considered to define or contribute to the "headedness" in compounds.

Either of these solutions is presumably workable. Each may bring different benefits to the overall description of compounds. In theories in which roots have no categorical marking inheritance has to be interpreted differently from the way in which it is interpreted in other theories, but the same comment is still valid.

3.3   Binarity

The minimum compound, being made up of lexemes (plural), contains two lexemes, as in *windmill*. It is thus trivial that if we want to draw a tree structure for such a compound, it will be a binary tree. But it is widely claimed that most compounds have a binary structure. Even a compound like that in (3) has a binary structure, which, in English, the hyphenation indicates.

(3)   He was the groundsman, handyman, **if-there's-any-sort-of-difficulty-ask-William-and-he'll-fix-it-for-you person** about the place. (Meynell, Lawrence. 1978. *Papersnake*. London: Macmillan, p. 10)

Here the two parts of the compound are the sentence, *if there's any sort of difficulty ask William and he'll fix it for you* and the noun *person*.

Perhaps strangely, the notion of compounds having binary structure does not seem to be controversial. The well-known exception is provided by coordinative compounds. Some examples are given in (4).

(4)   That's a question you cannot ask a lawyer. Or even teacher-lawyers. Or even builder-teacher-lawyers. (Vitachy, Nury. 2008. *Mr Wong goes west*. Crows Nest, NSW: Allen & Unwin, p. 83)
         . . . to bask in the painter-writer-musician glamour of the place. . . (Block, Lawrence. 1999. *The burglar in the rye*. Harpenden, Hants.: No Exit, p. 9)
         The best actors in the world, either for tragedy, comedy, history, pastoral, pastoral-comical, historical-pastoral, tragical-historical, tragical-comical-historical-pastoral, scene individable, or poem unlimited. (Shakespeare, William. 1603. *Hamlet* Act 2 Sc. 2)

While the first example in (4) seems to imply a structure [*builder* [*teacher lawyer*]], this is a local decision based on the context, not something based on the linguistic structure inherent in the elements. We cannot assume either [*painter* [*writer musician*]] or [[*painter writer*] *musician*] and must take it that all of the relevant items in these examples are on an equivalent level. This is generally also what is done in syntax when items are coordinated. We can thus see it as a general exception brought about by coordination, rather than a strange kind of compound.

A different kind of problem is raised by French examples such as *pomme de terre* 'apple of earth = potato', *chemin de fer* 'way of iron = railway'. If these were syntactic chains, they would have to be analysed as [*pomme* [$_{PP}$ *de* [$_{NP}$ *terre*]]] with no more than a binary division, but there is some dispute in the literature as to whether these constructions are lexical or syntactic, given the idiomatic nature of some of them, which implies listedness (in other words, the same controversy faces these constructs as faces compounds in English as to whether they are words or not). If they are morphological structures, the answer is less clear: the syntactic analysis might still rule, or different rules might apply. The same is presumably true of the examples like those in (5).

(5)   "'I'll be go-to-helled'" she said. (Buchanan, Edna. 1996. *Act of betrayal*. London: Simon & Schuster, p. 105)
         What was he? Her ex? Her erstwhile lover? Her lover-in-abeyance?
         (McDermid, Val. 2006. *The grave tattoo*. London: HarperCollins, p. 5)

... to indulge your carnal appetite in exchange for a little looking-the-other-way. (Hammond, Gerald. 2004. *Dead letters*. London: Allison & Busby, p. 87)

The example in (6) is more worrying. The compound is a cut-down version of the proverb *throw the baby out with the bathwater* and seems to be interpreted as [[*baby bathwater*] *tossers*], where *baby bathwater* is a coordinative compound and the whole is synthetic, but there is something odd with the construction, to the extent that I am not convinced it is grammatical. The interpretation above retains binary branching but might be erroneous.

(6)   Both ... were ... overly focused baby-bathwater-tossers. (Kellerman, Jonathan. 2003. *The conspiracy club*. London: Headline, p. 6)

A construction like *forget-me-not* also looks as though it might not be binary, since there is at least an argument that the negative and the direct object independently modify the verb. The question here is whether *forget-me-not* is a compound. We will return to this question later (see Section 3.5.3).

For the most part, then, binarity seems to be the rule. Adams (2001: 3) seems to imply that all coordinative constructions are phrases and not compounds. Her argument for this is that coordinative compounds are not right-headed (see the discussion in Section 3.2 above). For her, then, there would be no non-binary compounds.

If we include coordinative items such as *producer-director* as compounds, binarity seems less of a feature of compounds. We should also remember that for many syntacticians, all trees (except where coordination is involved) are binary, in which case the binarity of compounds is not surprising. We can link this back to the discussion of headedness in the sense that if compounds are made up of a head element and a modifying element, then binarity allows a representation of this. However, if compounds are said not to have a head, this justification would fail.

3.4   Recursion

If we assume a construction of the type given in Section 3.2.3 so that $N_x + N_y > N_z$, there is no apparent reason why N_x or N_y cannot be filled by an N which is the output of such a construction. That is, we might expect to be able to find compounds like [[*road-side*] *restaurant*] or [*computer* [*keyboard*]] and even more complex examples such as [[[*Rugby* [*World Cup*]] [*opening night*]] [*traffic chaos*]] (Radio New Zealand Morning Report, 13 Sept. 2011 – the bracketing may be disputed, but the binarity is not controversial). The fact that we readily find such examples in Germanic languages seems to justify the assumption. However, the Germanic languages are not necessarily typical. Mukai (2008: 194) lists Latin and the Romance languages as not having recursive compounds (though see examples below in this section), Štekauer et al. (2012: 97), while concentrating on languages that do show recursion, comment that recursiveness is 'is in principle unproductive' in Slavic (specifically in Slovak and Russian except in some compound adjectives).

If compounding as a process were purely syntactic, then we would not expect to be able to restrict the recursive principle. Recursion is perhaps the main means whereby languages can produce an indefinite number of sentences from a limited number of input elements ('infinite use of finite means' – von Humboldt). Since syntactic rules are not expected to be subject to idiosyncratic restrictions, a syntactic rule limiting recursion within some structures would be unusual. Pöll (2015) considers a number of factors which have been suggested as limiting recursion but finds that none of them seem to be decisive. We are thus left with a puzzle.

To indicate something of the extent of the descriptive problem here, standard descriptions of thirty-seven languages were considered. The languages concerned are presented in Table 3.3 and were chosen as having accessible descriptions but providing a genetic and geographic spread.

Of these languages, those marked with an asterisk were specifically said not to have compounds. The ones marked with a plus-sign were said to allow recursion or illustrated with an example of recursion. For the others, information on recursion was missing, although the languages had (at least some) compounds. This does not mean that none of these languages has recursive compounds. Despite the view espoused by Mukai (2008), cited above, that Romance languages do not have recursive compounding, Štekauer et al. (2012: 98) cite Spanish *limpia[para-brisas]* 'cleans-stops-breeze = windscreen wipers'. Bisetto (2010) adds Italian *porta[asciuga-mani]* 'carry dry hands = towel-holder', a construction she finds surprising.

If we take the findings of the small experiment described above at face value, we would have to conclude that there are at least some languages which do have compounding but do not have recursive compounding. This seems to imply that in such languages that compounds, once formed, are listed and then used as vocabulary items which are fixed and not extendable. We would need to ask to what extent compounds in such languages can be extended by derivational means. In the Slavic languages, for instance, this is perfectly possible: consider Russian *les·o·step'* 'forest·LE·steppe' gives *les·o·step·n·oy* 'forest·LE·steppe·ADJLZ·M.NOM.SG', or Slovak *slovotvorba* 'word-formation'

Table 3.3 *Languages used for the investigation of recursion* (for symbols see the text)

Abkhaz (West Asia)	+
Babungo (Africa)	+
Basque (Europe)	+
Cantonese (SE Asia)	+
Diyari (Australia)	*
Finnish (Europe)	+
Fore (Papua New Guinea)	
Hebrew (West Asia)	+
Hindi (S Asia)	
Hixkaryana (S America)	*
Japanese (SE Asia)	+
Kalkatungu (Australia)	
Kayardild (Australia)	
Khmer (SE Asia)	
Kiowa (N America)	+
Kobon (Papua New Guinea)	
Malayalam (S Asia)	+
Mam (S America)	
Mangarayi (Australia)	*
Maori (Pacific)	+
Nama (Africa)	
Osage (N America)	
Quechua (S America)	
Seroi (Papua New Guinea)	
Tariana (S America)	
Thai (SE Asia)	
Tiwi (Australia)	*
Toba-Batak (Pacific)	+
Tswana (Africa)	
Tümpisa Shoshone (N America)	
Turkana (Africa)	
Urarina (S America)	+
Ute (Central America)	
Welsh (Europe)	
West Greenlandic (N America)	*
Yidiɲ (Australia)	
Yimas (Papua New Guinea)	

gives *slovotvorný* 'word-formational'. It may well be the case that the availability of very productive adjectivalisation processes means that recursiveness in compounds is not needed: any compound that has to modify another word can be turned into the appropriate part of speech to allow the modification. Moreover, the use of adjectives provides information on constituency, which may be lacking in a compound.

In order to get recursion, it seems to me that two things are required: a very productive pattern of compounding and some very well-established (perhaps lexicalised) examples created from that same pattern. *Limpia-para-brises* is possible because *para-brises* is well-established and because this pattern of compounding is productive in Spanish. There are not many such examples because of the lack of an onomasiological requirement for the names of people or machines which do things to people or machines named by this process. With N + N sequences, this need tends to be greater. Bisetto (2010) suggests that recursion may also be limited by qualia roles in some languages but not in others. If this is true, it might help explain why so few of the languages listed above are said to allow recursion. It also opens up the possibility that there are other semantic constraints on recursion, also varying from language to language. Such points would merit further investigation.

3.5   The Interpenetration of Compounding and Syntax

There are several ways in which compounding seems to get mixed in with syntax, and three separate types will be considered here: the use of syntactic constructions in the modifying element of a compound, the interpenetration of noun phrases into compounds, and words which derive entirely from phrases.

3.5.1   Phrases as Modifiers in Compounds

An example like (4) has already shown that syntactic constructions can form the modifying part of a compound, and such examples are not unusual in many languages. Some examples are given in (7).

(7)   a. ... his white lab coat starched to the **it-could-stand-alone state** (Temple, Lou Jane. 1998. *Bread on arrival*. New York: St Martin's, p. 94)
           b. She was dressed all in black – not a scruffy, Camden, **it-doesn't-show-the-stains-and-hides-my-fat-black**, but a designer-label **it-allows me-to-express-my-elegant-simplicity sort** of black. (Henderson, Lauren. 1996. *Too many blondes*. London: Hodder & Stoughton, p. 151)
           c. kulturen-ud-til-folket-idealister (Danish: culture.DEF out to people.DEF idealists; cited in Bauer 1978)
           d. our fear-of-terrorist-atrocity society. (Francis, Dick. 2006. *Under orders*. London: Michael Joseph, p. 87)
           e. de wie-heeft-het-gedaan-vraag (Dutch: the who did it question; Booij 2002: 148)

   f. Berg-und-Tal-Bahn (German: mountain and valley railway, 'roller coaster'; Fleischer & Barz 2007: 123)

   g. komochtagmigomdukanminen (Swedish: come and get me if you can expression.DEF; cited in Bauer 1978)

   h. Hann er svona 'eg-veit-þetta-allt-typa' (Icelandic: He is such a 'I know everything' type; Þorsteinn G. Indriðason 2000: 191 fn)

Just how these items are to be dealt with is not clear. The English items are usually seen as compounds (see e.g. Bauer et al. 2013: 488), and that may be justified by appeal to the other Germanic languages, where the orthography shows these to be considered as single words (the hyphenation in the first example in (7b) seems to be an error in English, but the normal marking for other languages). It would, however, be possible to argue that in English these are rank-shifted adjectives (that is syntactic structures used as adjectives), and that the rank-shift, while it has the effect of creating words, is not a word-formation strategy. This solution is not possible in the other Germanic languages, where pre-nominal adjectives inflect, but words within a compound do not (to oversimplify). It is sometimes claimed that only fixed expressions can be used in compounds like this (Bresnan & Mchombo 1995: 194, Carstairs-McCarthy 2005), but the examples in (7) seem to show this not to be the case. Not only are the expressions not item-familiar, they are not always constituents (as is shown by the example in (7d) and the Danish example in (7c)). Indeed, more than that, they are not always whole syntactic structures. The example (7d) shows that with the lack of an article before *terrorist atrocity*, and we find similar examples in the examples in (8), all of which have no determiners where they would be required in the syntax. Example (8a) is standard French, (8b) is German, from Meibauer (2007), and (8c) is cited by Ménová (2012) from the British *Daily Mail*.

(8)   a. fin-de-siècle 'end of century'
      b. die Affe-auf-Schliebstein-Position 'the ape-on-grindstone position'
      c. teenage-boy-on-motorbike side

Because it is not entirely clear how such items are to be dealt with, just how they are modelled in the grammar is equally unclear. The phrasal modifiers may not be lexicalised, but are they seen as direct quotations, for instance? The examples in (8) argue against such a position. In any theory that has a modular approach to morphology and syntax, if these things are compounds and if compounds are morphological, then there must be a loop between the syntactic module and the morphological module, but again the examples in (8) argue against such a position. There are, of course, several escape routes here. Perhaps these are not compounds, perhaps they are compounds, but compounds are syntactic, perhaps the modifiers are simply embedded as phonetic strings in the larger word without any grammatical analysis. Some of these escape routes may be blocked by the fact that phrases are also found as bases in affixal word-formation (Bauer et al. 2013: 513–514), but there are enough for it to be difficult to draw firm conclusions on the basis of evidence of this kind.

Nevertheless, the very existence of expressions of this type does raise a question: where does the type stop? Are any of the examples in (9) examples of the same type, and is there a borderline between structures of the type in (7) and more straightforward recursive compounds? I have no answer to these questions, but they are clearly of importance in determining the extent of compounding in English or other languages.

(9)   I steered the **sick-parrot lady** into the entrance hall. (Francis, Dick. 1991.
        Comeback. London: Michael Joseph, p. 74)
        it is a simple **Yes-No decision** (BNC)
        This can be a **'strap-on' boss** or a self-locking boss (BNC)
        They can be added to **stir-fry vegetables** at the end of cooking (BNC)
        The Commission suggests setting up **red squirrel protection areas** (BNC)
        Atomic power stations to be built in areas of outstanding natural
        beauty (BNC)
        QEB considered a report on the **school teacher fellowship scheme** (BNC)

Giegerich (2015: 118) suggests that what he calls 'anaphoric compounds', and what ten Hacken (2013: 39) calls 'deictic compounds', following Downing (1977), behave differently from 'listed' compounds in respect of how much syntax they allow within them. Listed compounds may allow limited phrasal modification as long as the phrase is itself item-familiar (see Bell 2014), as in *atomic power station*, where *atomic power* is itself a familiar collocation. Because of the requirement that such modifiers should be item-familiar, they are unlikely to be long, and so sentence-length modifiers, for example, will be restricted to deictic compounds. This explains the Bresnan and Mchombo and Carstairs-McCarthy position and also the exceptions to it. Longer compounds, like longer phrases, are unlikely to be as item-familiar as short ones. Correspondingly, long compounds are likely to be deictic compounds, while short compounds may be listed or deictic. The same is true of derivatives. The word *dancer* is listed in (10) but deictic in the (unattested) (11).

(10)   Madonna caressed the thigh and slapped the buttocks of a lingerie-clad
        female dancer (BNC)

(11)   The dancers had just bowed to their partners at the start of the Dashing White
        Sergeant when the door burst open.

That does not allow us to distinguish between long compounds and compounds including syntactic phrases, so that it may not be clear which category the items in (9) belong to. All we can say is that the less familiar the modifier is, the more likely it is that the compound containing it is a deictic one.

Being a deictic compound, though, should not necessarily be interpreted as indicating that the fundamental rules of construction are any different from those of any other compound. Deictic compounds are nonce-formations par excellence, and, as pointed out by Brekle (e.g. 1973: 2, 1978: 70) nonce formations are the best guide to the way in which word-formation works. If the two are distinct, there is an implication that *catch-as-catch-can syndrome* is a possible listed compound, while *failed-back-surgery syndrome* is not (examples from Bauer et al. 2013: 488). If there is a real distinction here, it may well arise because once a compound is listed, all its elements are also listed.

3.5.2 Phrases in Non-Modifying Position

A rather different problem arises in studies following from Chomsky & Halle (1968), where stress is taken as being a defining feature of compounds. Even if we do not wish to view stress as criterial for compounding, we can see a difference in stress in *black bird* and *blackbird*, which Chomsky and Halle term a difference between 'main stress' and 'compound stress'. There is a difference between *black bird nest* 'a bird nest which is black' and *blackbird nest* 'the nest of a blackbird', which in this tradition is explained as in (12).

(12) [black [bird nest]$_N$]$_{NP}$ [[black bird]$_N$ nest]$_N$
assign primary stress to each relevant item

  1   1   1   1   1   1
[black [bird nest]$_N$]$_{NP}$ [[black bird]$_N$ nest]$_N$
in innermost brackets, confirm leftmost stress in N, and reduce other stresses by one

  1   1   2   1   2   2
[black [bird nest]$_N$]$_{NP}$ [[black bird]$_N$ nest]$_N$
remove internal brackets, confirm leftmost stress in N and rightmost stress in NP

  2   1   3   1   3   3
[black bird nest]$_{NP}$ [black bird nest]$_N$

Next consider the example in (13).

(13) the National Science Foundation's commitment to discovery-based learning is the National **Science Digital Library** (COCA)

If we deal with the item in bold in (13) in the same way, we get the result in (14).

(14)   [Science [Digital Library]_{NP}]_N

assign primary stress to each relevant item

$$1 \qquad 1 \qquad 1$$

[Science [Digital Library]_{NP}]_N

in the innermost brackets, confirm leftmost stress in N, and rightmost stress in NP, and reduce other stresses by one

$$1 \qquad 2 \qquad 1$$

[Science [Digital Library]_{NP}]_N

remove internal brackets, confirm leftmost stress in N and rightmost stress in NP

$$1 \qquad 3 \qquad 2$$

[Science Digital Library]_N

The system works and provides the correct output. However, we now have an NP with an N. Here compound and phrase have been defined phonologically, but the outcome is syntactically odd.

3.5.3   Words from Phrases

There is a small number of words which appear to be derived directly from phrases. Some examples from English are given in (15) (see also the examples in (5)).

(15)   altogether
attorney general
bullseye
couldn't-care-less (as in *a couldn't-care-less attitude*)
downunder
dyed-in-the-wool
forget-me-not
go-faster (as in *go-faster stripes*)
good-for-nothing
has-been
heartsease
into
jack-in-the-box
love-lies-bleeding
man of the moment
man-at-arms
mother of pearl
rough-and-tumble
thank you
touch-and-go
wannabe
whosoever

The examples in (15) are very varied in their word-class and composition, but they all seem to be instances of words whose structure is phrasal. For some authorities (e.g. Erben 1975, Neef 2009) these words are compounds, for others, (e.g. Carstairs-McCarthy 2002: 67, who calls them 'phrasal words') they are not. The German term for such constructions is *Zusammenrückung* 'jolting together, juxtaposition'. In the French literature these are called 'conglomerations' (*conglomorés*), following Benveniste (see Ballier 2015). The most common English term – a diachronic term which can also be used synchronically – seems to be 'univerbation'.

If items such as these are compounds, it is because they are lexical items composed of more than one lexeme. If they are not, it is presumably because they are created by a process other than composition. Just what that process is may well be controversial. In Systemic Functional Grammar, the phenomenon is known as 'rank-shift', a concept which has not transferred to other theories of grammar. But even if we accept the notion of rank-shift, its borders may be difficult to determine. Is *iron* in *iron bar* a rank-shifted noun, for example, or is it simply a noun (used in a recursive structure), or has it become an adjective? Without definitions which clarify these differences, it is not even clear that we can pose the question. Yet, again, it is crucial for the theory of compounding. If we view univerbation as a diachronic process rather than a synchronic one, then it is the result of frequency of collocation, a matter of perception, perhaps, more than a linguistic change. Whatever we decide here, we then really need to determine what a process of composition is, to draw the distinction.

The difference between 'being made up of two or more lexemes' and 'being produced by a process of composition' is of importance in other places as well. Marchand's (1969: 100) statement that '[v]erbal composition does not exist in Present-Day English' is possible only because an item like *stagemanage* is not created by modifying *manage* by *stage*, but by back-formation from *stagemanager*. That is, Marchand has perceived a compound as the result of a process of composition rather than as an output type. Either view is presumably perfectly justifiable, and it may not be possible to say that either is the only correct solution, but the difference to what 'a compound' is may be quite extensive. It so happens that in English we have sufficient information to distinguish the two diachronic processes: I would expect that in some languages such information is not available, and output form would be the only available criterion.

3.6 Exploiting Argument Structure

Some compounds exploit argument structure or verbal diathesis in the sense that they are produced using lexemes which are determined by the semantic structure of the verb involved (a case can be made for other word-classes showing argument structure, but we need not consider those in detail here) or interpreted in terms of the semantic structure of the verb. Although the semantic structure of the verb is lexically determined (as is well-known *give* allows an indirect object, while *donate* requires a preposition *to*: **He donated the museum his paintings*), the structure which arises from this is usually viewed as syntactic, since it involves syntactic roles such as subject and object. Argument structure intersects with compounding in two places: with so-called 'synthetic compounds' and with incorporation. Synthetic compounds will be dealt with in more detail later in terms of their semantic structure (see Section 4.5). In general terms I avoid discussion of incorporation in this book, since the subject is too involved and not crucial in the languages which are most in question in this discussion. However, in order to delimit my topic here I present a very brief comment on incorporation and its importance for the grammar of compounding.

There is wide agreement that incorporation is a type of compounding (Geerdts 1998: 84, Haspelmath 2002: 86, Bauer 2003: 44), although it involves some syntactic features. In canonical incorporation, the noun which would be the direct object of the verb in a syntactic construction is built into the verb. A simple example from Nahuatl (a Uto-Aztecan language of Mexico, taken from Geerdts 1998) is provided in (16).

(16)   a.   ni·c·qua   in   nacatl
            I·it·eat   the   flesh
            'I eat the flesh'
       b.   ni·naca·qua
            I·flesh·eat
            'I eat flesh, I am a meat-eater'

Canonically, incorporation is a feature of polysynthetic languages, but it is also found in others, including largely isolating languages like Maori (the indigenous language of New Zealand; W. Bauer 1997). What happens to the noun is, again canonically, that it loses any inflectional marking it might otherwise have carried, including case marking; it does not refer to any particular entity, but has generic reference, non-specific and indefinite; it cannot itself be modified or take determiners; and in many cases it is extremely productive, perhaps automatically so. In all these ways, incorporation behaves just like compounding. But, just as was shown earlier (in Chapter 2) that there are places where such canonical behaviour is not observed in compounds, so there are exceptions with incorporation. In Maori (W. Bauer 1997: 316) and Greenlandic (Sadock 1986: 23) the incorporated noun may be modified; in

Southern Tiwa (a Kiowa-Tanoan language of the United States, Mithun 2000: 925) the incorporated noun may take a determiner and so be referential (see also Sadock 1986); in Tiwi (an Australian language, Osborne 1974: 48, 50) not all nouns can be incorporated, and body part nouns can incorporate only with a very few verbs; and there are many languages which can incorporate words other than nouns (Mithun 2000) or where an incorporated noun need not be the direct object of the verb (Geerdts 1998: 86–87).

Incorporation appears rather more syntactic than other types of compounding (see Sadock 1986 and Geerdts 1998) in that

- The incorporated noun is usually chosen on the basis of its syntactic role;
- The process of incorporation typically makes a transitive verb intransitive;
- The incorporated nouns appears to be moved into the verb-word from elsewhere in the sentence;
- Incorporation can be used to highlight the words in certain syntactic positions and so acts similarly to syntactic topicalisation processes (Mithun 2000: 918);
- Incorporation sometimes allows otherwise syntactic phenomena such as gapping;
- The incorporated noun may be the head of an NP;
- The new verb has not only verbal meaning, but includes the meaning of one of its arguments; this argument, however, does not trigger object-agreement in languages which have such a feature (Geerdts 1998: 88). Because incorporation changes a verb from transitive to intransitive, it may also cause a change to the case-marking of the subject of the verb.

Some other kinds of compounding, especially synthetic compounding, and indeed some kinds of derivation, share some of these features, but the interplay of syntactic matters and lexical matters is particularly striking in incorporation.

3.7   The Grammatical Function of Compounds

The canonical modifier of a noun is an adjective, the canonical modifier of an adjective or of a verb is an adverb. While it is not the case in English, in many languages this canonical status is shown by specific morphology. Consider another Germanic language, Danish, for instance. Attributive adjectives are marked in definite constructions, in plural constructions, and in agreement with indefinite singular neuter nouns, as shown in (17).

(17) a. en rød bog
          a.NON-NEUT red book (*bog* is non-neuter, so *rød* is unmarked)
       b. et rød·t hus
          a.NEUT red·NEUT house
       c. rød·e hus·e
          red·PL house·PL
       d. det rød·e hus
          the.NEUT red·DEF house

Because word-classes are an intrinsic part of lexemes in Danish, only adjectives can take the adjectival inflection, so that no other word-class can be used to modify a noun. However, nouns and verbs regularly modify nouns. The only way they can do this, though, is by forming compounds (Klinge 2005). Thus we find examples like those in (18).

(18) *dag-bog* 'day book = diary', *hønse-hus* 'chicken house = hen house'
       gå-gade 'go street = pedestrian precinct', *sove-pose* 'sleep bag = sleeping bag'

In such a system, it might seem that there is no need for adjectives to modify nouns in compounds. But that has the function of changing a gradable adjective into a classifying adjective, as illustrated in (19).

(19) *en lille bil* 'a little car', *en lillebil* 'a taxi'; *en rød kål* 'a red cabbage' (could have been dyed red), *en rødkål* 'a red cabbage' (a specific type of plant, contrasted in Danish with *hvidkål* 'white cabbage'); *små kager* 'small cakes', *småkager* 'biscuits, cookies'.

This is a simplified view of the situation in Danish, which is complicated by other types of compounding and compounding with other types of adjective. Nevertheless, we can see this as the kind of input English might have inherited from Germanic. English, though, lost the morphological marking which delimits the system in Danish.

Clearly, this is not necessarily the only way in which compounding can arise cross-linguistically. Nonetheless, there may be some truth in the notion that we view constructions with non-canonical patterns of modification of one word by another as compounds. To the extent that this is true, then processes which allow for such outcomes are compounding processes. We shall return to this view of the function of compounds later (Section 7.1).

4   *The Semantics of Compounds*

4.1   Introduction

The semantics of compounding has always been a puzzle to linguists. The ancient Sanskrit grammarians provided a classification of compounds based on semantic factors; in the twentieth century, analysts tried to account for semantic differences with distinct underlying grammatical patterns; most classifications today still make important distinctions between endocentric, exocentric and coordinative compounds. Such distinctions are based on notions of headedness, which was discussed more fully in Section 3.2; in this chapter, the semantic effects of those distinctions will be considered. Most of the work that has been done of the semantics of compounding has been done on noun compounds; here verb and adjective compounds will also be considered (adverb compounds and preposition compounds are much rarer than these main three types, and thus harder to discuss). The leitmotif of the chapter will turn out to be variability of semantic interpretation.

Before looking at the semantics of individual patterns of compounding, though, attention will be given to those semantic features of compounds which seem to derive from the fact that compounding is a type of word-formation.

4.2   Semantic Features of Word-Formation

There are some semantic features which seem to apply equally to derivatives and to compounds, and which might thus be thought of as features associated with word-formation in general. In general terms these have to do with the lack of features of clauses, features like negation, tense, aspect and modality. In many cases it is possible to override the lack of these features in word-formation by specific lexical means, and these will be mentioned.

4.2.1   Negation
The relationships implicit in word-formation are positive unless specifically overruled by negative markers. That is, there are no forms such as *driver* which

mean 'a person who does not drive', nor compounds such as *library book* which mean 'a book which is not found in a library'. Where negation is required it has to be explicit, as in *unhappy, non-negotiable*, or, for compounds, as in the example in (1).

(1)   Since when did you do no-result no-fee jobs? (Hill, Reginald. 1999. *Singing the sadness*. London, HarperCollins, p. 111)

Even where the negation is explicit, it need not always mean precisely the same thing: a *non-person* is a person, *unhappy* is on a scale which also includes *happy, not happy* and *not unhappy* (and possibly *sad*), while *non-negotiable* is the converse of *negotiable* (see the discussion in Bauer et al. 2013).

I have found only one possible exception, for which I have no direct reference. I have come across the item *fuss bus* with the explanation that the bus meant that there was no fuss. (There are multiple hits for *fuss bus* on Google, often in the expression *no fuss bus*, which is unexceptional, but I cannot now find a negative explanation of *fuss bus*.) I take this to be a genuine exception, though it might be argued that there is an underlying relationship of 'saves': the bus saves fuss.

4.2.2   Number

The general principle is that meaningful number marking does not occur within the word. We cannot contrast a *vacationer* who takes just one vacation with a **vacationser*, who takes more than one, or a *balloonist* who rides in a single balloon with a **balloonsist*, who rides in more than one, or even a *mouser* which catches one mouse with a **micer*, which catches many.

Where compounds are concerned, there are hosts of apparent counterexamples to this claim. Consider, for instance, the examples in (2).

(2)   a. 'Missy, what are you looking for back there . . .?'
            And she said, 'I'm looking for mice manure'. (Hillerman, Tony. 1999. *The first eagle*. London: HarperCollins, pp. 60–61)
        b. sometimes Doyle found coyote scat inside, sometimes mouse droppings. (COCA)

At first glance, it might appear that only one mouse was responsible for the droppings, but several provided the manure, but that is not right. Given *coyote scat*, there is no possibility of *coyotes scat*. The plural form *mice* is only possible because it is irregular.

Having said, that, though, there are also plenty of examples with apparent regular plurals. Some English examples are presented in (3).

(3)   arms control, communications technology, companies legislation, drugs
          problem, examinations board, letters column, textiles industry, tradesman,
          yachtsman

In some of these cases, the plural is used for semantic reasons which are not
connected to plurality. *Arms control* is connected to weapons, not to a body
part, while *arm control* would probably mean the opposite. *Drugs* seems to be
used as a modifier when illegal drugs are involved rather than when legal drugs
from the chemist's shop are involved. A *yachtsman* does not necessarily crew
more than one yacht, but the plural marker seems to be partly a function of the
element *-man* (*craftsman, marksman, oarsman, salesman, sportsman*),
although there are also examples with no plural (*boatman, ferryman, nurseryman, seaman* etc.). But *linesman* and *lineman* are alternative names for the
same profession, not distinguished by the number of lines involved. Although
it is not clear precisely what function the plural marking in such position has, it
does not seem to be to mark plurals as such.

The same is true if we look away from English. In Danish both *barne-*
'child' and *børne-* 'children' can be used in modifying position in compounds.
Sometimes it seems as though the difference is meaningful: *barnefødsel* 'child
birth' probably deals with the birth of one child at a time, while
børnebegrænsning 'children limitation = birth control' presumably deals with
the prevention of the births of many children. But the difference between
barneskol 'child school = infant's class' and *børnehave* 'children garden =
kindergarten' is hard to explain, and *barnebillet* 'child ticket' and *børnebillet*
'children ticket' both mean 'a reduced-price ticket'. In Dutch, Booij (2002:
147) points out that there are some compounds such as *huizen-rij* 'houses
row = row of houses', where the plural really does seem meaningful. He
suggests that the modifier in such cases is an NP. But Don (2009: 381) prefers
an alternative analysis where there is no semantic plural element in such forms.
In German there are occasional pairs such as *Landes·kunde* 'land.GEN.
SG·knowledge' versus *Länder·kunde* 'land.PL·knowledge' where the number
of countries (lands) involved is relevant, but at the same time there is *Land-
es·grenze* 'land.GEN.SG·border', which is inevitably a border between two
countries even though the singular is used, or (perhaps better, since with a
border only one side of it might be relevant) *Wort·schatz* 'word·treasure =
vocabulary' where multiple words must be involved, and the plural form of
WORT is found in other compounds, but the singular is employed. Libben
et al. (2009: 154) report that most German compounds whose first element is
homophonous with a plural form 'have definitely no plural meaning'. Even in
Faroese and Icelandic, where the linking-elements are living genitive markers

which also show number, there does not appear to be any reliable link with semantic number (Thráinsson et al. 2004: 206–208).

Yet the generalisation about the lack of plural marking within the word is wrong, as is shown by the examples in (4).

(4)   a. [T]heir relationship is sort of **Lord-of-the-Flies**-esque. (Sims,
         Elizabeth. 2010. *On location*. New York: Minotaur, p. 44)
      b. We were all heavily travelled and armed with cast-iron stomachs full of
         veteran **kill-all-intruders** bacteria ... (Evans, Jon. 2004. *Trail of the dead*.
         London: Hodder & Stoughton, p. 294)

The point about such examples is that there is some syntax within the word, and that word-internal syntax may demand plural marking. This point is valid for the points made in subsequent discussion as well and should be noted at this point as a principled exception. Further discussion of English compounds with plural first elements in English will be found in Section 6.4.

More remarkable are instances such as (5), which do not seem to be covered by the same regularity. Examples (5) and (6) are from Maori. In (5) the plural word *tamariki* 'children' is incorporated into the verb, as is shown by the corresponding sentence in (6) where *tamariki* is not incorporated, and there has to be a preposition marking the direct object and a determiner for the noun phrase.

(5)   E   rua   tekau   tau   a   ia   e   whakāwhānau
      NUM   two   ten   year   PERS   3SG   CONT-   cause.birth

      tamariki   ana
      children   -CONT

      'For twenty years she has been delivering children [into the world]' (from *The
      Dictionary of New Zealand Biography*, glosses from Winifred Bauer,
      personal communication)

(6)   E   rua   tekau   tau   a   ia   e   whakāwhānau
      NUM   two   ten   year   PERS   3SG   CONT-   cause.birth

      ana   i   ētahi   tamariki
      -CONT   DO   these   children

      'For twenty years she has been delivering these children [into the world]'

The Maori example may not be entirely convincing for a number of reasons: (a) *tamariki* is exceptional in marking number on the noun – number is usually only marked on the determiner in Maori, (b) *tamariki* has no gender-neutral singular form, (c) Maori orthography makes it look as though the incorporated direct object is a separate word, though the *e...ana* continuous marker brackets the verb (as can be seen in (5)). Nevertheless, number does appear to be meaningful here. However, such cases appear to be rare, since a general feature of incorporation (as of word-formation in general; see Section 3.6) is that the elements do no not refer to specific entities (Mithun 2000).

4.2.3 Tense

It does not appear to be possible to have a distinction between, say, *lover* and **loveder* such that the second means 'a person who used to love, an ex-lover'. Neither can the relationship between the elements of a compound be past or future: a *windmill* is not a mill that was once driven by the wind, nor one which will be driven by the wind.

This does not mean that there is no time associated with the relationship between the elements of words. The relationship is one which is true now because it is expected to be true across time. It is universal. Bauer (1978) glosses this as indication that the relationship is habitual/inherent/permanent (with different glosses fitting different cases). In most languages with tense systems, this would be encoded as present tense, but it is not encoded with a tense marker within words.

This relationship shows itself in different ways. With *-er* derivatives in English, for instance, there is often an implication that the person so designated has a job or profession, as in (7). In other cases, the base of the *-er* derivative denotes a typical or permanent character trait of the person or thing involved, as in (8). Sometimes this permanence can be seen in that we have an object which is designed for a particular purpose, as in (9).

(7) commissioner, confectioner, designer, developer, driver, drummer, farmer, labourer, piper, programmer, repairer, slaughterer, treasurer, trooper, waiter, wholesaler

(8) bungler, cheater, gambler, malingerer, philanderer, shirker, sniveller

(9) beater, browser, cruiser, eraser, fastener, muffler, strainer, stroller, sweetener

Even in instances where the denotation of the base makes a profession or a general characteristic seem unlikely, the inherence of the relationship can still be seen. Some examples are in (10).

(10) accuser, escaper, murderer, sleeper, smiler, winner

Most murderers, despite popular crime fiction, murder only once, yet by that single act (rather than a repeated and characteristic act) they are seen as being inherently connected with murder. Being a winner is not, for most of us, a profession, but something that we become only rarely. Yet the word *winner* forces us to see the relationship between the person and the winning as somehow inherent. Chaucer's 'the smiler with the knife' makes the smiling a typical facet of the person, but *smiler* would often refer to a transitory event, as in (11).

(11)   His image peered out at her, smiling wide, mouth open like the smiler was
        singing a promise song she couldn't hear (COCA)

Consider the following rather more extended example, from a philosophy paper.

(12)   A promise is defective if the thing promised is something the promisee does
        not want done, and it is further defective if the promisor does not believe that
        the promisee wants it done ... (Searle, John. 1965. What is a speech act? In
        Max Black (ed.), *Philosophy in America*, pp. 221–239. Ithaca: Cornell
        University Press)

In this example, at one level it seems as though the promisor and the promisee are individuals on a single occasion; at another, this is a generalisation across all instances of promises and so the habitual label fits again.

Despite this strong generalisation, Luschütsky and Rainer (2013: 1303) discuss two examples where they claim that tense is relevant in word-formation. First they cite England (1983: 119) on the distinction between *poom·b'il* 'place where rites are performed' and *jus·b'een* 'place that has been burned' in Mam (a Mayan language of Guatemala). But England terms the second of these constructions a 'resultant locative': it denotes a place that is of importance in context because of its having been burnt. Since the result is important, the action must, of necessity, have already taken place. They also cite Aikhenvald (2003: 465) on Tariana (an Arawakan language of Brazil). There *dihpanimi* (3SG.NON-F.work.LOC.NOM.PAST) 'the place where he used to work, the result of his work' contrasts with *dihpaniri* (3SG.NON-F.work. LOC.NOM.NON-PAST) 'the place where he is working, his work (as object)'. But despite Aikhenvald's glosses, which appear to focus on tense, the former affix is clearly resultative in nature, and again a result can only arise from an action which is completed, so that it is possible to see the distinction as being the difference, fundamentally, between a resultative affix and a locative affix. I therefore do not consider these to be serious threats to the generalisation that tense is not involved in word-formation.

4.2.4   *Other Verbal Categories: Mood, Aspect, Voice*

In general terms, it seems that these other verbal categories work in much the same way, but less reliably so: there are more exceptions here. There is a default reading of the output of the word-formation process which is unmarked for these categories and whose reading takes only the unmarked value for these categories. This can be overridden by overt marking of the category in some form, such as the use of the suffix *-able* in English which leads to a form with some modal reading (not always that which would be carried by the free form *able*).

There are, though, some examples which merit further investigation.

Consider, first, the example of aspect in Russian word-formation. Russian verbs show imperfective or perfective aspect. The perfective form of the verb is usually a prefixed form of the imperfective, though other formation types are found, especially ablaut. The aspect marker often carries derivational meaning over and above a simple aspectual difference, so that *podpisat'* 'to sign' is a perfective of *pisat'* 'to write'. Most agentive or instrumental nouns derived from verbs are derived from the imperfective (unmarked) verbs. For example, *uchitel'* 'teacher' derives from the imperfective *uchit'* 'to teach', and *dvigatel'* 'engine' derives from the imperfective *dvigat'* 'to move'. There, are, though, such words derived from perfective verbs, such as *narushitel'* 'violator', which is derived from the perfective verb *narushit'* 'to violate'. Since a violator is a person who has broken a law, rather than a person who habitually breaks laws (see the discussion of *murderer* above), this could be seen as a matter of verbal aspect being meaningful. A particularly nice minimal pair is provided by *spasatel'* 'lifeguard' from the imperfective form *spasat'* 'to save' contrasting with *spasitel'* 'saviour' from the old perfective form *spasiti* 'to save'. A lifeguard is person who regularly or professionally saves (imperfective) while a saviour is a person who has, on a specific occasion, saved (perfective).

The only blot in this landscape is that there are places where the perfective might be expected but the imperfective is used. For instance, *poluchatel'* 'recipient, payee', presumably so-called because they have received something, is based on the imperfective verb *poluchat'* (data from Natalia Beliaeva and Liza Tarasova, personal communication).

Although the facts are not entirely clear-cut, Russian seems to be a language where aspect can function meaningfully in word-formation. However, aspect in Russian is derivational, and thus rather more lexical than, say, tense in the same language. Derivational material may be found inside derivatives (as in *compar·abil·ity*) and inside compounds (as in *knowledge revolution*) so that the existence of derivational aspect, mood etc. within a compound is not unexpected or problematic. It may be that only material from the lexical end of the lexical-grammatical cline can be used meaningfully in word-formation. Examples of clearly inflectional morphology underlying word-formation would be rather more surprising. Note that the Russian example deals with derivation rather than compounding, and that we would expect derived words to be able to form elements of compounds on a par with other words. Aspect can be marked in compounds only insofar as it is marked on the elements of the compounds concerned.

Next consider voice. Kornfilt (1997: 460) distinguishes between two distinct patterns in Turkish:

> The suffix **-A(K)** derives adjectives ... related to the active voice of the basic verb:
>
> tirk   '(to) start; (to) shy'   tir-ek   'timid'
>
> ...
>
> The suffix **-GIn** derives adjectives whose meanings are ... related to the passive voice of the corresponding transitive verb ...
>
> sür   '(to) exile'   sür-gün   'exiled'

But although voice is an important part of the interpretation of the relevant suffixes here, there is no voice marking within the base for these affixes. Rather the active/passive interpretation can be assigned to the suffixes under discussion, just as the modal interpretation (and, indeed, the passive interpretation) can be assigned to the suffix *-able* in English. So this Turkish example, which at first looks like a counterexample to our generalisation, turns out not to be.

In French, compounds of the form V + N, like *ouvre-boîte* 'open-box = can-opener', have been given various interpretations over the years. One of these interpretations is that the verbal element is an imperative (see Bauer 1980, Fradin 2009). Most recent analyses reject this solution, although there are still several potential analyses in the current literature. Villoing (2009) provides a very thorough analysis of such words, where she argues for a position in which these forms are not imperatives, but stems representing the verbal lexeme. So a position whereby mood is expressed within the compound has, in the light of further research, been rejected in favour of one where no mood is involved.

4.2.5   Discussion

Of the many criteria that differentiate canonical derivation from canonical inflection is one that says that where both are present, inflectional markers occur further from the root than derivational markers. Thus, for example, in *sermon·ise·s* the inflectional *-s* is further from the root *sermon* than is the derivational affix *-ise*. At first glance, it would seem that the results above are guaranteed by this criterion. Certainly, this cuts down the number of potentially relevant examples. However, that is not necessarily the whole story. There is an argument that plural-marking is, in many languages, derivational rather than inflectional (see e.g. Beard 1982), and the Russian example in

Section 4.2.4 shows that where the relevant categories are derivational, they may well be overtly marked within other word-formation categories. In rather more general terms, the distinction between inflection and derivation is language-specific, and we cannot necessarily assume that it will apply, or apply in the same way, in individual languages. That is, we cannot generalize from Standard Average European languages to others and simply assume we will meet the same patterns.

More subtly, we have seen with the Turkish example in Section 4.2.4 that the semantics which in some places is associated with a particular inflectional category can, in cases of word-formation, be re-associated with derivational affixes. This may have the effect of making the general claim in this discussion vacuous. Another way of looking at this, however, is as a kind of markedness constraint. There is a default reading within word-formation which does not imply number, tense, negation etc.; overt marking of these categories is not always meaningful, as a result, although it may be; such readings may be required, and if they are there is a possibility that they will be overtly marked. Any occurrence of either marking of these categories or semantic interpretation using these categories is unexpected, but not impossible.

That is, it would be expected that some of these categories should be found in word-formation. If they are, they may be marked but asemantic, semantically present, but not overtly marked, or both marked and meaningful. But the default assumption is that word-formation builds on relationships which are positive, not specified for number (because general), unspecified for tense, aspect, mood, voice except in instances where phrasal material is used within word-formation.

4.2.6 *Naming versus Describing*

It is often claimed that instances of word-formation name, while syntactic constructions assert or describe (Downing 1977: 1, Levi 1978: 61, Grzega 2009: 217–218, Rae 2010: 21 and many others). There is clearly something to this idea, and not only because it is so widespread. One of the major functions of word-formation is to provide names for things which have no name, as dictionaries of neologisms show. Such works also show that there are other ways of creating new names, for example by figurative usage, but we are not concerned with such matters here. (For a more generalised approach to naming, see the onomasiological approach deriving from the work of Dokulil.) However, it is less clear that syntax only provides assertions or descriptions, and this brings us back to the whole question of the limits of morphology and the lexicon discussed in Chapter 2.

Consider, for example, the term *capital punishment. Capital* is syntactically very restricted: it cannot be submodified, for instance, nor can it be used predicatively without changing its meaning. This leads Giegerich (2015: 27) to suggest that adjectives like *capital* do not head adjective phrases. Giegerich also sees such adjectives as being lexical in nature. It is less clear that this means they are not syntactic (especially for Giegerich, who allows things to straddle both modules). If we ask whether *capital punishment* is a name or a description/assertion, it is not clear that there is an answer. It is the name for a set of procedures established for state justice systems, but it asserts that the punishment 'involv[es] loss of … life' (*OED*). Similarly, *railway* provides a name for a network of paired lines with certain functions but seems to assert that the way is somehow connected to rails. So while I am convinced that word-formation has a function of naming, I am not convinced that is the only way in which this function is carried out, and not convinced that this can be used as a criterion to distinguish morphology (or the lexicon) from syntax.

In this context, it also needs to be pointed out that names need not be permanent. In Downing's (1977) famous example of the *apple-juice seat, apple-juice seat* provides a name for a particular place at a particular table, but that name is of value only under a temporary set of pragmatic circumstances. No set of apple-juice seats is implied for language-users in general by the use of this name. Hypostatisation implies that there is a referent for the name *apple-juice seat*, but does not require that that name should have general, wide-spread and permanent value.

4.3   Centred or Not: Endocentric versus Exocentric

One of the major semantic divisions of compounds has been between endocentric and exocentric compounds. This distinction has already been introduced in Section 3.2.3. Endocentric compounds are hyponyms of their centre, exocentric compounds are not. Thus *windmill* is an endocentric compound because *windmill* is a hyponym of *mill*, but *blackhead* 'type of pimple' and French *ouvre-boîte* 'open-box = can-opener' are exocentric because they are not, respectively, hyponyms of *black* or *head*, or hyponyms of *ouvre* or *boîte*. Note that while *blackhead* and *ouvre-boîte* contain elements which are nouns and might be thought to inherit their nominal nature from these nouns, some exocentric compounds like *send-off* have no element within them from which they can inherit their word-class: *send-off* is a noun, *send* is a verb and *off* is a preposition. Thus there are degrees of exocentricity. In the terms of Scalise and Fábregas (2010), a distinction can be drawn between semantic exocentricity and categorial exocentricity.

Bisetto and Scalise (2007) suggest that exocentricity is a feature of compounds but not of other word-formation processes. They term this the 'exocentricity principle'. I disagree with this analysis for a number of reasons, the main one of which is semantic. The word *revolver* does not denote an instrument which revolves, but a thing which has as a part an instrument which revolves. The gloss is thus parallel to the gloss of *blackhead* which is something which has as a part a head which is black. The two are both exocentric for the same reason. Similarly, though *carriage* can mean an 'act of carrying' (as in *carriage of goods*), it has another meaning according to which it is a 'vehicle used to carry things (usually people)'. There is nothing in the word to indicate that it is a vehicle, and so it is exocentric. This has implications for embedding the notion of exocentricity in a wider context, but here the focus is on exocentric compounds (for further discussion of the other cases, see Bauer 2016).

Compounds may be exocentric for a number of reasons. Bauer (2010b) lists five types, but we can probably list more.

1. BAHUVRIHI COMPOUNDS. Bahuvrihi is the Sanskrit name for compounds which canonically label a part of the whole which the compound denotes (see further Section 5.2.2). Thus *yellowtail* denotes a type of fish which has a yellow tail. The compound labels only the yellow tail, but it denotes the entire fish. Such compounds are sometimes called 'possessive compounds', because they label what is possessed. An alternative way to view this is to see these compounds as instantiating the part of speech synecdoche, or pars pro toto: the tail is the part, but it is used to refer to the entire fish.

Bahuvrihi compounds may be subdivided in several ways. The example *yellowtail* is a noun, but some bahuvrihi compounds are adjectives. In English, the closest we have to this is a form like *blue-eyed*, but strictly this is a derivative based on a phrase, [[*blue-eye*]*d*], and not a compound. The modifying element in such words may also be an adjective (as in *yellowtail*) or a noun, or a quantifier (including a numeral), or a verb. Some examples are provided in Table 4.1, mostly taken from Bauer (2008b, 2010b).

2. SYNTHETIC COMPOUNDS. Synthetic compounds will be discussed in greater detail in Section 4.5. They involve a verb and an argument of that verb.

Table 4.1 *Examples of bahuvrihi compounds*

Language	Form	Gloss	Translation	Pattern
Nouns				
Danish	lang·øre	long·ear	long-eared bat	A + N
Koasati	nakeó-baski	ear-long	mule	N + A
Warlpiri	langa-kirrindi	ear-long	donkey	N + A
Apache	c'is-tè[1]	body-be.wide	terrapin	N + V
Dutch	vier·kant	four·edge	square	Q + N
Adjectives				
Basque	txori-bru	bird-head	bird-headed	N + N
Finnish	partasuu	beard.mouth	bearded	N + N
Japanese	tuyo-ki	strong-mind	aggressively confident	A + N

Example from Warlpiri from Simpson (2009: 615), that from Japanese from Kageyama (2009: 515)

Table 4.2 *Exocentric synthetic compounds*

Language	Form	Gloss	Translation	Pattern
Babungo	mè-vɔ̀lú'	swallow-eggs	snake sp.	V + N
English	buzz-kill			N + V
French	ouvre-boîte	open-box	can-opener	V + N
Japanese	tsume-kiri	nail-clip	nail-clipper	N + V
Korean	sal-in	kill-person	manslaughter	V + N

The relevant ones here are those where there is no centre, so that there is no element in the compound of which the compound as a whole is a hyponym. This includes the Romance type of V + N compound. Some examples are provided in Table 4.2.

3. EXOCENTRIC COORDINATIVE COMPOUNDS. There are various types of exocentric coordinative compounds, as might be expected given the range of coordinative compounds that are found (see below, Section 4.6). Most coordinative compounds are exocentric in the sense that they fail the hyponymy test. Some examples are provided in Table 4.3.

4. EXOCENTRICITY BY LANGUAGE CHANGE OR SOCIAL CHANGE. In some cases our use of words changes so that a label no longer applies to the

Table 4.3 *Exocentric coordinative compounds*

Language	Form	Gloss	Translation	Pattern
English	blue-green			compromise
German	Schleswig-Holstein	id		additive
Italian	bagna-asciuga	soak-dry	wet, hard sand, below the high-tide mark	antonymic, transpositional
Khmer	khɔh trəw	wrong right	morality	antonymic, transpositional
Mandarin	cai-feng	cut-sew	tailor	additive, transpositional
Meithei	mítná	eye.nose	organs	co-hyponymic
Turkana	ŋi-kari-mɔjɔŋ	thin-old	The Karimojong tribe	additive, transpositional
Vietnamese	trời bể	sky sea	unending	compromise, transpositional

Italian and Mandarin examples from Scalise and Fábregas (2010: 123), Vietnamese from Panfilov (2004: 1548).

same set of denotata. The result can then be that a compound ceases to be endocentric. Some examples are given in Table 4.4.

Table 4.4 *Exocentricity by language change or social change*

Language	Form	Gloss	Translation	Comment
English	glow-worm			*Worm* no longer has the meaning 'insect'
English	killer whale		orca	An orca is a type of dolphin, not a whale
English	marshmallow			No longer made of mallow plants
English	shell-fish			Does not fit the modern definition of *fish*
German	Walfisch	whale fish	whale	A whale is a mammal not a fish

Note that a case like *blackberry* presents something of a conundrum (and the same may well be true of German *Walfisch*, at least for some speakers). Technically, a blackberry is an aggregate fruit, not a berry. This should make the word *blackberry* exocentric. But speakers would not be surprised to find blackberries in a dish of berries (although they would be surprised to find a banana, which is technically a berry, in such a dish). This makes *blackberry* seem endocentric. So *blackberry* is simultaneously endocentric and exocentric.

The distinction between this category and the next can be difficult to draw: a *hedgehog* and a *winter rose*, for example, seem to be metaphorical rather than a false classification, and it is not clear whether people ever thought that a koala bear was a bear or just resembled one.

4. METAPHORICAL COMPOUNDS. Where compounds have a metaphor in their non-modifying element, they automatically become exocentric. Metaphors in the modifying element do not have the same effect and are not illustrated here. Some examples of metaphorical exocentrics are provided in Table 4.5.

Table 4.5 *Metaphorical compounds*

Language	Form	Gloss	Translation
English	buttercup		ranunculus
English	firedog		andiron
German	Spaß·vogel	fun-bird	practical joker
Mandarin	tiān qì	heaven breath	weather
Turkish	altın-top	gold ball	grapefruit
Urarina	ahāaori-kwitɛana	turtle-blood	birth mark

Turkish example from Kasar (2004: 275)

The problem that these compounds raise is that if they become exocentric by virtue of a figurative interpretation, and if the bahuvrihis are exocentric for the same reason (albeit a different figure of speech), is there any reason to say that all so-called exocentrics should not be seen in the same way? In most cases, the figure of speech would be metonymy, but there are occasional exceptions where some other figure is involved.

Consider, for instance, the Danish *bjørne·tjenste* 'bear good.deed = disservice' (the word may well be a translation of the German *Bärendienst* with the same meaning; a version of the story can be found in the fables of La Fontaine). Behind the word lies a story of a bear who wanted to help a man by killing a mosquito which was pestering him. The mosquito landed on the man's forehead, and the bear squashed it, but, not knowing his own strength, killed the man with the same blow. The bear thought he was doing a good deed, but from the man's point of view, it turned out not to be one. The figure of speech involved here is irony.

Table 4.6 *French V + N exocentric examples*

Form	Gloss	Translation
croque-madame	crunch madam	toasted cheese with ham and a fried egg
ouvre-boîte	open box	can-opener
passe-partout	pass everywhere	skeleton key
porte-feuille	carry leaf	wallet
remonte-pente	reclimb-slope	ski-lift
réveille-matin	awaken morning	alarm clock

The distinction between figure of speech and exocentricity becomes particularly striking when we consider an example like *hand* meaning 'worker'. If we say (13a), we are using synecdoche to refer to the worker, but if we say (13b), then we have an exocentric compound but not a figure of speech. The distinction seems untenable in such situations, and we have to consider the figure-of-speech interpretation as the most parsimonious solution.

(13)   a. The hand is working in the field.
        b. The farm hand is working in the field.

This raises the question of whether all exocentrics can be treated as instances of figurative speech. In the sense that metonymy is extremely wide-spread and covers a large number of possible semantic relationships, it seems that this position is tenable (and it is argued for in Bauer 2016). If it does not work, the place where it is least satisfactory seems to be where we have categorial exocentricity. Two cases will be considered here: V + N exocentrics in French, and exocentric compound attributives in English.

French V + N exocentrics have been illustrate already, but some more examples are given in Table 4.6.

The examples in Table 4.6 illustrate that the N is not always the direct object of the verb (though that is the default) – and, indeed, may be replaced by an adverb. Some of these are so lexicalised that the meaning must be listed for the particular form (e.g. *croque-madame*). Others have a more predictable meaning. The question is whether the action can be metonymical for the person or thing which carries out the action (or, in the case of *passe-partout*, allows someone to carry out the action). Given English words like *cook* 'person who cooks' and *whisk* 'instrument with which one whisks', there seems no reason why not, and indeed Kövecses and Radden (1998) illustrate metonymy with such cases of conversion. Marchand (1969: 380) gives just such an analysis of the English V + N equivalents like *pickpocket*, which he then terms 'pseudo compounds' and, with a label that seems to stress the metonymical nature of these words, 'bahuvrihi substantives'. Of course, 'conversion' itself could be just another name for figurative interpretation by metonymy of this type. At some level this must become a personal choice on the part of the analyst: is conversion a better analysis than metonymy or vice versa? Such arguments are well-established in the literature for the choice between conversion and zero-derivation; figurative interpretation is just an extra possibility.

Within Construction Grammar, it is not even clear that we need to make such a decision. If we accept that we have a construction type [V N]$_N$, such that the N of the whole construction is not related to the internal N by hyponymy, then an interpretation of 'N which has something to do with V and N' (formulated loosely to allow for types like *réveille-matin*) requires no formal means of conversion, no zero-morph and no overt figurative reading, either.

Let us turn, now, to compound attributives in English. Some examples are presented in (14).

(14)   a fail-safe (device), a fifty-pound (charge), a go-go (dancer), a hang-dog (expression), a no-fly (zone), a real-time (display), a ten-acre (site), a tow-away (zone), a yes-no (question)

The examples in (14) are formally varied. In some of the instances, the attributive form can stand alone (e.g. *real time*, though with a different stress), in others it cannot (e.g. *no-fly*). Some of the patterns are clearly very productive (e.g. *fifty-pound*), others probably not at all (e.g. *go-go*). There are several questions that these forms give rise to: are the forms compounds or not? Are they adjectives or not? If they are compound adjectives, they must be exocentric, but can they be viewed as figurative readings of the words?

The forms certainly fit the definition of compounds, although whether they are formed by a process of compounding is perhaps more dubious. They could be elements within a larger compound, so that *no-fly zone* could be [[*no fly*]$_N$ *zone*]$_N$, or they could be compound adjectives in their own right. Bell (2014) argues that such items are compound adjectives, in that they are item-familiar. The productive patterns like *fifty-pound* appear to be totally literal, but nouns rather than adjectives. In contrast, the type *yes-no* does not appear to have any counterpart in word-formation which does not lead to attributive forms. Perhaps there is not a single class of items here, and they should not all be treated alike. If *fifty-pound charge* is a complex compound, and *yes-no* is an exocentric compound adjective based on a coordinative compound with an alternative reading ('either yes or no'), metonymy could account for the categorical exocentricity in *yes-no* (it is related to a choice between the elements), and no metonymy would be required for *fifty-pound*. The matter is not simple, and not resolved; it seems likely, though, that exocentricity can, where necessary, be explained in terms of figurative readings.

4.4   Variable Semantics in Centred N + N Compounds

One of the features of N + N compounds that has been most frequently commented on in the literature is the unpredictability of the meaning relationship that exists between the two nouns. This can be illustrated in many ways. Consider, for example, the relationships between the elements in the examples in (15).

(15)   fire alarm   alarm which warns of a fire
        fire ball   ball made of fire
        fire-bomb   bomb which causes fire
        firefly   insect whose tail resembles fire
        firelight   light that originates from a fire
        fire line   a line in vegetation cleared to prevent a fire from spreading
        fire service   group of people dedicated to extinguishing fires
        fire trap   a place which would be dangerous in the event of a fire

Occasionally, the lack of semantic specificity is exploited, often for comic effect.

(16)   ... fire escapes were unknown in in Ankh-Morpork and the flames generally had to leave via the roof. (Pratchett, Terry. 1996. *Feet of clay*. New York: HarperTorch, p. 290)

(17)   My wife is a great shopper. One time she went out window shopping and brought back several windows. (*The Observer*, 21 Oct. 1973)

(18)   Do we have a cake-tin?
        Yes, under the table in the corner.
        No, I don't mean a tin for keeping cakes in, I mean a tin for making them in. (Reported in Bauer 1978: 77)

(19)   Calling me a *housewife* makes it sound as though I'm married to a house (widespread)

Accordingly, a compound like *rain snake* cannot necessarily be interpreted in isolation: it could be a snake which emerges in the rain, a snake which resembles rain, a snake which causes rain (compare *rain maker*) and so on. Only in context does its meaning become clear:

(20)   Rainy days ... the sliding doors that led to the deck were crawling with rain snakes. (McBain, Ed. 1986. *Cinderella*. London: Hamish Hamilton, p. 223.)

All of this gives rise to at least two questions. How can these semantic relationships best be classified? What mechanism allows compounds to be generated when their semantics is so variable? Recall Aronoff's (1976: 39) statement that 'the surer one is of what a word will mean, the more likely one is to use it', so that insecure semantics should lead to lack of use.

There is a huge number of classifications of these semantic relationships available in the literature. For a sample, consider Jespersen (1942), Hatcher (1960), Lees (1960), Brekle (1970), Adams (1973), Levi (1978), Ryder (1994) and Szubert (2012) (on Danish). Almost any description of the word-formation of a Germanic language will provide some kind of classification, and equivalent lists are available in the descriptions of other languages in which compounding is important. Some of these classifications include meanings based on syntactic relationships ('subject-verb', including *bee-sting*; Adams 1973: 64), others are based purely on semantic relationships, frequently glossed by prepositions or verbs ('is', 'from', and so on, including, respectively, *soldier ant* and *olive oil*; Levi 1978: 76–77). All of them suffer from similar problems.

1. What is the purpose of the classification? It is not entirely clear what purpose is served by providing a classification of this type. Is it simply a way of trying to provide an overview of a very complex area of semantics, or is it supposed to have some implication for the production of relevant forms? If the former, then any classification is helpful to some degree; if the latter, then it would be nice if there were some evidence for the psychological reality of the classification.

2. How useful is a classification if individual items are not assigned uniquely to one of the established classes? Is, for instance, a *police dog* 'a dog owned by the police', 'a dog from the police', 'a dog in the police', 'a dog used by the police', 'a dog associated with the police' or something else entirely? In any classification where 'from' and 'in' and 'instrument' are different categories in the classification, how is the linguist to associate *police dog* with one or the other of these categories? If it really does not matter which category the compound is associated with, then what is the point of the classification?

3. Is an exhaustive classification possible? A claim that it is not goes back at least as far as Carr (1939: 329) and is repeated in Jespersen (1942: 138) and Bauer and Huddleston (2002). Take the Danish example of *bjørne·tjenste* 'bear good.deed = disservice', discussed above. If we try to gloss the relationship between the bear and the good deed in this compound, we get something like 'the so-called (or ironically named) good deed done by the bear in the story with which I presume you to be familiar'. Other instances which create similar problems of unusual semantic links between their elements, but from English, include *cottage cheese, credibility gap, dogwood, gravy train, light year, milk tooth, monkey wrench, polka dot, spaghetti western, tree line* (some of these

examples are from Bauer and Huddleston 2002, some from Jackendoff 2016).
If there are examples which do not fit a particular classification, so that there is
a miscellaneous category at the end of the classification, the classification is
never testable, because anything which fails to fit into the other categories can
always fit into the miscellaneous category.

4. How fine-grained is the ideal classification? Related to this question is
another: what linguistic evidence is there for borderlines to the categories?
This is, of course, related to the first question in this series, but not quite the
same thing. Consider the examples *morning coffee, kitchen appliance, bone
cancer, orange juice, head shot.* Does *morning coffee* represent a temporal
relationship that is different from the locative relationship illustrated by the
other examples, or are both subtypes of locative relationship, with the well-
known metaphor of using location to represent time being applied? Do *bone
cancer, orange juice* and *head shot* all illustrate a single locative relationship,
or do they illustrate locative, ablative and illative respectively? Do *kitchen
appliance* and *bone cancer* both illustrate the same locative relationship, or
does the fact that *appliance* is an instrument but *cancer* is not mean that there
are two distinct relationships here? More generally, what makes a given
analysis of the semantic relations better or more valid or preferable to one that
is more fine-grained or to one that is less fine-grained? I take it that these
questions have no answer outside a particular theory of grammatical description. If we expect to find relationships corresponding to particular case relationships (compare Beard 1981), then we might have an answer here, but in the
lack of such a framework, any classification seems equal to any other. But
I know of no evidence to tell us whether the relationship in *bone cancer* and
that in *orange juice* are or are not the same relationship. If that is the case, these
classifications may be no more than rough and ready guidelines dependent
upon the fantasy of their creators rather than important linguistic categories.
Such a conclusion is reinforced by the fact that inter-rater reliability on the
assignation of such relations to individual compounds is apparently poor
(Bell & Schäfer 2016: 177).

A second position is thus that there is only one relationship between the
elements in a compound. This comes in two variants. The first is that there is
one relationship but it is a variable relationship, with the details of the variation
being determined by the particular elements put together in the compound
(Lees 1970, Allen 1978). Allen terms this relationship 'variable-R', a label
which has become current in discussions of this point. The variable-R analysis
avoids some of the problems outlined above, but assumes that an appropriate

relationship is computable from the meanings of the lexemes compounded. The example of *cake tin* cited above suggests this is not true.

For this reason, Bauer (1978) suggests that there is only one relationship which holds between the elements of a compound. This relationship may be loosely paraphrased as 'In any endocentric nominal compound of the form $N_1 + N_2$, N_1 denotes something which pragmatically allows for an appropriate subclassification of the class of N_2 and an appropriately mnemonic label for the class'.

There is a possible argument against this mnemonic theory of internal semantic relationships from places where it seems that speakers use a more detailed level of information. We can consider two, both of which turn out to have the same solution. They are the assignment of stress in English and the productivity of compound patterns. A third possible argument, coordination in compounding, seems to be harder to pin down.

If we make the assumption that all N + N compounds in English belong to the same class (see above, Section 2.7), then we have to explain the distribution of stress patterns across that class. There are two relevant patterns, often called 'compound stress' and 'phrasal stress' (though that terminology makes many assumptions which we might not wish to endorse), or more neutrally 'forestress' and 'end stress'. We find forestress in examples like *applecake, birthday party, Maddison Street, toy factory* ('factory where toys are made'), and end stress in words like *apple pie, Christmas party, Maddison Avenue* and *toy factory* ('factory which is itself a toy') (see further below, Section 6.1). It has long been noted that certain internal semantic relationships predispose words to particular stress patterns. For example, a temporal relationship as in *summer day* or an appositional relation as in the second example of *toy factory* above tend to lead towards end stress (Fudge 1984, Giegerich 2015). Even in the most recent corpus discussions of such matters, the internal semantic relationship remains one of the relevant statistical factors in assigning stress to such compounds (Bell & Plag 2012). If speakers relate specific meanings with specific stress patterns, it would seem to follow that they are aware of specific semantic relationships.

The second point is to do with the productivity of compounding patterns. It seems that, in a language like English, at least, it is not the N + N pattern of compounding which is productive, but patterns with individual lexemes within that. For instance, the noun *product*, usually occurs with a noun denoting the purpose of the product (*beauty product, cleaning product, office product*), followed by a series where the modifier indicates the composition of the product (*animal product, fish product, milk product*) and finally a set where the modifier indicates the origin of the product (*farm product, forest product*) (Tarasova 2013: 148–149). While other patterns may be possible, these are the most productive ones. Such productive patterns are different for elements in modifier position and elements acting as semantic centres. Again the question is whether speakers need to know a series of internal semantic relationships in order to exploit them in this way.

In both cases, I believe that the answer is in the negative. Rather than working with abstract relationships, speakers only need to know about individual exemplars. Where there are sufficient exemplars showing a particular pattern, speakers can see a pattern without necessarily being able to label that pattern, and without necessarily knowing whether that pattern overlaps with the pattern for some other element in their vocabulary. That is, whatever you do with *product* or *factory* is independent of the way in which you might calculate the stress on *toy house* or the productivity of *farm milk*. Rather there are many parallels with already familiar expressions, and the strongest of those links will affect the way in which new compounds are produced. There does not have to be a specific set of internal semantic relationships, there simply has to be similarity between some familiar words and a potential new word.

The argument from coordination may have much the same solution. It is clear that in English (and also in other Germanic languages) it is possible to coordinate elements within compounds. Thus we find examples like that in (21).

(21)   The question is can we keep this kind of huge **troop and money investment** to try to and make this government succeed? (COCA [*sic*])

It seems that one of the prerequisites for such a construction is that the relationship between the coordinated words and the other element in the compound should remain constant. *Salt- and pepper-mills* seems unobjectionable, *wind- or water-mills* also seems unobjectionable, but *pepper- and wind-mills* – where the mill grinds pepper but wind drives the mill – sounds distinctly odd. Here, I think, the solution lies in the nature of coordination. We coordinate things which we perceive as belonging together. The more closely they belong together in our world, the more closely we can coordinate (see Wälchli 2005). For them to belong together, it is more likely that the two compounds are linked by a similar internal relationship. We can, in appropriate pragmatic situations, break that expectation. There is a famous drawing of Don Quixote on his horse in a landscape which is dotted with windmills. It would not be beyond possibility that a surrealist painter, illustrating a pun, would add some pepper mills to this painting. Under such circumstances, it becomes rather less odd to say *The landscape is dotted with pepper- and windmills.* The pragmatics of the situation is paramount, not the semantic relationship between the elements.

Most of the discussion of variable internal semantic relationships in compounds assumes that this is some kind of oddity of compounding, perhaps of word-formation, that is different from what we would expect to find in syntax. That is far from true.

If we take the viewpoint, already mentioned above (see Section 3.7), that one of the functions of an N + N compound is to allow nominal modification of a head noun in languages where that is not a canonical modification pattern, then we find that creating a compound is just one of several possible strategies for doing this. Others involve use of the genitive (or equivalent), use of a denominal adjective, use of a specific attribute-creating word-formation process or use of some other means of word-formation (Bauer & Tarasova 2013).

The use of the genitive is self-explanatory. The genitive is often said to be the adnominal case par excellence. Not all genitives are equal, though. Rosenbach (2006) illustrates the fact that some genitive + N constructions are more compound-like than others, and she is by no means the first to note that there are different kinds of genitive relation. All of the non-pronominal genitives put a noun adjacent to another noun (it is tempting to write 'modifying', but in some models of grammar the genitive is in head position), and very often genitives and compounds are synonymous alternatives, as in the examples in (22) from the *OED*.

(22)	*genitive*	*compound*	*meaning*
	bull's nose	bull nose	'angle in architecture'
	dog's breath	dog breath	'halitosis'
	dog's chop	dog chop	'fig marigold'
	dog's standard	dog standard	'ragwort'
	dog's trick	dog trick	'despicable trick'
	frog's hornpipe	frog hornpipe	'dancing step'
	hare's thistle	hare thistle	'sow thistle'
	robin's wheat	robin wheat	'a moss'
	tailor's tack	tailor tack	'large marker stitches'

Alternatives to the genitive include the use of construct case (Borer 1988, 2009) and the use of prepositional phrases. Borer (1988) specifically comments on the closeness of construct case and compounding in Hebrew, and N + P + N phrases are often considered to be compounds in French (Lombard 1930), perhaps because of the degree of lexicalisation many of them show, as illustrated in (23).

(23)　　*French*　　　　　*gloss*　　　　　　　　*translation*
　　　　avion à réaction　　plane with reaction　'jet plane'
　　　　chemin de fer　　　way of iron　　　　'railway'
　　　　jus de fruits　　　juice of fruit　　　　'fruit juice'
　　　　pomme de terre　　apple of earth　　　'potato'
　　　　vie d'étudiant　　　life of student　　　'student life'

Despite their syntactic structure, many of these are treated as vocabulary items, and they act as translation equivalents of Germanic compounds (Bauer 1978: 190–191). English has some equivalent structures, as illustrated in (24).

(24)　　attorney-at-law, father-in-law, heart-to-heart, lady-in-waiting, man-about-town, man-at-arms, man-of-war, part of speech, pay-per-view, point of view, print-on-demand, stock-in-trade

By a denominal adjective I mean an adjective like *elemental* from *element* or *alcoholic* from *alcohol*, However, for present purposes I would like to include so-called collateral adjectives (Koshiishi 2002) which function as denominal adjectives but whose form is borrowed rather than directly derived: these are adjectives like *canine* related to *dog* or *dental* related to *tooth*. These often pair with compounds in English or with N + P + N phrases in French to provide synonyms (or, sometimes, non-synonymous readings of the same basic element – for example, *tache de soleil* 'stain of sun = dappling' is different from *tache solaire* 'sun spot', just as *fish market* is different from *fishy market*). Examples with English compounds are given in (25), and with French N + P + N phrases in (26) (Wandruszka 1972, Bauer 1978).

(25)　　*compound*　　　　　　*adjective*
　　　　atom bomb　　　　　atomic bomb
　　　　dog tooth　　　　　canine tooth
　　　　language development　linguistic development
　　　　noun compound　　　nominal compound
　　　　tooth floss　　　　　dental floss

(26)　　*N + P + N*　　　　*adjective*　　　　　　*gloss*
　　　　formalités de douane　formalités douanières　customs formalities
　　　　panneau de publicité　panneau publicitaire　billboard
　　　　titre de prince　　　titre princier　　　princely title
　　　　vie d'étudiant　　　vie estudiantine　　student life

Other forms of word-formation that may involve the same kinds of semantic relationships as compounds include the use of neoclassical compounds and blends in English, while Hungarian appears to have an affix specifically for marking attributives (Kenesei 2014).

The existence of these various competing patterns does not mean that all of them can be used on any given occasion. Some may be canonically central with particular meanings, such as the genitive with the meaning of possession. Mostly, the choice between the patterns seems to be regulated by collocational frequency and idiomaticity. That is, although there are undoubtedly underlying patterns, it is called a *family business* and not a *familial business* (or *family's business*, or *fusiness*) because that is the label it happens to have. Where the label is less fixed, there is greater flexibility, as shown by the examples in (27) from the same novel.

(27)   a. . . . you can't just arrest them on coply intuition?
        b. Judges hate to issue them [warrants] on cop intuition.
           (Parker, Robert B. 2003. *Stone cold*. London: Murray, pp. 229 and 240)

I would suggest that it would not have been shocking to find (27c) in place of (27b).

(27)   c. Judges hate to issue them on a cop's intuition.

The overall point here, though, is that syntactic structures can show the same semantic variability in their internal relationships that compounds do. Corresponding to the semantic variability shown with *fire* in (15), we can find examples like the following, based on examples from COCA.

(28)   the city's budget   passed/accepted by the city
        the city's dependence   of the city (*city* is the subject of *depend*)
        the city's letter   from the city
        the city's mall   in the city
        the city's problems   which the city has
        the city's temptations   which the city offers

(29)   civic auditorium   in the city
        civic duty   to the city
        civic imagination   of the city (*city* is the subject of *imagine*)
        civic leaders   of the city (*city* is the object of *lead*)
        civic research   about the city

In other words, the so-called problem of the neutralisation of meanings in compounds is not the result of the fact that compounds are involved, but the result of the fact that nominal modification of nouns is involved. Correspondingly, this is not a feature of compounding, or even of word-formation. The problem would exist even if only syntax was involved and there was nothing that could be classed as a compound. If nothing else, this moves the question of how to deal with such matters from the realm of compounding specifically to a much more general area of semantics or pragmatics.

There are implications here. If we look at a list of semantic relationships that can hold between the elements of compounds in, say, Mandarin, such as that given by Packard (2000), and compare it with the list of relationships given for English by Levi (1978) or by de Haas and Trommelen (1993) for Dutch, the chances are that any mismatch between them does not reflect a genuine mismatch between the possible relationships in the languages. To the extent that there is a genuine mismatch, we would expect it to be covered by some other, possibly syntactic, construction.

It is less clear whether accepting the notion that there might only be a single relationship here would also imply that more compounds are transparent in their semantics. I suspect that it does, but precisely what counts as transparency in this context is always rather fraught (see above).

4.5 Relatively Fixed Semantics in Verb-Based Compounds

The apparent plethora of meanings for most N + N compounds contrasts with those instances where one of the elements of the compound contains a verb as its base. In such instances, it is often the case that argument structure of the verb is filled by other elements in the compound, and that the meaning of the compound is extremely constrained. Such compounds are sometimes called 'synthetic compounds', sometimes 'secondary compounds', sometimes 'verbal-nexus compounds'. The main problem with such compounds is in determining which compounds might fit under this heading.

The clearest of the verb-based compounds in English are those which have an *-er* derivative as the second element. Typically the modifying element provides the direct object of the verb, and the *-er* affix represents the subject of the verb, so that a *bus driv-er* is 'one (*-er*) who/ which drives (nonspecific) buses'. Some further examples of the type are presented in (30).

(30)   ant-eater, bee-keeper, child murderer, coal-miner, deer-hunter, dish-washer, file-sharer, fire-fighter, hand-drier, home owner, office-bearer, rabble rouser, safe-cracker, tongue-twister, typesetter

In other instances, where there is nothing to denote the subject, we find the compound as a whole denoting an action or event, but still with the modifying element being the direct object of the verb. This is most productive with *-ing* forms, as in (31).

(31)   bear-baiting, bed-wetting, coal-mining, dressmaking, house-painting, house-warming, price-fixing, sabre-rattling, talent-spotting, typesetting

In a number of cases, as can be seen from the examples above, there is an *-ing* verb-based compound corresponding to an *-er* verb-based compound.

The nominalizers *-er* and *-ing* are the most productive suffixes in this construction, but it is not surprising to find parallel examples with other nominalizers (including conversion), as illustrated in (32).

(32)   consumer protection, cost containment, garbage disposal, pollution control, prisoner swap, subdivision development, tiger enclosure (*Dominion Post*, 21 and 23 Sept. 2015 and Bauer et al. 2013: 467)

Once we get beyond this, we start getting into controversial territory. Many authorities argue that the nouns which can appear in first position in words like these must be arguments of the verb. For some but not all authorities, arguments exclude adjuncts which tell us about the time and location of the event, for example. Some, but not all, also exclude the external argument of the verb, the subject, from occurring in such forms. (For a good summary and analysis of some of the argumentation here, see Spencer 1991: 324–343.)

First consider what happens with intransitive verbs, where there is no direct object to be used as the left-hand element in the compound. We find examples like those in (33).

(33)   a. cinema-goer, globe trotter, grass-hopper, night crawler, road runner, stilt-walker, town crier
        b. homecoming, island hopping, pole dancing, seabathing, sleepwalking

Here we see locative elements appearing in the modifier, and we have to ask whether these are arguments of the verb. The verbs involved in (33b) are largely unergative verbs which take part in locative inversion (Levin & Rapport Hovav 1995), but the verbs do not demand a locative element. If we look further afield, we find first elements with other kinds of semantic relationships to the head, as in (34).

(34)   *instrument*:   kick-starter, tape recorder, vacuum cleaner
        location: shop lifting, sky-writing; desk dispenser, Sunday driver
        subject: spirit writing
        other: baby-sitter, chest freezer, figure skating, king fisher, pattern bombing, prize-fighting, skin diver

Again, some authorities see synthetic compounds as being limited to those which denote events (Spencer 1991), so that many of the examples in (34) would be considered irrelevant; but the examples in (30) denote persons, animals and things, not events, yet they are central to synthetic compounds.

In any case, we find examples like that in (35), where an event is denoted, but we find the subject of the verb in the modifier position.

(35)   ... prior to protectee movements in the vicinity of the White House
              (*Dominion Post*, 23 Sept. 2015)

The point that I wish to make here is that there does not seem to be a simple way of recognising synthetic compounds as such, and that the language-user is faced with a number of patterns in which the modifier in an apparently relevant compound is not simply the direct object of the verb. To be sure, that is the majority pattern, but it is not the only pattern, and with some head nouns, it is not even the majority pattern. For example, a fairly superficial analysis of N + *participation* compound types occurring more than once in COCA suggests that slightly more of them have a first element denoting who participates (the subject of the verb: *peer participation, teacher participation*) than have a first element saying what they are participating in (possibly the object of a prepositional verb: *recreation participation, seminar participation*). With *treatment*, the number of compound types identifying the treatment used (*estrogen treatment, iron treatment*) is nearly as great as those where the first element denotes who or what was treated (*glaucoma treatment, sewage treatment*). In both cases there are other patterns as well, but they are minority patterns. For instance, with *treatment* we find locatives (*surface treatment, home treatment*) and subjects (*parent treatment, police treatment*).

It is clear that the semantic patterning in compounding is related to the meaning of the verb, but it is less clear that it is determined by the semantic class of the verb, as opposed to the individual lexeme concerned and the pragmatics of the situation, alongside the patterns which are expected because of item-familiar compounds with the same verbal element. If we start with the verb, and ask how to predict what will occur in the first element, it seems likely that we will get a different answer from that which we get if we start with an overall average pattern across verbs, or if we start with the compound and ask how we should interpret it. There is at least a possibility that the range of semantic interpretations available for items which have a verb-base in the righthand element can be accounted for by precisely the same factors which account for the interpretation of non-verbal N + N compounds.

This possibility is only strengthened by two other types: compounds containing relational nouns and compounds containing a verb-based element in the modifier.

A relational noun is a noun which can take an argument (Bauer et al. 2013: 472). Examples with such nouns in their centres include *club member, moon surface, cancer victim.* A member has to be a member of something, and that something can easily appear as the modifier in a compound (and similarly with the other examples). The meaning of the compound as defined by the relationship between its elements thus seems to be more restricted than, say, the examples in (15). Yet other relationships are possible with *member* (just as they are with verb-based righthand elements). Consider, for example, *core member, freshman member, life member, signature member* (all COCA). Again we see a pattern where a particular interpretation dominates with a given element, but is not used exclusively.

Where the verbal element is in the first element, we find instances with verbal stems like *driftwood* ('the wood drifts') and *punch card* ('someone punches the card'), but in English, and especially in British English, a lot of the instances with alternative interpretations get *-ing* forms in the first element: *coughing fit, driving licence, falling sickness, freezing level, growing pains, heating bill, killing field, learning curve.* In other Germanic languages, and to a certain extent in American English, such words often have a verbal stem, too. Where other nominalisation markers are used in a first element, we also see a range of potential semantic relationships between elements, not necessarily ones limited to the argument structure of the verbs concerned. Consider the examples in (36).

(36)   acceptance speech, administration plan, arrival date, arrival delay, ascent
        vehicle, assessment criterion, clearance sale, closure issue, closure time,
        departure tax, divorce lawyer, protection racket, protection officer, residency
        permit, survival skills, withdrawal symptom

What all of these types show is a great deal of variability in the relationship between the elements of a compound, whether or not they contain one element with a verbal base. Allen's (1978) 'Variable R' is not restricted to a class of N + N compounds: it is wider than that. While it may be true that having a verbal element in one of the elements is likely to reduce the number of available interpretations of the compound, it does not guarantee a particular relationship, and there are other factors which also reduce the available readings.

4.6   Variability in the Semantics of Coordinative Compounds

Although I find the term 'co-compound' (from Wälchli 2005) a neat piece of terminology, it fails to provide a contrast with subordinative compounds of the type that were discussed in Section 4.5. Thus I shall use the label 'coordinative compound', as has been used so far in this book. An alternative label is provided by the Sanskrit label 'dvandva', though that label has often been misused (Bauer 2008a). As this shows, this is an area where terminology has been very confused. Moreover, there is a great deal of dispute as to what compounds count as being coordinative compounds, what constructs count as being compounds and what the semantics of the constructs might be. In this section an inclusive approach is taken to listing potential coordinative compounds, and it will be suggested that some of the constructs may not belong in this category.

The fundamental point about a coordinative compound is that it contains two elements which are on an equal footing, not one which is subordinate to the other. It will be shown that even this is not always clear. Coordinative compounds may be nouns, adjectives or verbs, with nouns the most frequent category. Although Western European languages do have some coordinative compounds, such constructs are poorly represented in them, and oriental languages seem to have far more of them (Olsen 2001, Wälchli 2005). The classification here is based on Wälchli (2005), Bauer (2008a) and Renner (2008) but does not completely follow any of these. See also the classification in Detmold and Weiß (2012). Some examples are also from Bauer (2010a).

Given the definition of coordinative compounds above, it might seem that their semantics would be trivial: a compound of form [X Y] has a meaning 'X and Y'. Because coordination is typically between items with the same function, we would expect X and Y to belong to the same word-class, and the compound as a whole therefore to share that word-class. We will see that this is not necessarily the case at all.

We begin with what Renner (2008) calls 'heteroreferential compounds', that is, compounds where the two elements do not refer to the same entity. Where proper nouns are concerned we find at least three distinct types here, which we might term commercial, personal and geographical, and then we find some marginal types.

The commercial type arises through business mergers and includes examples like *Hewlett-Packard, Time-Warner, Mercedes-Benz, A. P. Møller-Mærsk, Mouton de Gruyter*. This type is clearly recursive, so that we can get *AOL-Time-Warner*, but the historical structure of the longer compound is not evident in the compound itself.

The personal type can be seen in *Creutzfeldt-Jakob (disease)*, which is presumably the same as arises with "double-barrelled" family names, whether written with or without a hyphen, like *Mayer Rothschild, Vaughan Williams,*

Kennedy Onassis. In the Spanish tradition, such names are sometimes linked by *y* 'and', which makes them look like good coordinations, but only one of the names is inherited, so that there seems to be some functional difference. The inherited name is on the left in Spanish, but on the right in Danish, following the direction of modification in those languages, and thus making these names look as though they are subordinative rather than coordinative compounds. In given names created from the juxtaposition of two names, such as Italian *Giancarlo*, French *Jean-Paul, Jean-Marie*, English *Maryann* (variously spelt and pronounced) there is no independent reference of the two names, and such words do not fit within the category.

Geographical examples include the names of cities (*Budapest, Minneapolis-St Paul, Napier-Hastings, Newcastle-Gateshead, Ålborg-Nørresundby*) and larger areas (*Alsace-Lorraine, Nelson-Marlborough, Schleswig-Holstein* and *Bosnia-Herzegovina*). There are superficially identical constructions whose interpretation is rather different, though. Consider *Hamburg-Altona* (the Altona suburb of Hamburg), *Leipzig-Halle, Dallas-Fort Worth* (the airport which serves two distinct cities), *London Gatwick* (the airport at Gatwick which serves London), *Edinburgh-Turnhouse* (the only airport for Edinburgh, which happens to be at Turnhouse), *Rhein-Main* (the airport at Frankfurt near the confluence of the two rivers, or a navigable waterway which involves the two rivers), *London-Edinburgh* (in English, an adjective showing the end points of a journey or transition), *Kassel-Köln* (in German an adverb showing a direction or a stage in a journey). While some of these may count as coordinative compounds, they are not of the same type as *Budapest*.

Many of these coordinative compounds can be used attributively or as one of the elements in another compound which is not a coordinative compound (*Rhein-Main-Donau-Kanal*). An adjective like the one illustrated in the French (*guerre*) *franco-allemand* 'Franco-German (war)', on the other hand, does seem to be formed as an adjective rather than derived from the names of the countries. Presumably, it is an adjectival coordinative compound using a bound element.

The examples above all involve names, and it may not be the case that the rules for names are the same as the rules for non-names. Although English allows a few toponyms based on the principle of naming something by the coordination of its elements, it does not seem to allow the naming of sets of family members by the same principle, as is common in other languages (see (37) below for some examples). I include examples with names here for completeness, but it does not automatically follow that such examples are canonical examples of coordinative compounds, or even that they should be classed in that way at all.

When we turn to heteroreferential compounds including common nouns, we are in the area that is traditionally covered by the label 'dvandva'. We can see some subdivisions here, but the fundamental requirement is natural coordination (Wälchli 2005) so that the denotata or the two nouns are regularly, naturally or traditionally found together. One obvious type here is pairings of family members, as illustrated in (37), but the type is much wider, as shown in (38). In many languages these compounds take dual or plural agreement, depending on the referent. Renner (2008) calls these 'additive' compounds.

(37) | Basque | aitona-amona-k | grandfather-grandmother-PL |
	Japanese	oya-ko	parent-child
	Lezgian	buba-dide	father-mother
	Mandarin	zĭ nǔ	son daughter
	Tamil	aɲɲan-tampi	elder.brother-younger.brother
	Turkish	karı koca	wife-husband

(38) | Basque | zer-lur-ak | heaven-earth-PL |
	Hunzib	mesed-okro	gold silver
	Malayalam	rapakalə	night-day
	Sanskrit	ajāváyaḥ	sheep goats

In some instances, the relationship between the two elements, while coordinate, is a matter of alternatives rather than addition, as in (39).

(39) | Marathi | pāp-puṇya | sin merit |
| | Punjabi | such-dukh | happiness sorrow |
| | Sanskrit | jayaparājaya | victory defeat |

In some instances, the two words that are compounded are synonyms or near-synonyms, and the compound as a whole is another near-synonym. Examples of such co-synonymic compounds are in (40).

(40) | Lezgian | kar-k'walax | job work | 'business' |
| | Punjabi | maar-piTT | beating beating | 'assault' |
| | Vietnamese | đường sá | road street | 'roads' |

In other cases, we find co-hyponyms rather than co-synonyms, and the compound as a whole denotes the superordinate category. Examples are in (41).

(41) | Chantyal | nɦe tɦara | milk buttermilk | 'dairy products' |
	Mandarin	huā mù	flower tree	'vegetation'
	Marathi	tikhaṭmīṭh	pepper salt	'spices'
	Vietnamese	bàn ghế	table chair	'furniture'

There are cases here where the meaning of the whole is unpredictable, as in Punjabi *daal-roTii* 'lentils bread = livelihood'. I take it that these are cases of

idiomatisation, rather than a separate category, though they might be interpreted as a rather more exocentric type than those illustrated in (41).

We now proceed to some more marginal types. First among these we
have instances where the compound as a whole denotes a hybrid, cross or
compromise between the two things denoted by the individual elements.
Renner (2008) calls these 'hybrid' readings, while Bauer (2008a) calls them
'compromise' readings. The labels fit slightly different instances, but it is
not clear that we are dealing with more than one type. Some examples are
provided in (42).

(42)	English	bull-terrier	bulldog terrier	
	English	northwest		
	French	roman-poème	novel poem	
	French	whisky-soda		'whisky and soda'
	German	Zebra-Pferd	zebra-horse	'zorse'
	Italian	leontigre	lion tiger	'liger'

French examples from Arnaud & Renner (2014). Italian example from
Wikipedia.

Repeated-element compounds or reduplicative compounds (Levi 1978: 94,
Bauer et al. 2013: 457) have the same element twice and denote some prototypical instance of that element. These are things like *salad-salad* contrasted
with, perhaps, a Waldorf salad, and implying the presence of typical salad
ingredients like lettuce, cucumber or tomato. Although these are clearly used in
English and German, I have no information on their wider use. But there is a
question mark as to whether these formations are actually compounds, and
whether they are coordinative compounds, even if they are compounds. They
do not appear to become established, they seem to have a similar intensifying
meaning to syntactic repetition such as *very very*, as in the example from
COCA in (43). In any case they are to be distinguished from examples like
win-win (situation) and *go-go (dancer)*, whose function is very different.

(43)   He's very very very clever, very very brave, and he loves you ever very much

Similar problems beset tautological compounds, composed of a hyponym
and its superordinate, as in *elm tree, tuna fish*. Benczes (2014) deals with these
in some detail and treats them as coordinative compounds. I am not totally
convinced by this: *elm* reduces the potential referents of *tree* in *elm tree* in
much the same way that *red* reduces the potential referents of *book* in *red
book*. In the additive coordinative compounds illustrated in (38) above, that is
not the case. While there are other readings to coordinative compounds, as has

been shown, the reading used here is one associated with subordinative compounds. I do, however, agree with Benczes that these are not strictly redundant. Benczes (2014: 445) argues that they are non-redundant because they are

> ... used to dignify and upgrade concepts via the conceptual metaphor MORE OF FORM IS MORE OF CONTENT ...

Benczes points out that there are also tautological compounds made up of two synonyms, and these do look like coordinative compounds. Her examples are *courtyard* and *subject matter*. These may be the same as the co-synonymic compounds illustrated in (40). Part of the function of such compounds, according to Benczes, is that the juxtaposition of the two elements cuts down the possible number of relevant polysemes of each of the elements. Again this argues against the use of the label 'tautological compounds'. The same argument could be used for the *elm tree* type.

The next type, Renner (2008) calls 'multifunctional', which is probably a clearer piece of terminology that the traditional 'appositional'. Here an entity is named by two distinct aspects of that entity. We can divide these up into those denoting people and those denoting other objects. The first are illustrated from English in (44) and from other languages in (45). Note, however, that if these truly are appositional, then there is an argument that they are not compounds (Radimský 2015: 40–44, who argues that apposition is a syntactic phenomenon).

(44)   hunter-gatherer, owner-occupier, singer-songwriter, translator-interpreter

(45)   French   boucher-charcutier   butcher pork.butcher
         German   Arzt-Kosmonaut   doctor-cosmonaut
         Norwegian   sanger/komponist/tekstforfatter   singer/composer/songwriter
         Spanish   filosofo economist   philosopher economist

         French example from Renner (2008), German example from Fleischer & Barz (2007), Spanish example from Fábregas & Scalise (2012)

The second type are possibly more controversial, at least as far as what counts as a member of the set is concerned. Examples like *café-restaurant* and *fighter-bomber* seem to be well-accepted as members of the group. They denote, respectively, something which can function as a café or as a restaurant, something which has the features of a fighter and of a bomber. A *washer-drier* could be a member of the same set, but a *fridge-freezer* has two separate units within the whole, and seems to be an additive example. A *fighter-bomber* could be interpreted as a bomber which has some resemblance (perhaps some of the functionality) of a fighter, in which case it would be subordinative.

In either case, Adams (2001: 82) suggests that these structures are not compounds, though unfortunately without arguing the point. Presumably, the possibilities of asyndetic coordination (i.e. coordination without an overt coordinator) or apposition would allow for these constructions in syntax, and there is no need to set up a special kind of compounding to cover them as well. However, the stress and intonation of these forms does not seem to match that in asyndetic coordination, or in apposition, contrast (46a) and (46b) and (46c).

(46)   a. The singer-songwriter fell to the floor.
        b. Humbugs, chocolates fell to the floor.
        c. The minister, Thomson, fell to the floor.

One type that is often included among the multifunctional compounds is that where the first element is a gender marker. Examples from English are given in (47).

(47)   boy-child, bull-calf, dog-fox, gentleman-farmer, girl-friend, hen pheasant, maidservant, man-servant, she-devil, woman-doctor

Although these could be glossed using the word *and* ('he is a boy and a child' etc.), the real function is ascriptive (Bauer & Huddleston 2002) or attributive (Scalise & Vogel 2010), as if using the adjective *male* or *female* (see also Radimský 2015: 102 on the difficulty of distinguishing coordinative compounds and these other types). The real question here is whether this is an independent category, and if so, what it includes. Bauer and Huddleston (2002: 1648) include *apeman, houseboat, pathway, washerwoman* in this category, while Benczes (2014) includes *pathway* as a tautological compound, and Renner (2008) would see *apeman* as a hybrid coordinative compound. Even from these few examples it becomes clear that the borders of coordinative compounding are not clear, but are controversial. Perhaps most surprisingly, the existence of a gloss with *and* is not a sufficient defining characteristic for coordinative compounds.

We must also consider the status of numbers like *eighty-four*. Since these translate into a language like German as *vierundachtzig* 'four and eighty' (which is also possible, though dated, in English, and in some languages like Czech, both possibilities are available), and can be glossed as meaning 'eighty and four', we have a semantic link with *and*, but we have just seen that this is not necessarily sufficient. The *and* here is a marker of arithmetical addition, not simply a marker of grammatical coordination. Bauer (2008a) concludes that these are not coordinative compounds (see also Bauer et al. 2013: 484), but the matter is not straightforward.

The classification above may not be exhaustive. For example, Renner (2008) divides additive compounds into those which denote the union of two things and those which denote the addition of one thing to another (e.g. *tractor-trailer*). I have not made such a distinction, and it might be difficult to draw the distinction under all circumstances. Renner (2008) also distinguishes between synchronous and asynchronous events, so that *murder-suicide*, for instance, is asynchronous since the murder necessarily precedes the suicide. While I agree that this is the case, I am not necessarily convinced that it is a separate linguistic subdivision of coordinative compounds.

Adjectival coordinative compounds can be found in many of these same categories, and there is one category that seems to apply only to compounds formed from the coordination of adjectives. The new type is illustrated in (48), where two antonymic adjectives together provide a noun. These have been discussed earlier as instances of categorial exocentricity.

(48)	Khmer	khɔh trəw	wrong right	'morality'
	Mandarin	hòu báo	thick thin	'thickness'
	Old Uygur	ulug·i kičig-i	big·its little·its	'size'

Additive compounds include examples such as English *obsessive-compulsive*, German *taubstumm* 'deaf dumb', Mandarin *yuán huá* 'round smooth'. Co-synonymic compounds include English *teeny-tiny*, Mandarin *měi li* 'beautiful beautiful', Vietnamese *do-bẩn* 'dirty dirty = filthy'. Co-antonymic compounds may indicate alternation between two states (English *manic-depressive*) or the simultaneous presence of both qualities (English *bitter-sweet*). With the latter type, it is not clear whether these are to be taken as additive or as multifunctional. More importantly, there are many compound adjectives which could be read as coordinative compounds or as subordinative compounds. These include *red-hot* ('red and hot' or 'so hot that it is red'), *squeaky-clean* ('squeaky and clean' or 'so clean that it reaches the degree of squeakiness').

Colour terms seem to be particularly difficult to classify. A compound such as French *bleu-blanc-rouge* 'blue-white-red', designating the colours of the French flag (and there are equivalent compounds in many other languages, including Dutch, German and Slovak), are clearly additive, as are terms such as German *schwarz-weiß* 'black and white' or Cantonese *hāk-baahk* with the same meaning (Matthews & Yip 1994). On the other hand, a term such as English *blue-green* is clearly a compromise reading (something we also find with terms such as *medium-rare, north-west*). Dutch and German appear to distinguish between the two readings in terms of stress, while English strongly disfavours additive compounds of this type, though they are occasionally found, as shown in (49).

(49)   Croatia's decision to reinstate its ancient red-white checkerboard coat of arms (COCA)

It might seem that three-term labels automatically exclude compromise readings, as do terms using colour-labels that refer to non-adjacent colours in the spectrum. But in principle *schwarz-weiß* could mean 'grey', *red-white* could mean 'pink' and even *red-green* could feasibly mean 'brown'. Accordingly, there is no obvious reason why *red-white-blue* could not mean 'pale purple', though I know of no case where this happens, perhaps because of the amount of computation it requires from the listener.

Terms such as *light-green, dark-blue* are even harder to deal with. Are they coordinative compounds ('dark and blue') or are *light, dark* degree markers, so that these are subordinative compounds? De Haas and Trommelen (1993: 432) treat the Dutch equivalents as parallel to compromise readings, but I am unconvinced by this analysis. It does, however, show that the semantics of this particular area is not clear to speakers. Even cases like *red-brown* are controversial. Bauer and Huddleston (2002: 1658) see these as subordinate, and equivalent therefore to *reddish brown*, while others see them as compromise readings or perhaps even as additive readings (with the addition of *red* and *brown* giving a red-brown colour).

In English, there are many coordinative compounds that are used attributively and which might, therefore, be considered compound adjectives. In some of these the elements are adjectives, so that we would expect the compound to be considered an adjective, but in other cases, if these are considered to be adjectives, they must also be considered categorially exocentric. Consider the examples in (50)

(50)   a. Edinburgh-London train
         b. father-daughter dance
         c. French-Spanish dictionary
         d. go-go dancer
         e. pass-fail test
         f. Syrian-Israeli talks
         g. the push-pull tension inherent in drone design (COCA)
         h. the stop-go pattern of growth (COCA)
         j. yes-no question

Bauer (2008a) terms examples like (50a, c) 'translative' and those like (50b, f) 'co-participant' compounds. Those whose elements are nouns create adverbs rather than (or as well as) adjectives in some other languages, such as Danish, as shown in (51).

(51)   På strækningen Aalborg-Hjørring kører der mellem 6.900 og 11.100
         personbiler i døgnet. (KorpusDK)
         Between 6,900 and 11,100 cars use the section from Aalborg to Hjørring
         every twenty-four hours.

The interesting thing about the items in (50) is that they are mainly patterns which occur only attributively, and so most of them are not easily analysed as longer compounds which contain a coordinative compound element, although we might expect such an analysis to make fewer presuppositions.

Repeated element compounds are also found with adjectives, as illustrated in (52).

(52)   'Mine is green'. 'Green green? Or more like olive green?' (Block,
         Lawrence. 2000. *Hit list*. London: Orion, p. 118).

We also find coordinative compound verbs, though the greatest problem here is in determining which of them are genuinely coordinative compounds and which of them show a subordinative structure.

Consider examples such as *blow-dry, stir-fry, trickle-irrigate*. For Renner (2008) such verbs are coordinative compounds ('blow and dry' etc.), while for Carstairs-McCarthy (2002: 60–61) these are subordinative compounds ('dry by blowing' etc.). The very fact that this is an overt debate illustrates the difficulty involved in determining the classification of such forms, and the problems in deciding whether verbs are or are not coordinative compounds.

Other examples are, however, less controversial. *Drop-kick* and *freeze-dry*, for example, refer to two distinct actions which follow each other in time, and the compounds thus look like additive compounds which are asynchronous. Many V + V compounds are used attributively and might therefore be categorially exocentric (as well as semantically exocentric): *roll-on roll off, stop-start, win-win*. Other languages provide a greater range of verbal coordinative compounds, including additive (Japanese *naki-sakebu* 'read write'), co-hyponym (Vietnamese *ăn-uống* 'eat drink = get nourishment'), co-synonym (Korean *olk-mayta* 'bind tie = fasten') and compromise (Erromangan – a language of Vanuatu – *avan alou* 'walk run = half walking, half running').

Coordinative compounds are occasionally found in other parts of speech, too. Numerals have been mentioned, and adverbs can be illustrated by

Mandarin *zǎo-wān* 'early late = sooner or later' and Mordvin *t'ese-toso* 'here there = everywhere'.

The survey given above is almost certainly not exhaustive, even if only because subtypes of the various types can be found. Overall the range of interpretations is striking, as is the amount of categorial exocentricity. One of the big questions all this raises is how far the various readings of coordinative compounds are a feature of grammar, and how far they are merely a pragmatic factor associated with the vagueness of coordination (or the polysemy of *and*). Is it a matter of linguistics, in other words, that in *stir-fry* the stirring and the frying take place simultaneously, while in *freeze-dry* the freezing and the drying take place consecutively? Is it a matter of linguistics that Khalka (a language of Mongolia) *end tend* 'here there' does not mean 'everywhere' (as in the Mordvin – a Uralic language from central Russia – example above), but 'scattered' as in English *here and there*? My answer would be that these various shades of meaning are not linguistically distinct, but pragmatically imposed by usage in the individual language and by the nature of the event. That does not mean that they are not real, but it may mean that we do not need to have a model of grammar that forces us to distinguish between them.

This also raises the question of whether the semantic relationships which hold between the elements of coordinative compounds are categorially different from those which hold between subordinative compounds, or whether there is simply a single relationship/set of relationships. Given that, for instance, Levi (1978: 76) lists the relationship between the elements in *consonant segment, soldier ant, target structure* as 'be', is this or is it not the same as the relationship between the elements in *gentleman-farmer* ('the farmer is a gentle-man') or *secretary-treasurer* ('the treasurer is a secretary')? Levi (1978: 93) draws a distinction. Adams (2001: 82) appears to see them all as the same thing. Levi justifies her position on the grounds that the two elements in coordinative compounds are semantically equivalent: *secretary* and *treasurer* denote two roles in an organisation, while *soldier* and *ant* are not equivalent words in the same way, they are not co-hyponyms in some hierarchy. Even if we accept that, though, it seems that there might be an alternative analysis whereby when the two words are appropriately equivalent we tend to read the resultant compound as if it is linked by *and* rather than by *is*. That is, the question remains open as to whether these categories of compound are actually distinct in terms of their semantics or not. Consider the example of *killer whale*. Is this a coordinative compound ('the creature is a whale and a killer') or a subordinative compound ('this whale species is a species that kills')? In general terms, the assumption in the literature has been that we are dealing with distinct categories here, and the position is rarely argued overtly, but an example like *killer whale* suggests that it may be impossible to draw a firm line. Even if the case can only be made within a particular model of compound structure, it would be desirable if an overt position were taken on questions like this.

4.7 The Semantics of A + N Compounds

It was suggested above (Section 3.7) that one of the grammatical functions of a compound was to allow non-canonical forms of modification. Since, however, adjectives canonically modify nouns, it would seem that there is no role for A + N compounds. In this section, this point will be considered. The discussion here will be primarily in terms of what happens in Germanic languages, since it is difficult to be sure precisely what happens in unfamiliar languages. While it would not be surprising if the same types of relationships were found in other languages, other factors might also play a role.

We can begin with consideration of the English *black bird* versus *blackbird*. The former is taken to be a normal noun phrase with *black* modifying *bird*, while the second is a compound. Various things follow from this, as illustrated in (53).

(53) black bird   blackbird
      a very black bird   *a very blackbird
      a blacker bird   *a blackerbird
      *this black bird is brown this blackbird is brown

> (Note that the last example here is not only grammatical, but true when *this* refers to a female blackbird in Europe or New Zealand. The North American blackbird is a different bird – or set of birds – with different colorations.)

Similar facts arise in other Germanic languages, but the adjective also loses inflections. The examples in (54) are from Danish.

(54) et højt hus   a tall.NEUT   et højhus   a tower block
                           house
      det høje hus   the tall.INFL   højhuset   the tower block
                           house
      et meget højt hus   a very tall house *et meget
                                              højhus
      det højeste hus   the tallest house *højestehuset
      *det lave, høje   the low tall   det lave højhus   the low tower
      hus   house   block

> (Notes: (a) I have marked *højstehus* as ungrammatical, though there are forms such as *højesteret* 'supreme court'. *Højestehus* could not be a superlative of *højhus*. (b) Apparently contradictory adjectives may be used syntactically to

modify a single head noun, but only when they have non-contradictory readings. Corresponding to *lille·bil* 'little·car = taxi', *en stor, lille bil* 'a big little car' might be possible if *stor* was read as 'great' and *lille* read as being a marker of affection.)

All this follows from the fact that while *black bird* provides a description of the bird in question, *blackbird* provides a classification of birds (see above, Section 4.2.6 on naming more generally). That is, *a black bird* is a bird whose colour happens to fall within the black range, and we can therefore be more precise (*a jetblack bird, a mostly black bird, the blackest bird I've ever seen*) if required. With *blackbird*, the precise colour is not at issue, all that is at issue is that a blackbird is a type of bird which can be seen as having its colour as an important identifying factor.

There are various complications with this view. The first is that, in English, there are also expressions like *red squirrel* which are not stressed on the first syllable, not written together, but which are classifying, just like *blackbird*. The important thing about a *red squirrel* is not that it is red (it might not even be considered to fall within the prototypical domain of red), but that it is not a *grey squirrel* or a *black squirrel* (or any other species of squirrel). Expressions such as *red squirrel* are not usually considered to be compounds, because of their stress (and possibly orthography and syntactic behaviour – see the Appendix). I would like to claim that they should be considered to be compounds, and that the stress distinctions are a consequence of their relative frequency (Bauer 2004b): only the most common expressions have forestress.

The next complication is provided by adjectives which are variously termed 'non-predicate' (Levi 1978), 'associative' (Pullum & Huddleston 2002, Giegerich 2015) or 'relational' (Bally 1950, see Rainer 2013). These adjectives tend not to occur predicatively, are often denominal and in their fundamental meanings are usually ungradable. In English, many of them are Romance loans. Different Germanic languages deal with these differently as far as compounding is concerned.

In German, most such adjectives are not used in compounds (Neef 2009: 388, although there are notable exceptions). In Danish, these appear to be able to form compounds as well as ordinary noun phrases: *Den private kunde, privatkunden* 'the private customer' are both found, though precisely what the semantic difference between the two might be is not clear. In English, such adjectives can be found with end-stress or with forestress in the relevant construction, but forestress is usually associated with classification or with specific readings of the adjective. Compare, for example, the instances in (55), where the collocation in the first column takes end-stress, while that in the second column takes forestress.

(55)   a dramatic increase   a dramatic society
              a medical disorder   a medical journal
              dental decay   dental treatment
              nervous energy   nervous system
              primary production   primary school
              solar energy   solar system

Some of these differences might also be frequency-related (*nervous system* is the most common collocation with *nervous* in COCA, for instance), some may be to do with analogies driven by the noun (*dramatic society* and *operatic society* and *co-operative society* all take forestress).

In other words, there are places where the precise correlates of these adjectives are not well understood. This may imply that we are not yet in a position to argue for the status of constructions involving them. Levi (1978) calls them 'complex nominals' along with compounds, and this seems to me to be a reasonable and defensible stance. Whether they are compounds, as some suggest (e.g. Giegerich 2005), is an open question (Giegerich 2015 suggests that they have the possibility of being compounds and that those with forestress are compounds). Where English is concerned, this may be another area where stress has to be seen as being irrelevant to the status of the construction as a whole, though scholars have not overtly accepted such a position previously. Rainer (2013) presents a good discussion of the difference between N + N and relational adjective + N and genitive + N, showing how the various patterns may be exploited in different languages. In my view, we have to see these patterns as alternatives, but not necessarily all as compounds. As alternatives, they are likely to prefer particular parts of the continuum they divide between them, and may divide it in more or less regular ways, with more or less predictable semantic effects. Classificatory versus descriptive use of adjectives is likely to be a relevant consideration in all of this where we have a clear distinction between [A + N]$_N$ and [A + N]$_{NP}$, but in this section I have shown that this distinction is easier to see with simple adjectives than with complex adjectives.

4.8   The Semantics of Compound Verbs

The delimitation of compound verbs in the literature is not particularly clear. On the one hand, compound verbs are usually distinguished from incorporation, although incorporation is taken by some to be a sub-type of compound (Bauer 2004a; see above, Section 3.6). On the other hand, compound verbs are not necessarily clearly distinguished from serial verbs. And in principle, compound verbs also need to be distinguished from sequences of auxiliary and main verb.

Auxiliary verbs require the presence of a main lexical verb (unless there is elision) and mark grammatical or functional categories such as aspect, modality, mood, tense or voice. Auxiliary verbs form a closed class and may differ syntactically from main verbs, as when an auxiliary can be fronted to form a question in English, but not (or not any longer) a main verb, as is shown in (56).

(56)   Will the president attend the meeting?
        Did the president attend the meeting?
        *Attended the president the meeting?

Haspelmath (2016) indicates that there is very little agreement in the literature as to precisely what constitutes an instance of serial verbs. He proposes (2016: 296) the following definition of a serial verb construction, which is largely in agreement with the criteria proposed by Aikhenvald (2003: 423):

> A serial verb construction is a monoclausal construction consisting of multiple independent verbs with no element linking them and with no predicate-argument relation between the verbs.

The lack of predicate-argument relation between the verbs would distinguish a serial verb construction from an instance of incorporation. The lack of a linking element might distinguish serial verb constructions from verbal compounds, but not necessarily in all languages (and since linking elements often derive from inflections, it might not always be clear whether an element has acquired the features of a linking element or not). The requirement that the verbs should be 'independent' is intended to distinguish serial verb constructions from constructions with auxiliaries. However, the other elements of this definition do not distinguish serial verbs from verbal compounds, and it is perhaps better to say that serial verb constructions, like incorporation, provide a sub-type of compounding, albeit with special features.

Aikhenvald (2003: 446–448) takes care to distinguish verbal compounding from serial verb constructions in Tariana (an Arawak language of Brazil), which has both. However, it is not necessarily clear that the same criteria would work for other languages or across languages. Crucially, for Aikhenvald, serial verb constructions consist of independent phonological words strung together, while compounds are single phonological words, and compounds have one of their verbs from a closed class. The two constructions also have slightly different functions in Tariana. While these criteria suggest that languages may have different kinds of V + V construction, and that the labels of 'serial verb' and 'compound' may be useful in stating such distinctions, the criteria for distinction may well be local and not universal. This means that any list of verb compounds may include items which would be just as validly described as serial verb constructions, just as some of them may be validly described as instances of incorporation. Note, for instance, that Baker and Fasola (2009: 595–596) call V + N compounds where the N is the direct object of the V 'compounds', but say they are 'a kind of noun incorporation'. Nevertheless, we can note some common patterns that are reported in the literature.

When the verb compound is categorially endocentric, we might expect any other element in the compound to be an argument of that verb or an adjunct modifier of that verb (which, in some cases, may be an argument). We certainly find such examples, as illustrated in Table 4.7.

Many languages have verbal compounds where one element is a preposition/particle/adverb. In other languages, such forms are replaced by forms which look like V + V coordinative compounds, and these are exemplified below. Examples with particles are given in Table 4.8.

It is not surprising that there are also exocentric verb compounds, usually because of some figurative interpretation. Some examples are given in Table 4.9.

Verb + verb compounds also fall into several clear groups. The coordinative compounds have already been dealt with in Section 4.6 and will not be considered here. With subordinative compounds, we find those where the verb acts as a causative marker or inchoative marker or other similar quasi-aspectual marker. Examples are given in (57). We also find examples where one of the verbs is a direction marker, more or less semantically equivalent to the compounds with preposition/particles in Germanic. Examples are given in (58). And we find resultative compounds, where one action results from another (as illustrated in (59)). When a state results, an adjective is used in languages which have adjectives.

(57)	Mandarin	chàng wàn	sing finish	'to finish singing'	Li & Thompson 1981
	Turkish	kullan-ıl- a-gel-mek	use-PASS- GERUNDIVE- come-INF	'be in constant use'	Kornfilt 1997

Table 4.7 *Endocentric verbal compounds with arguments and adjuncts*

Language	Form	Gloss	Translation	Source
Modifying element is subject of the verb				
Japanese	ti-asiru	blood run	'to get bloodshot'	Kageyama 2009
Korean	kep-nata	fear come.out	'to be scared'	Sohn 1999
Mandarin	tái téng	head ache	'to have a headache'	Li & Thompson 1981
Toqabaqita	lio-dora	mind-forget	'to forget'	Lichtenberk 2008
Modifying element is object of the verb				
Basque	hitz egin	word do	'to speak'	Hualde & Ortiz de Urbina 2003
Cantonese	tàuh-jī	throw resources	'to invest'	Matthews & Yip 1994
Danish	lov-give	law give	'to legislate'	
German	rad-fahren	bicycle-ride	'to cycle'	Neef 2009
Kannada	dukkha paDu	sorrow feel	'to regret'	Sridhar 1990
Lezgian	fikir awun	thought make	'to think'	Haspelmath 1993
Mapudungun	kintu-mara·n	look.for-hare·1NF	'to hunt hares'	Baker & Fasola 2009
Thai	ɔ̀ɔk kamlaŋ	put.forth strength	'to do physical exercise'	Iwasaki & Ingkaphirom 2005
Toqabaqita	dada lifo	brush tooth	'to brush one's teeth'	Lichtenberk 2008
Turkish	alay et	mockery do	'to ridicule'	Kornfilt 1997
Modifying element is prepositional object of the verb				
Danish	råd-spørge	counsel-ask	'to seek counsel'	Bauer 2009
Japanese	su-datu	nest-fly	'to fly from the nest'	Kageyama 2009
Modifying element is adjunct to the verb				
Basque	gurutz:iltza-tu	cross nail 1NF	'to crucify'	Hualde & Ortiz de Urbina 2003
Japanese	sato-gaeri	home return	'to come home'	Kageyama 2009
Mandarin	lì yòng	profit use	'exploit'	Li & Thompson 1981
Thai	cam khúk	confine-prison	'to be imprisoned'	Iwasaki & Ingkaphirom 2005
Toqabaqita	kafi-boro	lift.clothes-bottom	'to moon'	Lichtenberk 2008
Modifying element is an adjective with adverbial meaning				
Basque	ezkon-berri	married recent	'just married'	Hualde & Ortiz de Urbina 2003
Danish	fast-gøre	firm-make	'to bind'	Bauer 2009
Japanese	tika-yoru	near approach	'to go near'	Kageyama 2009
Mapudungan	ngellu-miauw-n	difficult-walk-inf	'to walk with difficulty'	Baker & Fasola 2009

98

Table 4.8 *Compound verbs with particles*

Language	Form	Gloss	Translation	Source
Cantonese	chēut-māau	out-cat	'cheat' (in examinations)	Matthews & Yip 2004
Danish	op·tage	up·take	'to record'	Bauer 2009
Danish	under·vise	under·show	'to teach'	Bauer 2009
Dutch	op·bellen	up·shout	'to call up'	Don 2009
Finnish	ylläpitää	above hold	'to maintain'	Sulkala & Karjalainen 1992

(58)	Korean	chy-eta-pota	raise-INF-see	'to look up'	Sohn 1999
	Mandarin	păo-shang	run ascend	'to run up'	Packard 2000

(59)	Danish	løs-rive	loose tear	'to tear loose'	
	Mandarin	dă-pò	hit broken	'break'	Li & Thompson 1981
	Turkish	pişman ol-	regretful become	'to feel remorseful'	Kornfilt 1997
	Udihe	xekui b'a-	warm get	'to get warm'	Nikolaeva & Tolskaya 2001

There are also compound verbs whose elements do not include a verb. Mandarin *wù sè* 'colour thing = to hunt for' or *xiǎo biàn* 'minor convenience = to urinate' (Packard 2000) are examples of this type.

A common comment on verb compounds is that they are somehow rare or restricted. For instance, Hixkaryana (Derbyshire 1979) is described as having compound verbs (or incorporation) only when the object noun is a body part; Mandarin is described (Li & Thompson 1981: 65–66) as having only five verbs which take part in 'phase' compounds; in Basque (Hualde & Ortiz de Urbina 2003: 357) most subordinative compound verbs are made with just one verb (meaning 'do'), though smaller numbers employ another four – other head verbs are rare; Kham is described (Watters 2002: 107) as having only five verbs which take the head role in serial verb constructions; Finnish is described (Sulkala & Karjalainen 1992: 363) as having very few compound verbs, something that is also often said of English, and also of Udihe (Nikolaeva & Tolskaya 2001: 325) where only one head element is widely used. Although such comments on rareness can involve incorporation (see the comment on Hixkaryana), incorporation is often the exception to this rule, frequently being extremely productive. Part of the distinction between serial verbs and compounds might be the level of productivity, with serial verbs being seen as

Table 4.9 *Exocentric verbal compounds*

Language	Form	Gloss	Translation	Source
Cantonese	haap-chou	sip-vinegar	'be jealous'	Matthews & Yip 2004
Finnish	mustamaalata	black.paint.INF	'to defame'	Sulkala & Karjalainen 1992
Korean	sok-thaywuta	inside-burn	'to worry oneself'	Sohn 1999
Thai	tòp taa	slap eye	'to deceive'	Iwasaki & Ingkaphirom 2005
Toqabaiqita	qoo-qae	break-leg	'to walk a long way'	Lichtenberk 2008

syntactic and thus productive. Even serial verbs can be idiomatised, however (Haspelmath 2016: 297).

4.9   The Semantics of Compound Adjectives

If compound verbs are often said to be rare, the problem is even greater with compound adjectives. Not only are there many languages which either do not have a recognisable class of adjectives or have very few adjectives (see e.g. Dixon 1982: 2–3), in many cases something that is compound in form may actually be a derivative on a compound base (some forms where this is probably true are included below). Even instances where the base is not adjectival but there is adjectival inflection may be considered to be made adjectives by that inflection and so fall into this category.

Despite this poverty of data, there are several clear types of compound adjective, and there are also rather more idiosyncratic types which are not specifically mentioned here.

The first type is where the adjective in the centre is graded or scaled by its modifier. One way to do this is to compare the adjective to something which protypically is described by that adjective. Some examples are in (60).

(60)	English	sky-blue			
	Dutch	fluister·zacht	whisper·soft		Don 2009
	Finnish	säkkipimeä	sack-dark	'pitch dark'	Sulkala & Karjalainen 1992

In some instances this comparison becomes idiomatic or figurative, so that we get examples like Danish *sten·rig* 'stone·rich = very rich', Dutch *ape·trots* 'ape proud = very proud' (Booij 2002), or English *piss-poor* 'very poor'. Note that in a number of Germanic languages, these items have two stresses, so that we can find a contrast in German between *blút·árm* 'blood·poor = extremely poor' and *blút·arm* 'blood·poor = anaemic'. This might be a reason for treating this set of items differently from other compounds, or even treating them as non-compounds. Hoeksema (n.d.) calls these forms 'elative compounds' and discusses them with particular reference to Dutch, showing how they differ in behaviour from other compounds. One such difference is that the elative compounds do not allow subsequent affixation (e.g. nominalisation): *piss-poor* does not give rise to **piss-poorness* or **piss-poverty*. Note, though, that other compound adjectives tend to avoid nominalisation as well, although we can find occasional examples like (60).

(60)   the current study examined whether African-American college students score
         higher on three self-report scales of **psychosis-proneness** (COCA)
         Swann will now offer **AfricanAmericana** annually in February in honor of
         Black History Month (COCA)
         I was admiring the shiny **blue-blackness** of its eyes (COCA)

We also find very occasional items like (61), which seem to show the difference is not absolute.

(61)   a shirt that had previously been another color but was now **blood-
         reddish** (COCA)

In other instances, the gradation or scaling is indicated by an adjective (sometimes with adverbial import) or adverb. Some examples are provided in (62).

(62)

Danish	ny·født	new born		Bauer 2009
Dutch	dicht·bevolkt	thick·peopled	'densely populated'	Don 2009
Dutch	diep·droef	deep sad	'very unhappy'	Don 2009
English	light green			
French	malpropre	ill clean	'dirty'	Fradin 2009

Another major class of adjectival compound is the type where the modifier is an argument of the adjective. Where the adjective is a participle, then the argument will be an argument of the underlying verb, but there are also non-participial adjectives which take arguments. The argument itself may be a noun, a verb, an adjective or an adverb. Examples are presented in (63).

(63)

Danish	fri·t·stående	free·ADV·standing		
Danish	mad·glad	food·happy	'fond of good food'	Bauer 2009
Dutch	doel·bewust	target·aware		Don 2009
English	houseproud			
German	herz·zerreißend	heart·tearing.up	'heart breaking'	Neef 2009
German	treff·sicher	hit·sure	'accurate'	Neef 2009
Greek	petr·o·xtistos	stone·LE·built		Ralli 2009

The third major class is the class of bahuvrihi compounds, where the compound adjective denotes something which the head noun of the NP has (or in one case below, does not have). These are illustrated in (64).

(64)

Basque	begi-gorri	eye red	'red-eyed'	Hualde & Ortiz de Urbina 2003
Cantonese	hāk-sām	black heart	'malicious'	Matthews & Yip 1994
English	blue-eyed			
Japanese	kuti-gitanai	mouth dirty	'foul-mouthed'	Kageyama 2009
Korean	pay-puluta	belly-bulgy	'be full, satisfied'	Sohn 1999
Margi	kəla tlər	without work	'unemployed'	Hoffman 1963
Polish	dług·o·nos·y	long·LE·nose·SUFF	'long nosed'	Szymanek 2009
Russian	p'atiugol'nyi	five corner	'pentagonal'	Ward 1965
Thai	cay rɔɔn	heart hot	'short tempered'	Iwasaki & Ingkaphirom 2005
Turkish	aç·göz·lü	hungry·eye·with	'greedy'	Kornfilt 1997

While these compounds are largely exocentric, there are also compound adjectives which are exocentric for other reasons, both categorial and semantic. Examples are given in (65).

(65)

Basque	ipurt-erre	buttocks burnt	'grumpy'	Hualde & Ortiz de Urbina 2003
Cantonese	tóuh-ngoh	stomach-hunger	'hungry'	Matthews & Yip 1994
Damana	tua-kuaga	see liveᵥ	'visible'	Amaya 1999

| Karachay | suw baš | water head | 'brainless' | Seegmiller 1996 |
| Zhuang | ta^1 ?din^1 | eye red | 'jealous' | Luo 2008 |

As well as compounds of these types, some languages, of which English is one, have a host of forms which could be interpreted as attributive adjectives but which do not contain an adjective in their make-up. These forms were previously discussed in Section 4.3. While such forms are potentially adjectives in English, they are not in other languages. Consider, for example, the English *three-week* in *a three-week holiday*. Contrast this with what we find in Danish (examples from KorpusDK) in (66) and in German (examples from various net sources accessed on 10 October 2016) in (67):

(66)   a. parret var på en treugersferie på Filippinerne
         the.couple were on a three.weeks.LE.holiday in the.Philippines
    b. i den kommende tre-ugers periode
         in the coming three-weeks.GEN period

(67)   a. Arbeitnehmer nehmen maximal 3 Wochen Urlaub am Stück
         Workers take maximally 3 weeks leave in the piece
         'Workers may take a maximum of three weeks' leave at a time'
    b. Manfred Meier geht in seinem 3-wöchigen Urlaub klettern.
         M.M. goes in his 3-week.ADJLZ leave climbing'
         'M.M. goes climbing in his three week leave'
    c. Im Spätsommer leisteten wir uns einen Drei-Wochen-Urlab an der
         bulgarischen Schwarzmeerküste
         In the late summer we afforded ourselves a three-week-holiday on the
         Bulgarian Black Sea coast.

In Danish, either the whole of the three-week holiday is a single compound, or 'three-week' is put in the genitive. In German, in (67a) we have an independent noun phrase which cannot be an adjective because it does not inflect as an adjective, which seems to have adverbial function; in (67b) we have an overt derivation to make the 'three week' constituent into an adjective; and in (67c) we have a compound. Only in English is the question of whether *three-week* is an adjective or not a relevant question to ask.

The example makes the point that what counts as an adjective may depend on the criteria that are used to define an adjective (function or position in the English case, inflection in the German case), and that these criteria have to be language-dependent. Accordingly, no overarching answer can be provided as to how to deal with such forms, so that any analysis of what is happening in English demands a justification from the analyst.

4.10   Psycholinguistic Approaches

There is a huge psycholinguistic literature on the understanding of (usually nominal) compounds and how meanings are assigned to unfamiliar compounds. A magisterial overview is provided by Gagné (2009), on which I draw freely here.

One factor which has been discussed at length is whether the processing of a compound involves the processing of the individual elements of that compound. It goes without saying, perhaps, that nonce compounds can only be processed through their elements, but it might be expected that there would be a difference between, for instance, *butterfly* on the one hand (where no butter is involved) and *milk bottle* on the other, where both milk and bottles are involved. To some extent, this is reflected in the literature, but there seems to be a development of ideas over time. The consensus at the moment seems to be that even in *butterfly, butter* is activated, but very briefly, while in *milk bottle, milk* and *bottle* are both fully activated (see e.g. the summary in Bauer 2001: 110). So we can say that the elements of a compound are used where they are semantically and conceptually useful for the interpretation.

Certain factors seem to make compounds easier to interpret. The frequency of the constituent words in the compound is one such factor. There is some discussion as to whether the first element or the second is more crucial, but both seem to have influence (Gagné 2009: 261). Another relevant factor is family size. The more often the elements of the compound are found in different types, the easier it is to process compounds containing them. This is clearly related to the matter of frequency. Recency of exposure is also a relevant factor. Not only do speakers react more quickly to a compound element after having recently processed the compound, the implication goes in the other direction, too. That is, hearing (or seeing) *milk* makes it easier to process *milk bottle*, and hearing (or seeing) *milk bottle* makes it easier to process *milk*. Even *butter* can help process *butterfly*, though not as much as *milk* helps process *milk bottle*. But while prior exposure to *cream* might help process *milk bottle*, prior exposure to *bread* does not help process *butterfly*. This relates to the processing of the individual elements referred to above.

Moreover, it appears that compounds are easier to process when the elements are in an expected semantic relationship to each other (Gagné & Shoben 1997). For example, *winter cloud* is easier to understand than *gas cloud* because both *winter* and *cloud* regularly appear with a 'during' relationship, while *gas* and *cloud* do not both regularly appear with a 'made of' relationship. This finding seems to give credence to the notion of a limited number of semantic relationships between the elements of a compound, which was discussed previously (see Section 4.4). It is thus worth some reconsideration here.

If we consider the coining of new compounds from the speaker's point of view, which we might also term the onomasiological point of view, the aim is to produce an expression which will act as a label for the entity to be denoted. The speaker does not need to know or think about a particular semantic relationship between the elements of the compound being formed, because the speaker has an exemplar of the relevant entity available to the senses. All the speaker needs to know is whether (at least in the case of an endocentric compound) the modifier will act as a suitable mnemonic for the sub-type of head that is to be named. Various factors, no doubt, influence the choice of a suitable mnemonic. Some of these factors are phonological, which might lead to *screen queen* being considered a better mnemonic than *cinema queen*, for example; some will be paradigmatic in the sense that known compounds with the same head will lead to expectations as to the kind of modifier a given head is likely to co-occur with. But whatever these factors are, they do not have to involve specific semantic classes, because the speaker is perceiving a relationship between the head and the modifier, not trying to describe it.

The listener's role is different. The listener has to decode the speaker's form, and arrive at a mental image of the appropriate entity. In face-to-face interaction, this process is helped by the fact that what is present for the speaker is probably also present for the listener. The listener has to see a relationship between *screen* and *queen* for the entity in the field of perception. When there is no face-to-face interaction, matters become more problematic, although even then the entity being named may be available to the listener (reader) in the previous text. The listener has to use whatever strategies are available, and knowledge of known structures will be one of those strategies. However, that does not imply that there is a fixed and known set of relationships which are possible between compound elements. All the listener needs are hints which push in an appropriate direction for an interpretation. The presence of *chocolate bar, chocolate cake, chocolate biscuit, chocolate chip, chocolate mousse* and so on does not necessarily mislead us when we come to *chocolate poodle* or *chocolate skin*, and those do not mislead when we come to *chocolate industry, chocolate shop*. The listener is playing the odds, but *chocolate donut* and *chocolate almond* might be close enough to the pattern set up by *chocolate chip* to work, even if one means 'made of' and another means 'covered with' (and *chocolate mousse* means 'made with'). The only reason we would need to set up a particular exhaustive list of relationships is if we need to catalogue the patterns for some (probably linguistic) purpose.

Thus Verhoeven (2012), for example, uses such relationships to test the reliability for determining the meanings of compounds computationally (see Johnston & Busa 1999 for an alternative approach which specifically denies the need for such relationships).

In brief, I would suggest that the use of a fixed number of relationships between the elements of compounds is a useful fiction for allowing classification of compound meanings, but not necessary for the coining or interpretation of compounds in usage.

4.11   Summary

The semantics of all kinds of compounds seems to be variable. To phrase it another way, in order to find a compound construction with fixed semantics, you have to look at quite specific patterns. This variability has always been a problem in the description of nominal compounds, where it is most obvious, but the analysis here has shown that it is also there for other types of compound. Compound adverbs have not been specifically considered here, nor compound adpositions, since they are rarer than the types that have been considered. But there is no reason to suppose that they would show fixed semantic relationships where they occur.

In theoretical terms, this variability has to be dealt with somehow. The preferred way in the past has been to create a list of possible semantic relationships that can occur in compounds, but such solutions have themselves shown great variability in the perception of the relationship on the part of the analyst and have also inevitably left an unanalysed residue that does not fit the classification.

In most of the analyses of the last century, there was also a distinction made between those 'semantic' relationships which were based on argument structure (and might thus be considered syntactic) and those that were not. The question has been raised here as to whether a distinction along these lines is really useful to the analyst.

The distinction between endocentric and exocentric is also important in terms of the semantics, but it has been suggested here that the difference might not be grammatical.

There is also a question as to whether subordinative compounds and coordinative compounds are clearly distinct categories, or whether they merge into each other and can be dealt with in much the same way. This question was discussed in Section 4.6 and will be taken up again in the next chapter.

5 *The Classification of Compounds*

5.1 Introduction

The question of how compounds are best classified has received a lot of attention in recent years, due largely to the work of Scalise and his colleagues (see e.g. Bisetto & Scalise 2005, Scalise & Bisetto 2009, Scalise & Vogel 2010). One of the reasons for this focus has been the observation that scholars have been very inconsistent in their classification of compounds: the inconsistency is not only in the classes considered important, but also in the nomenclature used for the classes.

In this chapter the question of classification will be taken up for closer scrutiny. First the Sanskrit classification will be considered, not because it is a particularly good classification, but because it has been so influential on all later work on compounding. Subsequently, a more contemporary approach to classifying compounds will be discussed.

5.2 The Sanskrit Classification

The Sanskrit grammarians recognise four major types of compound – tatpuruṣa, bahuvrīhi, dvandva and avyayībhāva – the first type having two major sub-types, one of which is the karmadhāraya. Each of these types will be considered in turn, and then we will turn to other types.

5.2.1 *Tatpuruṣa*

Tatpuruṣa (literally: 'his servant') compounds are what we would now call endocentric subordinative compounds. They denote a hyponym of the element which is the centre of the compound, which in Sanskrit is the right-hand element. Tatpuruṣa compounds are recursive, especially in later Sanskrit (Whitney 1889: 480). Killingley and Killingley (1995: 45) give the example in (1), and Lowe (2015: e80) gives an even more dramatic example, extending over many lines.

(1)   [aneka-vyāghra-nakha-prahāra-kupita]-[vana-gajam]
       several tiger claw blow angered forest elephant
       'a forest elephant, angered by several blows from tiger-claws'

The karmadhāraya (literally: 'action carrying' – Killingley & Killingley 1995: 46 – or 'office-bearing' – Whitney 1889: 489 – though the reason for the name is not clear) subset of tatpuruṣa compounds are those where the modifier and the head refer to the same entity (Killingley & Killingley 1995: 46), so that, for example, a *blackbird* refers to a bird and refers to something black. In turn, this can be broken down into cases where the modifier is an adjective, as in *candrámās* 'bright moon', *kṛṣṇaśakuní* 'black bird = raven', *mahāvīrá* 'great hero' (Burrows 1973: 210), and those where the first element is a noun, as in *puruṣamṛgá-* 'male antelope', *ūlūkayātu-* 'owl demon' (Burrows 1973: 210–211). Note that when applied to English, this would include types such as *blackbird, woman-doctor* and *singer-songwriter*, which are most usually classified as belonging to different sets in English, the last usually being seen as coordinative. Most of these karmadhārayas correspond to the attributive endocentric compounds of Scalise and Bisetto (2009).

The other main branch of tatpuruṣa compounds does not seem to be given a special name. It is the group where one noun is said to modify another in a relationship which would normally be expressed by a case. The case is not normally overtly marked, although some cases were marked for a period in the history of Sanskrit. This, therefore, looks like an early attempt to provide a list of relationships holding between the elements of a compound (compare above, Section 4.4). Given that the meanings of the genitive, in particular, are so general, a limitation to case-meanings may not exclude a great deal; nevertheless this provides a method of classifying the relevant compounds. Examples illustrating three different semantic case relationships (there is no overt case marking) are *brahmagavī* 'Brahmin's cow' (genitive), *apsaraḥsambhava* 'descent from a nymph' (ablative), *jalakrīḍā* 'sport in the water' (locative) (Whitney 1889: 490).

There is also a minor subtype of tatpuruṣa compound called 'dvigu' ('two cows'). This type has a numeral in first position.

5.2.2   *Bahuvrīhi*

The bahuvrīhi ('much rice = possessing much rice, rich') type has been discussed previously in more general terms (see Section 4.3). Note that I mark the macron here when I am citing it as a Sanskrit word, although I do not use a macron elsewhere.

Whitney (1889: 502) comments on these that their peculiarity lies in the fact that 'any compound with noun-final may be turned without alteration into an adjective, while to a simple noun must be added an adjective-making suffix'. This means that, if we follow the Sanskrit pattern closely, English *red-eyed* is not a bahuvrīhi, because it has the adjective-making suffix *-(e)d*, while *red-eye* (a noun in English, not an adjective) is closer to the prototype. In Sanskrit some of the bahuvrīhi 'come to be used as substantives' (Macdonell 1926: 175). Though the primary usage is adjectival in Sanskrit, in many other languages, the label is used for compounds which function as nouns rather than those that function as adjectives. Some examples are *bṛhádratha* 'having great chariots', *dugándhi* 'of ill savor', *yajñākāma* 'having desire of sacrifice' (Whitney 1889: 502).

5.2.3 Dvandva
The class of dvandva ('pair, couple') compounds is not precisely the same as the class of coordinative compounds discussed in Section 4.6, since some of the coordinative compounds are, as was shown above, karmadhāraya compounds. The prototypical dvandva is an additive coordinative nominal compound, shown in (2).

(2)   a. *hastyavçvāu* 'the elephant and horse'
       b. *prāṇāpānāú* 'inspiration and expiration'
       c. *vrīhiyavāú* 'rice and barley'
       d. *devāsurās* 'the gods and demons' (Whitney 1889: 485)

Note that the examples do not all show the kind of natural coordination (Wälchli 2005) that one might expect to find here. Dvandva compounds may be nouns or adjectives, and may involve more than two elements, at least in the later periods of Sanskrit. Dvandva compounds are dual (2a) and (2c) or plural (2d), depending on the meaning (Whitney 1889: 485).

5.2.4 Avyayībhāva
The avyayībhāva compounds are adverbial compounds, sometimes adjectival forms with adverbial usage, sometimes, especially in later Sanskrit, forms which were created as adverbs (Burrows 1973: 217). Examples are *pratyagni* 'facing the fire', *upararājam* 'near the king', *yāvajjīvam* 'as long as one lives' (Burrows 1973). The indeclinability of the first element of the compound was seen as criterial to this class (Whitney 1889: 513). This class is not much discussed in later classifications, probably because other languages do not have a distinctive class defined by precisely the features that define it in Sanskrit.

5.2.5   *Other Compound Types*

Apart from the avyayībhāva, the compounds classified above have been nouns and adjectives. Sanskrit also had compound verbs made up of a preposition or adverb and a verb, with a restricted number of prepositions and adverbs available (Macdonell 1926: 166).

There are also various sub-types of each of the major types given above, depending on whether they are nouns or adjectives, whether an ordinary adjective or a participle is used, the stress or the sandhi phenomena involved and so on. The classification given here is thus only the top-level classification, not a full classification. Lowe (2015: e73) notes that some thirty types of Sanskrit compound can be distinguished if it is relevant. One marginal sub-class of dvandva compounds worthy of note is the class with the same word repeated twice, as in *çváḥ-çvaḥ* 'further and further', *dyávi-dyavi* 'from day to day', *vayáṁ-vayam* 'our very selves' (Whitney 1889: 488, who says that these 'are not properly copulative compounds').

5.2.6   *Discussion*

The influence of the Sanskrit classification has been widespread, not only in terms of the classification it provides, but also in terms of the terminology – a terminology which has often been extended or misapplied in later discussions. Its main weakness as a more general classification is the fact that it is firmly based on the patterns of a single language; that is why, for example, it does not have a class of compounds like the French *porte-parole* 'carry-word = spokesperson', Italian *lavapiatti* 'wash-dishes = dishwasher'. Ironically, it does not even give us terms for classes of compound verb, even though such classes exist in Sanskrit. In other words, it cannot be used as a complete classification, even if it gives us hints as to what a more complete classification might look like. More recent classifications tend to attempt to provide a series of language-universal categories.

The terminology has long been, and continues to be, problematic. Many of the Sanskrit classes have labels in English, and sometimes those labels have been extended as much as the Sanskrit labels themselves have been extended. Some modern equivalents have been given in the discussion above, but it seems worth trying to draw this together.

The tatpuruṣa compounds are termed 'determinative' by Whitney (1889), and are now often called, as in this book, 'subordinative' (sometimes 'subordinate', as in Scalise & Bisetto 2009). Sometimes the subordinative aspect of these compounds is ignored in favour of their endocentricity, and they are simply termed 'endocentric' (Fabb 1998). This makes assumptions about headedness in other types of compound; see the discussion in Section 4.3.

The karmadhāraya sub-class of tatpuruṣa compounds is called 'descriptive' by Whitney (1889) and 'attributive' by Scalise and Bisetto (2009). They are largely ignored by other scholars (e.g. Bauer 1978).

The non-karmadhāraya sub-class of tatpuruṣa compounds is called 'dependent' by Whitney (1889), but this is not a good label, since all of the tatpuruṣa and bahuvrīhi compounds are dependent, in the sense that they have an internal structure that shows a modifier-head structure. We might call this class 'non-attributive', but that carries the implication that the attributive class is the default class, which is not the case in all languages. Perhaps, taking the label from the classification of adjectives discussed in Section 4.7, we might call this sub-class 'relational'. These are therefore forms like *water sport* (see the Sanskrit form in Section 5.2.1) where the *sport* has some relation to water, but *water* does not describe the sport in the way that *black* describes the bird in *blackbird*.

The term 'bahuvrīhi', which Whitney (1889) glosses as 'possessive', has largely been equated with the term 'exocentric', though the term 'exocentric' covers a much wider range of constructions that does 'bahuvrīhi' (see Bauer 2008b). There is a German tradition of calling these 'Dickkopf' ('thick-head') compounds, using an example of the type (just as *bahuvrīhi* is an example of the type); note, however, that the Sanskrit example acts primarily as an adjective, the German example as a noun. In any case 'possessive' seems more usual in modern German descriptions (e.g. Fleischer & Barz 2007). The widespread use of 'bahuvrīhi', even in English texts, may be due to the perceived lack of a suitable English language term.

Whitney (1889) calls the dvandva compounds 'copulative', a label which goes back to the Latin grammarians. This label has also been widely used in recent times. The overt relation of *copulative* with *copulate*, which is now restricted to sexual congress, makes the term seem less suitable today (although that was its origin), but if it is understood as 'forming a couple' is less worrisome. The *singer-songwriter* type is often termed 'appositional', or 'appositive' (Scalise & Bisetto 2009), and the term 'multi-functional' was used earlier (see Section 4.3), but, as we have seen, falls within the set of karmadhāraya compounds rather than the set of dvandva compounds for the Sanskrit grammarians. More recent labels such as 'co-compound' (Wälchli 2005), 'coordinate compound' (Scalise & Bisetto 2009) or 'coordinative compound' (Bauer et al. 2013) cover far more than the term 'dvandva' covers (see Section 4.6).

Finally, in this section, I should like to draw attention to the work by Lowe (2015). He argues in great detail that Sanskrit compounding is open to syntactic description. Similar points have been made about (some of) English

SUB				ATAP				COORD	
ground		verbal-nexus		attributive		appositive			
endo	exo	endo	exo	endo	exo	endo	exo	endo	exo
windmill mushroom soup	sans papiers sottoscala lavapiatti	bookseller tree eater street seller	pickpocket	high school blue- eyed	redskin	snailmail swordfish mushroom cloud	?	poeta- pintor	mother-child Bosnia- Herzegovina

Figure 5.1 Scalise & Bisetto's (2009: 50) classification of compounds

compounding, for instance, by Payne and Huddleston (2002: 448–51). Although Lowe does not deny the word-like status of many compounds, he prefers to see compounding as having a 'somewhat intermediate status ... between full phrasal syntax and morphology' (Lowe 2015: e109). The suggestion is, in itself, not new, though such a complete argument is rarely presented, but it does lead to the question of how typical the compounds of Sanskrit might be. I cannot answer this question, but leave it as a potential problem with basing a classification on the Sanskrit system.

5.3   Exploring Scalise's Approach

The discussion in this section is based on Scalise and Bisetto (2009). The authors point out that the classification of compounds given in the standard works on morphology shows a complete lack of agreement. Attributive compounds are sometimes but not always distinct from other subordinative compounds, for instance, and the terminology is variable, as is the way in which these categories interact with categories like exocentric and endocentric. Some authors present a very flat classification, with few subtypes, while others present a very hierarchical classification. Perhaps inevitably, some classifications include categories that are ignored in others. Scalise and Bisetto (2009) themselves provide a classification with three major types (subordinate, attributive/appositive and coordinate) with endocentric and exocentric subtypes much lower down the hierarchy (reproduced in Figure 5.1). For Booij (2007), they report endocentric and exocentric being top-level distinctions (in a much flatter classification).

When phonologists and semanticists were faced with similar problems of cross-classification, they used features to provide a solution. While it is true that phonological and semantic features are often used in the formulation of rules, and here the features are simply being used to classify, the same solution

Table 5.1 *Summary of proposed feature system*

Feature	Values
±subordinative	subordinative vs. coordinative
±attributive	attributive vs. relational
±endocentric	endocentric vs. exocentric
±argumental	argumental vs. free
word-class	name, noun, verb, adjective, adverb, etc.
head word-class	name, noun, verb, adjective, adverb, etc.
headedness	right, left, both

seems called for. Qualities such as subordinative and endocentric are not hierarchically arranged but are values of equal standing which may apply to compounds. The features may be viewed as unary or binary and may have values other than plus or minus. Because there is no hierarchy, the features can be presented in random order. A summary of the features to be used is presented in Table 5.1. Note that not all the features presented are necessarily of value, either in particular languages or, possibly, universally.

The first feature to be considered here is [± subordinative] (or [subordinative] versus [coordinative]). Subordinative includes tatpurusa and bahuvrihi compounds, which are distinguished by other features; coordinative includes many more types than just dvandva compounds.

The next feature to be considered is [± attributive] (or [attributive] versus [relational]). Subordinative attributive compounds include those with A + N structure such as German *Rotwein* ('red wine'), coordinative attributive compounds include forms like *singer-songwriter*. Subordinative relational compounds include forms such as *windmill*, coordinative relational compounds are the dvandvas.

The third feature is [± endocentric] (or [endocentric] versus [exocentric]). The various cases and types have been previously mentioned, but we can set them out for clarity:

- subordinative, attributive, endocentric compounds include *Rotwein*
- subordinative, attributive, exocentric compounds include *redcap* 'porter, military policeman'
- subordinative, relational, endocentric compounds include forms like *windmill*
- subordinative, relational, exocentric compounds include forms like *egghead*

- coordinative, attributive, endocentric compounds are those like *singer-songwriter*
- coordinative, relational, endocentric are those like *stir-fry*
- coordinative, attributive, exocentric compounds would probably include *blue-green*
- coordinative, relational, exocentric compounds would include examples like Vietnamese *bàn ghế* 'table chair = furniture'

The next set of features is concerned with word-class. First, we need to know about the word-class of the compound as a whole. There are various ways in which word-class could be introduced. One of these would involve using the features [±N], [±V] as introduced by Chomsky (1970) and set out in (3).

(3)   .   +N   −N
+V   Adjective   Verb
−V   Noun   Adposition

These features, though, allow for only four word-classes – noun, verb, adjective and adposition. It seems likely to me that compounding in some languages would also involve adverbs where these might contrast with either adpositions or with adjectives. Certainly, if this never happens, it would be an interesting claim, and one that would have to be carefully justified. Also, the two-feature system does not allow proper nouns/names to be a separate category, although this may be useful in the classification of coordinative compounds, as was seen in Section 4.6. For these reasons, it seems to me to be preferable to have a feature [word-class] with values of name, noun, verb, adjective, adverb, adposition (and possibly numeral or quantifier and pronoun).

I would also propose that a feature marking the word-class of the head of the construction would be useful. In endocentric constructions, this would be totally predictable (and so redundant), but in exocentric constructions the head may or may not be of the same word-class as the construction as a whole (see the discussion of head versus centre in Section 4.3): in *lavapiatti* 'wash-dishes = dishwasher', for instance, the construction is a noun, but the head of the compound internally is *lava*, a verb. Thus we need a feature [head word-class] with the same possible values as the feature [word-class]. It is not clear to me whether a feature with the word-class of the modifier is required or not. It is clear one could be added, but the amount of gain does not seem to be valuable enough when set against the added complexity of the system.

If we compare English *postage stamp* with its French equivalent *timbre-poste* 'stamp-post(.office) = postage stamp', or the two Vietnamese compounds *xe lửa* 'vehicle fire = train' *hỏa xa* 'fire vehicle = train' (the first native Vietnamese, the second representing a Chinese pattern; Thompson 1965: 130), we see that we need to know whether the head of the compound is on the right or the left. We could do this with a feature [± right-headed] (since right-headedness seems to be the default) or with [right-headed] versus [left-headed], but if we want to allow for other options such as double-headedness, then we need a feature [headedness] which can have values left, right or both (and possibly neither).

Finally, for compounds which are [subordinative] and [relational] there is an option that they might be [± argumental] (or [argumental] versus [free]). Argumental exocentric compounds include things such as *lavapiatti*, and argumental endocentric compounds include things like *taxi-driver*. The examples given above, such as *windmill* and *egghead*, were free rather than argumental. (The label 'free' might not be the best terminology but seems appropriate. If the argumental compounds are restricted in meaning by virtue of their argument structure, the complementary set is unrestricted, and so 'free'.)

In any given language, it might be that not all of these features are required, or not all values of these features are required. For example, it may be that some languages have compound nouns, but no compounds in other word-classes, or might have only endocentric compounds, and so on. So this set of features will provide more categories than are required in most languages. At the same time, they might not be sufficient to distinguish between the various types of coordinative compound discussed in Section 4.6.

To show how this classification system might work, examples of English compounds in the various classes established by the system are illustrated in an appendix to this chapter. Because so many feature-combinations give rise to categories which are not found in English, only those combinations which are found, or may be found, are listed. The entire list should be taken as explora-tory rather than definitive: not only is it often difficult to determine which category a particular example fits (or at least, I find it so), it is difficult to be sure about the existence of some categories. The reader may thus disagree with categorial assignment without thereby disagreeing with the system as such and may be able to find examples for categories that I have not included. Note that I have called coordinative compounds right-headed unless there is reason to do otherwise, rather than double-headed – this is a controversial ad-hoc decision. The great benefit of a classification of this kind is that it forces the analyst to consider the range of types that may be found.

5.4   The Value of Classifications

A classification in isolation has little value: we need to know what the classification is supposed to do. The Sanskrit classification in Section 5.2 had as its goal to tell learners of Sanskrit how to interpret the various patterns they might find in texts. It was appropriately language-specific. The Scalise type of classification (and certainly the one I have produced here based on Scalise's work) has a much wider purpose: to allow for comparison of compound structures across languages. To do that it has to be fine-grained enough to ensure that comparisons match equivalent to equivalent, but not so fine-grained that it creates an unnecessary proliferation of types.

I have already suggested that the classification system provided above might be truncated for individual languages. For example, Dutch seems to be aggressively right-headed where compounds are concerned (Booij 2002: 143) and probably does not need to consider the [headedness] feature. A less clear case is illustrated with English: although it is clear that one can distinguish between attributive and other subordinative endocentric compounds in English, it is not clear to me that anything hangs on this distinction beyond the marginally different semantic interpretation. I suggested earlier that the fact that it can be hard to draw the distinction between the two classes may be evidence for such a position (see also Radimský 2015: 89–92 on Italian). However, any two classes that differ in respect of only one feature (or feature value) may be difficult to distinguish, and part of the problem with having a relatively detailed classification is that it leads to a large number of borderline cases. Thus the difficulty at the borders of the two groups may not indicate anything more than that there is a superordinate class – scarcely a surprising conclusion. Cross-linguistic comparison requires that both the superordinate and the subordinate class be compared; single-language descriptions may find some of the subclasses more useful than others.

It has already been argued that exocentricity may be a matter of interpretation rather than a matter of structure (see above, Section 4.3). If that point is accepted, then the whole [±endocentric] feature becomes redundant. There are instances which would be made much easier to deal with if that were the case. For example, the araucaria tree, native to Chile, is sometimes in English called a *monkey-puzzle tree* and sometimes just called a *monkey-puzzle*. Deletion of a head is one potential reason for an exocentric reading, so that we would expect *money-puzzle* to be exocentric, and to the extent that a monkey-puzzle is a tree, that is the case. However, there is a case to be made for a monkey-puzzle being something which is a puzzle, 'a difficult problem' (*OED*), at least for the putative monkey, and therefore it might be considered endocentric. Or it might be that this meaning of *puzzle* is seen as arising by metonymy from the older meaning, '[t]he state or condition of being puzzled' (*OED*), and that *monkey puzzle* has a structure similar to *barkeep* and is exocentric on those grounds, rather than on the grounds of elision. It is not clear that a definitive answer can be given as to whether *monkey-puzzle* is endocentric or exocentric.

A case which requires rather more consideration is the distinction between synthetic and free compounds. For many scholars it is self-evident that a compound like *bus-driver* is different from one like *windmill* because one of the elements in *bus-driver* fills one of the arguments in the verb *drive*, present in the other element, while there is no argument-filling in *windmill*. Conversely, there is no modification in *bus-driver*. Yet there are a number of reasons why this obvious answer may not be the only answer:

- Linguists seem to disagree on whether it is strictly argument structure which is reflected in synthetic compounds or whether adjuncts are also involved. Everyone agrees that *street cleaner* is a synthetic compound, but people do not agree about *street seller* (see above in Figure 5.1) where *street* indicates where the selling takes place rather than what is sold. This might seem to be no more than a matter of definition. However, if *street seller* is a synthetic compound, then what about *weekday delivery* (which still has a verb in the root of *delivery*) or *house party* (where there is no verb explicit in the compound)? To the extent that there is a distinction to be drawn here, it is not a semantic one, it is one based on whether or not there is overtly a verb in the compound. Even then there might be disagreements as to whether *speech synthesis* contains an overt verb, for instance (see e.g. Lieber 1994), or as to whether arguments of nouns are also included, as in *garage roof*. If the difference is the presence or absence of a verb, then there are two things to say. The first is that it is implicit in the formal make-up of the compound and does not need a special construction type. The second is that it seems to run counter to the lexical integrity hypothesis, because all we should know about *delivery* by the time we compound it with *weekday* is that it is a noun.
- There is also disagreement in the literature as to whether subjects can form part of synthetic compounds (or perhaps only subjects of ergative verbs). Thus Radimský (2015: 130) comments that under this interpretation *police protection* will be argumental if the police are protected, but not if they do the protecting. Lieber (2016) argues that

subject interpretations are part of the range of synthetic compounds, and she cites examples like *family celebration*, but points out that this is contrary to earlier statements on the subject. Again, this could be seen as merely a dispute over definition, but it influences the degree to which the interpretation of synthetic compounds is restricted.

- The most general interpretation of what counts as a synthetic compound is that it must contain a deverbal head (Lieber 1994: 3608), and this is viewed as the most common pattern. But more recent treatments (e.g. Bauer et al. 2013: 466) also consider instances where the verb is in the modifier, such as *cry-baby* and *draw-string*. Bauer et al. (2013: 473) acknowledge, with reference to these, that they might be interpreted as non-argumental. Again, it is not clear what compounds fall within the scope of synthetic compounding.

- Under the most restrictive interpretation of synthetic compounds, such as that given by Roeper and Siegel (1978), the interpretation of an argumental compound is unambiguous: *bus-driver* must mean 'one who drives buses' because *buses* is the first sister of *drive* in the corresponding syntactic tree. Even then, different arguments are put in modifier position by different compound patterns: *man-made* uses a subject, while *bus-driver* uses an object. Once we move away from this very narrow interpretation of what a synthetic compound might be, any novel compound has to be interpreted to discover what role the modifier plays in relation to the verb: subject (*police protection*), object (*bus-driver*), temporal locative (*weekend delivery*) and so on. Somehow we have to determine that a *street seller* is not selling streets. This interpretation process is no different from that which is involved in compounds like *windmill* versus *flour mill* (where no verb is involved), and saying that there are two construction types here may simply lead to the same fundamental process of interpretation having to be spelt out twice in different places in the grammar, which is not economical.

- An argument may be made that *bus-driver* does show modification, just like *windmill, bus* indicating what kind of driver is involved, contrasting with *car-driver, engine-driver, truck-driver* and even *pile-driver, screw-driver* and so on.

- Like any other subordinative compound, synthetic compounds may be ambiguous. Not only can they be ambiguous in terms of which argument they involve (like *police protection*), they can be ambiguous between a reading where they are argumental and a reading where they are not. *Street seller* might be such an example, if locative adjuncts are not part of the range of argumental compounds. *Car charger* is listed in the *OED* with two meanings, 'one who charges or loads railway cars' and 'a charger of electrical devices taking power from a motor car'. The examples in (4), all from COCA, illustrate a range of potential meanings with a single head, only a few of which are potentially distinguishable by stress. One point of interest here is that the compound can be interpreted even without the information as to whether *basketball* or *target*, for example, is the direct object of *shoot* (do you *shoot the target* or *shoot at the target?*).

(4)   a. basketball shooting, drive-by shooting, gang shooting, mass shooting, perimeter shooting, police shooting, precision shooting, rifle shooting, slug shooting, target shooting, trap shooting, trouble shooting, weekend shooting
       b. That cat – looks like it set off the gun that killed its owner. There's a tuft of fur in the trigger housing, and paw prints all over. "# I sat back on my haunches. Not many men can take my stare; Creighton only shifted slightly. "Look, Pru, I can't get into it. Just take it on faith, for once. Okay? Call it an accident. A real freak accident. "# So that's what he'd meant by a cat shooting. Death by feline.
       c. Pass shooting wood ducks means lurking between the roost and the food along a stream course, treeline, or some other feature the birds use for navigation.

In summary, there are two major problems here. The first is the definition of a synthetic compound. Theoretically this might not matter much, in that there may be more or less canonical types of synthetic compound, but it seems to indicate that there is no agreement as to what the crucial features of a synthetic compound are and thus where the core lies. The second problem is whether synthetic compounds are clearly a separate type from free compounds. The vital point here is that explanations of the semantics of free compounds through variable-R or through a mnemonic approach are already powerful enough to encompass synthetic compounds as well, and two distinct routes of interpretation are unnecessary, uneconomical and contrary to Ockham's razor.

The same argument can be raised against distinguishing coordinative and subordinative compounds, as has already been discussed in part in Section 4.6, and as is argued by Breindl and Thurmair (1992) and Eisenberg (2006: 232), as cited in Detmold and Weiß (2012: 423) – though these authors do not accept the conclusion. In general, the classification of compounds is dependent upon the goals of the classifier, and differing aims can lead to a need for a classification with differing grain size.

Appendix: Classification Applied to English

Features	Example(s)	Comment, reference, etc.
[subordinative], [attributive], [endocentric], [headedness: right], [word-class: name]	Fiery Fred	The nickname of the Yorkshire cricketer, Fred Trueman (1931–2006). There is little reason to consider this a compound, but it is classificatory, like *red squirrel*.
[subordinative], [attributive], [endocentric], [headedness: right], [word-class: noun]	blackbird	
[subordinative], [attributive], [endocentric], [headedness: right], [word-class: adjective]	well-chosen (words)	If this is a compound; Bauer et al. (2013: 438) exclude such examples.
[subordinate], [attributive], [endocentric], [headedness: right], [word-class: verb]	deep-fry	
[subordinative], [attributive], [endocentric], [headedness: right], [word-class: preposition]	into	If this is a compound and not coordinative
[subordinative], [attributive], [endocentric], [headedness: left], [word-class: noun]	governor general	Not counted as a compound, see Section 3.5.3.
[subordinative], [attributive], [exocentric], [headedness: right], [word-class: noun], [head word-class: name], [argumental]	peeping Tom	Possibly not a compound
[subordinative], [attributive], [exocentric], [headedness: right], [word-class: noun],	long John	

(cont.)

Features	Example(s)	Comment, reference, etc.
[head word-class: name], [free]		
[subordinative], [attributive], [exocentric], [headedness: right], [word-class: noun], [head word-class: adjective], [free]	big red	This used to be the name used for the buses in Wellington
[subordinative], [attributive], [exocentric], [headedness: right], [word-class: noun], [head word-class: noun]	dimwit	Standard bahuvrihi
[subordinative], [attributive], [exocentric], [headedness: right], [word-class: adjective], [head word-class: noun]	blue-collar (worker); backstage (areas)	(*backstage* can also be an adverb, though with different stress)
[subordinative], [attributive], [exocentric], [headedness: right], [word-class: adjective], [head word-class: adverb]	not-quite (candidate)	COCA
[subordinative], [attributive], [exocentric], [headedness: left], [word-class: noun], [head word-class: verb]	go-slow	
[subordinative], [attributive], [exocentric], [headedness: right], [word-class: adverb], [head word-class: noun]	backstage; off-side	Quirk et al. 1985: 453; *off-side* may be left-headed
[subordinative], [attributive], [exocentric], [headedness: left], [word-class: adjective], [head word-class: verb]	win-quickly (mentality)	COCA
[subordinative], [relational], [endocentric], [headedness: right], [word-class: name], [free]	Poker Steve Fox	COCA
[subordinative], [relational], [endocentric], [headedness: right], [word-class: noun], [argumental]	taxi-driver; cancer victim	For *cancer victim*, see Bauer et al. 2013: 472
[subordinative], [relational], [endocentric], [headedness:	windmill	

(*cont.*)

Features	Example(s)	Comment, reference, etc.
right], [word-class: noun], [free]		
[subordinative], [relational], [endocentric], [headedness: right], [word-class: adjective], [argumental]	houseproud	
[subordinative], [relational], [endocentric], [headedness: right], [word-class: adjective], [free]	colour-blind	Might be argumental: *blind to colours.*
[subordinative], [relational], [endocentric], [headedness: right], [word-class: verb], [argumental]	head-hunt	
[subordinative], [relational], [endocentric], [headedness: right], [word-class: verb], [free]	window-shop	
[subordinative], [relational], [endocentric], [headedness: right], [word-class: preposition], [free]	in between	
[subordinative], [relational], [endocentric], [headedness: left], [word-class: noun], [free]	end-game	
[subordinative], [relational], [exocentric], [headedness: right], [word-class: noun], [head word-class: noun], [argumental]	house-warming, glow worm	
[subordinative], [relational], [exocentric], [headedness: right], [word-class: noun], [head word-class: noun], [free]	downfall	the *fall* element could be a verb
[subordinative], [relational], [exocentric], [headedness: right], [word-class: noun], [head word-class: adjective], [free]	swimming blue	www.hertford.ox.ac.uk/news accessed 11 Nov. 2015

(cont.)

Features	Example(s)	Comment, reference, etc.
[subordinative], [relational], [exocentric], [headedness: right], [word-class: noun], [head word-class: verb], [free]	uptake	
[subordinative], [relational], [exocentric], [headedness: left], [word-class: noun], [head word-class: verb], [free]	show-down	
[subordinative], [relational], [exocentric], [headedness: left], [word-class: noun], [head word-class: preposition], [argumental]	underground	*underground* can also be an adjective and an adverb
[subordinative], [relational], [exocentric], [headedness: right], [word-class: noun], [head word-class: preposition], [free]	sun-up	
[subordinative], [relational], [exocentric], [headedness: right], [word-class: adjective], [head word-class: noun], [argumental]	turtle-neck (sweater); three-syllable (word)	
[subordinative], [relational], [exocentric], [headedness: left], [word-class: adjective], [head word-class: noun], [free]	oestrogen-only (pill)	Bauer & Renouf 2001
[subordinative], [relational], [exocentric], [headedness: right], [word-class: adjective], [head word-class: verb], [argumental]	quick-change (artiste)	
[subordinative], [relational], [exocentric], [headedness: left], [word-class: adjective], [head word-class: verb], [free]	fail-safe (device)	
[subordinative], [relational], [exocentric], [headedness: right], [word-class: verb], [head word-class: noun], [free]	machine-gun	An alternative analysis here would be based on conversion.

(cont.)

Features	Example(s)	Comment, reference, etc.
[subordinative], [relational], [exocentric], [headedness: right], [word-class: verb], [head word-class: verb], [argumental]	hen-peck	
[subordinative], [relational], [exocentric], [headedness: left], [word-class: adverb], [head word-class: noun], [free]	centre stage	If this is a compound
[coordinative], [attributive], [endocentric], [headedness: right], [word-class: name]	Prince Charles	If this is a compound
[coordinative], [attributive], [endocentric], [headedness: right], [word-class: noun]	woman-doctor	
[coordinative], [attributive], [endocentric], [headedness: right], [word-class: adjective]	icy-cold	
[coordinative], [attributive], [endocentric], [headedness: right], [word-class: verb]	blow-dry	
[coordinative], [attributive], [endocentric], [headedness: right], [word-class: adverb]	urgently-quietly	COCA
[coordinative], [relational], [endocentric], [headedness: right], [word-class: name]	Fotherington-Smythe	If this is a compound
[coordinative], [attributive], [endocentric], [headedness: right], [word-class: noun]	singer-songwriter	
[coordinative], [relational], [endocentric], [headedness: right], [word-class: adjective]	linguistic-philosophical (discussion)	
[coordinative], [relational], [endocentric], [headedness: right], [word-class: verb]	stir-fry	
[coordinative], [relational], [endocentric], [headedness: right], [word-class: adverb]	herewith	
[coordinative], [relational], [endocentric], [headedness:	onto	If this is a compound

(cont.)

Features	Example(s)	Comment, reference, etc.
right], [word-class: preposition]		
[coordinative], [attributive], [exocentric], [headedness: right], [word-class: name], [head word-class: name], [free]	Nelson-Marlborough	
[coordinative], [relational], [exocentric], [headedness: right], [word-class: noun], [head word-class: noun], [free]	ape-man	Possibly attributive
[coordinative], [relational], [exocentric], [headedness: right], [word-class: noun], [head word-class: verb], [free]	fly-drive	BNC
[coordinative], [attributive], [exocentric], [headedness: right], [word-class: adjective], [head word-class: adjective], [free]	blue-green	
[coordinative], [relational], [exocentric], [headedness: right], [word-class: adjective], [head word-class: verb], [free]	stop-go (economics)	
[coordinative], [relational], [exocentric], [headedness: right], [word-class: adjective], [head word-class: adverb], [free]	yes-no (question)	
[coordinative], [relational], [exocentric], [headedness: right], [word-class: adverb], [head word-class: adjective], [free]	north-east	

6 *Facets of English Compounding*

6.1   Questions of Stress

If we consider the difference between *black bird* and *blackbird*, we have seen that there are various reasons for considering *black bird* to be a sequence of two words, while *blackbird* is a single word (these reasons were canvassed in Chapter 2). Although stress is just one of the reasons for postulating the difference, it is an easily observable difference and correlates fairly well with spelling – at least for examples containing a sub-set of English adjectives. If we then look at the difference between *motor boat* and *motor neurone*, apparently the same difference is again audible, and there is a reason to see the two kinds of construction as parallel: forestress reflects compound status, end-stress reflects phrasal status (see e.g. Chomsky & Halle 1968). This view is also supported by parallels from other Germanic languages. In Dutch, German and peninsular Scandinavian, forestress is one of the defining features of compounds, marking them as being single words (see e.g. Dansk Sprognævn 2015).

However, the situation in English is not the same as the situation in these other Germanic languages. In English, but not in the other languages, there are systematic or quasi-systematic stress distinctions between pairs such as those in (1).

(1)	*forestress*	*end-stress*
	applecake	apple tart
	glass case (case to display glassware)	glass case (case made of glass)
	handball (a game)	handball (an offence in soccer)
	Madison Street	Madison Avenue
	shooting stick	shooting star
	toy shop ('shop where toys are bought')	toy shop ('shop which is a toy')

Once forestress has been labeled 'compound stress' and end-stress has been labeled 'phrasal stress' (Chomsky & Halle 1968), the natural assumption is that the examples in the first column in (1) are compounds, and those in the second column are not compounds. It is for that reason that I have avoided this terminology here, in favour of 'forestress' and 'end-stress', which makes fewer assumptions. Quite apart from the difficulty of explaining in what way *apple-cake* differs from *apple tart* (or *Christmas cake* from *Christmas pudding*) that would be a correlate of any such a categorial distinction, there is an alternative influence from Germanic, where almost any N + N sequence is a compound.

I have called the distinction between forestressed constructions and those with end-stress 'systematic or quasi-systematic', and it has to be asked just how systematic the distinction really is. There are some well-known examples which differ between British (especially older British) and American varieties of English, for example, British English having forestress in *ice-cream* and end-stress in *olive oil*, while American English shows the reverse. Scottish English has more end-stress than the English from south of the border (Giegerich 2004, 2015). More seriously, Fudge (1984: 144–146) lists items which might show variation, including those in (2). Fudge's list is by no means exhaustive.

(2)   armchair, baby doll, bargain basement, channel swimmer, part-owner, stage-manager

Bauer (1983b) reports that individuals vary in the stress they report on individual items, as well as dictionaries differing in the stress they assign to particular items. Kunter (2011: 198) agrees that 'we have to conclude that across-speaker variability is a common feature of compounds in naturally occurring speech' and cannot be put down to random variation. In New Zealand news readers' style, Bauer (2015c) finds the overuse of end-stress on items which might be expected to carry forestress. Despite such evidence, Kunter (2011) finds that most examples do have a relatively fixed stress pattern across speakers – and this is no doubt why dictionaries feel that they can (and should) mark stress in the N + N constructions that they list, and why there is such a large literature making the assumption that individual examples have a fixed stress-pattern in English.

Recent examinations of the question, using advanced statistical techniques, have shown that stress is largely predictable, providing that the appropriate factors and sufficient factors are taken into consideration (Plag 2006, Plag et al. 2008, Giegerich 2009, Bell & Plag 2012). Bell (2011) concludes that in the face of such evidence there is no reason to assume two different classes of compound (as is done by Giegerich 2004 and many others); rather there is a class of compounds with stress being distributed across them in a largely predictable manner. This seems incontrovertible: stress which is predictable on any given item cannot create two contrastive item types, unless those types are defined by the stress itself. A slightly different perspective is brought by Arndt-Lappe (2011) who argues that stress can be modelled as being assigned by local analogies with other exemplars of similar compounds (with what counts as similar being potentially variable). This again argues for there being a single class of compounds, but makes some attempt to explain the variability of stress assignment that can occur within that class.

In other words, although the point is not universally accepted, there is a growing consensus that distinct stress patterns in (especially N + N) compounds do not represent two distinct construction types, but largely predictable variation within a single construction-type.

The difficulty with this is that we are used to the notion of compounds being defined by their stress; if they are not, we need an alternative definition. Such a definition has been suggested earlier (see Sections 3.7 and 4.7). A compound is a structure which allows for non-canonical modification patterns which act semantically in a classificatory function. We will need to add to this, to allow for non-canonical compounds which are not formed by a process of compounding (things like *before-tax, baby-sit*), that a compound may also be a form which looks like a form created for these purposes. By such a definition, all the examples in (1) are compounds, independent of stress. This is not the main problem, though. This still does not allow us to call *blackbird* a compound, because adjectives canonically modify nouns. This problem was considered in Section 4.7, where it was suggested that an instance like *blackbird* provides classificatory rather than descriptive semantics for the adjective (with resultant inaccessibility of the adjective to, for example, comparison and with the possibility of having *a brown blackbird*). As was pointed out there, it is not only forestressed A + N constructions which show this semantic behaviour. There are also a host of other constructions, like *red squirrel*, which show the same behaviour but with a different stress pattern. It was suggested at the time that stress might have to be taken to be non-defining for A + N compounds, as well. In other words, just as stress does not distinguish one set of N + N compounds from another, so stress does not distinguish one set of A + N compounds from another.

However, the factors which determine stress in A + N sequences are not the same as those which determine it in N + N sequences. Bauer (2004b) suggests frequency as a prime determinant of stress in the A + N cases. This is consistent with variability in the stress of A + N sequences. In the two weeks preceding the writing of this section, I heard *hígh cloud, fóul play* and *blúe whale* in news broadcasts: since the semantics in these cases is potentially classificatory, the stress makes sense. In the case of *high cloud*, where the semantics might be expected to be descriptive, we must consider that in weather forecasts, where this was heard, only *high cloud* and *low cloud* get special mention, and both are relatively common.

Even this does not resolve the question, though. In Section 4.7 the case of things like *atomic bomb* was raised. Some people see these as compounds, others do not. If classificatory semantics (and inability to inflect) is all that matters, then constructions like *atomic bomb* should also be considered compounds (see Giegerich 2015 for some discussion). The question is whether the use of an adjective which is inherently classificatory (like *atomic*) is equivalent to the classificatory use of an adjective which is fundamentally descriptive. My proposal here is that the two are distinct. That compounds lead to non-canonical modification, but that canonical modification of an adjective like *red* is descriptive, and only classificatory modification is non-canonical, while with an adjective like *atomic* classificatory modification is canonical. Thus *atomic bomb* is an instance of canonical modification, and not a compound, but a noun phrase.

This also accounts for the stress difference between *dramátic society* and *dramatic appéarance*. Where the adjective is non-gradable and classificatory there is forestress. But it does not account for the difference between *prímary school* and *primary educátion*. Although I do not have definite answer here, it seems to me that the distinction, apart from a matter of frequency, is that *primary school* is nearly always overtly or covertly in opposition with *secondary school*. There are also questions of patterns from relevant exemplars. If there were such a thing as a *tertiary school,* it would have to be stressed on the first element, while *tertiary education* takes end-stress. Such questions would have to be tested on larger numbers of examples, but there is some kind of justification here which is in line with what has been found for N + N compounds.

Stress in other compound types is very variable. Bahuvrihi nominal compounds like *redcap* and *egghead* seem to take forestress. But where exocentricity arises from metaphor, we would not expect stress to correlate with exocentricity. We find forestress in *fire dog* and end-stress in *knuckle sandwich* 'a punch in the mouth'. V + N compounds like *spoilsport* seem to take forestress reliably, as do N + V nominal compounds like *buzz-kill* (see examples in (3), also the *OED*).

(3)   You're such a buzz-kill, Roadrunner. (Tracy, P. J. 2012. *Off the grid*. New
       York: Putnam, p. 71)
       A prick-tease at fourteen, a runaway at fifteen, that girl was nothing but trouble.
       (Robotham, Michael. 2012. *Say you're sorry*. London: Sphere, p. 195)

Multifunctional (appositional) coordinative nominal compounds like *singer-songwriter* take end-stress. This is also true of many other types of coordinative compound: *cough-laugh, stir-fry, blue-green, historical-philosophical, Nelson-Marlborough, HarperCollins, murder-suicide*, and translative and co-participant compounds like *Edinburgh-Glasgow, Dutch-English, Arab-Israeli*. Note that *dive-bomb, sleepwalk*, though, have forestress, and it is not clear why or how widespread the pattern is.

Compound adjectives of the form N + A which can be glossed as 'as A as (a) N' (*snow-white, dirt-cheap*) take end-stress, but these are often subject to iambic reversal (aka 'the rhythm rule', 'stress-shift') so that we perceive *A snów-white shirt*, but *This shirt is snow-whíte*. Other N + A adjectives like *air-tight, love-sick, work-shy*, which cannot be glossed the same way, take forestress (Fudge 1984: 148).

Compound verbs normally take end-stress when they are made up of Particle + V (*outwit, undergo*) or other Adv+ V (*freewheel, illtreat*) (Kingdon 1958: 173). Other subordinative compound verbs usually take forestress (*browbeat, hitchhike, ringbark*).

Endocentric adverbial compounds with a noun in first position seem to take end-stress: *all-in, head-first, head-on* (Kingdon 1958: 169). With other structures, there is often a difference in stress between a form used as an adjective and the same (orthographic or segmental) form used as an adverb, as in (4).

(4)   *Adjective*   *Adverb*
       ínside   insíde
       néar-by   near bý
       fár off   far óff
       óutright   outríght
       wórldwide   worldwíde

How far this is a matter of word-class and how much a matter of position is perhaps hard to determine. In some of these cases the reason for forestress in attributive adjectives is iambic reversal, with end-stress being found in attributive usage (which prosodically is more like the adverbial usage). This seems to be true at least of *far-off, inside* and *worldwide* in the list in (4). However, there are also examples which do not work the same way, as in (5).

(5)   *Adjective and Adverb*
       whólesale
       fréelance

Compound prepositions vary in their stress. This is illustrated in (6). Those listed here with end-stress might be argued not to be compound.

(6)   *forestress*   *endstress*
       apart from   throughout
       as to   underneath
       because of   within
       due to   without
       except for
       into
       off of
       onto
       out of
       upto

More complex examples, which are built from phrasal structures, seem to maintain the phrasal stress: *by means of, in comparison with, in exchange for, on behalf of.*

All this is summarised in Table 6.1.

Table 6.1 *Stress in English compounds: a summary*

Category	*Stress*	*Example*
N + N endocentric	variable, but largely predictable	*Christmas cake, Christmas pudding*
A + N endocentric, descriptive A used as a classifier	variable	*blackbird, red squirrel*
A + N endocentric, associative A	forestress, but not clear when forestress arises	*primary school*
N + N or A + N exocentric (except where the exocentricity is due to metaphor)	forestress	*bonehead, red head*
V + N]ₙ and N + V]ₙ exocentric	forestress	*spoilsport, kill-buzz*
N + N coordinative, multifunctional	end-stress	*singer-songwriter*
Other coordinative	mainly end-stress (some counter-examples)	*blue-green, cough-laugh*
N + A endocentric, elative	end-stress	*grass-green*
Other N + A endocentric	forestress	*airtight*
Particle + V endocentric	end-stress	*undergo*
Adv + V endocentric	end-stress	*illtreat*
Other endocentric verb	forestress	*hitchhike*
Adv endocentric	end-stress	*all-in*
P + P	variable	*because of, within*

Overall, there is huge variability in stress in things that look like compounds, and little evidence for taking stress to be definitional of a compound. We do seem to find certain recurring patterns. Forestress tends to be associated with items of high frequency, and with items which fit into productive series with forestress; end-stress occurs where there is productive use of an end-stress pattern, but also in unfamiliar combinations. Some of the patterns are associated with particular meanings or formal patterns, but it would seem that rather than seeing these as being determined by meaning, we should see them as being determined by local parallels, where the meaning is part of what makes cases parallel. In other words, I would see the approach championed by Arndt-Lappe (2011) as being the most useful way of looking at stress patterns in compounds across word-classes, and this has the related effect that we do not need to consider stress as a feature specific to compounds at all.

6.2   Phrasal Verbs

Verbs like *fall over, look up, look up to, put up with, shoot down* are often termed 'phrasal verbs' (Strang 1968; Palmer 1987; Sinclair 2005; Crystal 2008: sv *verb*), though other terminologies are often found: Quirk et al. (1985: 1150) call them 'multi-word verbs', with 'phrasal verb' being one subtype; Huddleston (2002a: 274) specifically avoids the term 'phrasal verb', seeing the various categories of verb involved here as syntactic combinations. Also, *pace* Jespersen (1927: 252), I shall call the elements that are not verbs in such constructions 'particles', avoiding the problems associated with the terms 'preposition' and 'adverb' in such constructions.

The relevant instances are those where:

A pronominal direct object must occur between the verb and the particle, and an NP direct object may occur in the same position:

(7)   a. He looked it up. She looked the answer up.
        b. *He looked the chimney up (*sensu*: 'he looked through the chimney in an upwards direction')

An adverb cannot intervene between the verb and the particle:

(8)   a. *He looked quickly up the answer.
        b. He looked quickly up the chimney.

If the verb is intransitive, the particle cannot be preposed for focus:

(9)   a. *In he gave.
        b. In he came.

If the verb is transitive, the particle cannot be preposed in a relative clause.

(10)   a. *This is the answer up which he looked.
          b. This is the chimney up which he looked.

In each of these cases, the (a) example shows the behaviour of a phrasal verb, and the (b) example shows the behaviour of a verb followed by a prepositional phrase or adverb (tests from Strang 1968: 178; Palmer 1987; Quirk et al. 1985: 1153).

Typically, phrasal verbs are treated as syntactic combinations in English rather than as compounds. Corresponding verbs in other Germanic languages are usually treated as compounds, and in English they have some features of wordhood. There is a real question, therefore, as to whether these are or are not compounds. Given other findings in this book, we might expect to discover that the question is not answerable in the abstract, but only within a specific theory. That does not mean, however, that the question is not worthy of consideration.

The most obvious way in which phrasal verbs resemble words is in their lack of semantic transparency. It has already been noted (see Section 2.5) that items other than words can be idiomatic, so that the existence of idiomatic phrasal verbs is not surprising. It is also the case that not all phrasal verbs are idiomatic. For instance, *shoot down* is a phrasal verb (see the examples in (11)) but is nevertheless transparent in its meaning.

(11)   a. They shot it down. They shot the plane down.
          b. *They shot quickly down the plane.
          c. *This is the plane down which he shot.

The factor of being idiomatic is not as strong a criterion for the wordhood of phrasal verbs as might be thought.

Another argument for the status of phrasal verbs as words might be that they act as the base in word-formation. While not all phrasal verbs have corresponding nominalizations (except with *-ing*, which is universal), and not all apparent nominalizations are based on phrasal verbs (things like *teach-in* and *uproar*, for example, have no verbal base), there are many instances of nominalizations formed from phrasal verbs, as shown in (12) or adjectives, shown in (13). Note the variability in the order of particle and verb in the derived forms, which is not obviously predictable.

(12)   *verb*   *noun*
          to blow out   blow-out
          to dress up   dress-up

to drop out	drop-out
to lap over	overlap
to rise up	uprise
to shoot out	shoot-out
to show off	show-off
to take out	out-take
to take up	uptake

(13)   *verb*   *adjective*

to drop in	drop-in (centre)
to put off	off-putting
to seek after	sought-after

However, the same is true of V + Particle constructions which are not phrasal verbs, as shown in (14).

(14)   *verb*   *noun*

to come in	income
to drive through	drive-through
to fall down	downfall
to hang over	overhang; hangover
to lift up	uplift
to pass under	underpass

The nominalizations can have several meanings, the order of particle and verb is not consistent in either pattern, and the derivative is often idiomatized and no longer means the same as the verb; nonetheless there is a pattern here.

However, given that we know that words can be formed on the basis of phrases (Bauer et al. 2013: ch. 22), and that we have evidence here (in the examples in (14)) of words being formed on the less lexicalized of the V + Particle constructions, evidence from this that phrasal verbs are 'words' seems weak.

It is clearly the case that some patterns of phrasal verbs are productive, just as some patterns of word-formation are productive. Consider, for instance, the examples in (15) of the V (by conversion) + *out* construction, particularly in the passive.

(15)   a. You get all cathedraled out and museumed out (Overheard, 2010).
         b. By the time Cap returned to the hotel at nine, Lou was conferenced out.
            (Palmer, Michael. 2014. *Resistant*. Farmington Hills, MI: Wheeler, p. 83)
         c. When I was moused out, I blagged a cleaning job. (Christer, Sam. 2011.
            The Rome prophecy. New York: Overlook, p. 11)
         d. I'm all Madonna'd out. (Hilary, Sarah. 2015. *No other darkness*. London:
            Headline, p. 152)

e. I'm all caffeined out. (Hilary, Sarah. 2015. *No other darkness*. London: Headline, p. 203)

f. I also had four days to be nervous and by the time the big day arrived I was all nervoused out. (BNC)

This is not evidence for wordhood, either, however. It is simply evidence that phrasal verbs are constructions – something which does not seem at all controversial.

The strongest evidence that phrasal verbs might be syntactic objects is provided by the fact that they can be interrupted, and, indeed, must be interrupted by a pronominal direct object (see (7) above). It is not entirely clear, though, that this counts as 'free' interruption. As was shown in (8), adverbs cannot be inserted between the verb and the particle. So although interruption is common, it is very constrained, neither like canonical syntax nor like canonical word-formation. Intransitive phrasal verbs (such as *give in* 'yield', *pass away* 'die') cannot be interrupted and seem more word-like than transitive ones on this measure.

It seems likely that phrasal verbs can be coordinated. (15a) could have read as (16).

(16)   You get all cathedraled and museumed out.

Real examples are hard to find, since the more usual pattern is that in (17) where one non-phrasal verb is coordinated with a phrasal verb.

(17)   We're all overworked and stressed out, after all (COCA)

An example like (18) is ambiguous.

(18)   ... all principal Gentlemen, freely **picked and culled out** by the People themselves, for their great Abilities, and Love of their Country, to represent the Wisdom of the whole Nation (Swift, Jonathan, *Gulliver's travels*. Google Books)

At the same time, it is not clear that the particles can be coordinated. An invented example like *She plumped for and up the red cushion* sounds odd, as does *He threw on a jacket and I off my flu* (note the zeugma which is at least part of the problem), although the general pattern of coordinated particles is perfectly ordinary when phrasal verbs are not involved: *comprising three official members and four elected by and from the Legislative Assembly* (BNC). The evidence here is weak but seems to point in the direction of the wordhood of phrasal verbs.

While we can use *do* to refer back to a phrasal verb, it does not appear to be possible to use it to refer to the verbal part of the phrasal verb without the particle. In (19), *did* has to mean 'shot through' and cannot mean 'shot'.

(19)   Shirley shot through, and so did I.

Similarly, (20) is impossible (quite apart from any zeugma) because we would expect the deleted predicate to be *throw up*, rather than just *throw*.

(20)   He threw up his lunch and I a party.

In general terms, then, whether phrasal verbs are syntactic or morphological constructs is not particularly clear, with the evidence in either direction not being very strong, but a syntactic analysis probably being the best supported. If we take the point of view espoused by Payne and Huddleston (2002: 449), then the satisfaction of any one of the criteria for being syntactic is sufficient to make the construction syntactic, and we would conclude that phrasal verbs are syntactic. On the other hand, it is not clear to me why that position is justified. It would seem just as valid to claim that the satisfaction of any one of the criteria for wordhood would be sufficient to make the construction lexical rather than syntactic, with a cline leading from clearly syntactic constructions to the most lexical. More obviously, perhaps, it might be argued that it requires a preponderance of evidence in one direction of the other to reach a conclusion.

In either case, we must distinguish phrasal verbs from another set of verbs which look similar: those with particles in the first element, like *download, oversee, understand.* These will be considered in the next section on compound verbs.

6.3   Compound Verbs

As has already been noted (Section 3.5.3), Marchand's (1969) claim that English does not have compound verbs has gained a certain currency in the literature. And it is certainly true that large numbers of the items that look like compound verbs we find in English are formed by conversion or by back-formation. Adams (2001), who accepts Marchand's position here, is a good source on these majority patterns. She cites, as established examples of conversion, the cases in (21), and as established examples of back-formation the examples in (22).

(21)   *Conversion*: to handcuff, to honeymoon, to machine-gun, to mastermind, to pitchfork, to rubber-stamp, to short-circuit, to snowball

(22)   *Back-formation*: to brainwash, to deep-fry, to dive-bomb, to drink-drive, to ghost-write, to globe-trot, to sleep-walk, to spoonfeed, to stage-manage, to window-shop

Moreover, Adams (2001) illustrates the continued productivity of these formation types, with examples like those in (23) and (24).

(23)   *Conversion* (from Adams 2001)
   a. [They] elected to litmus-test the first night of their new lives with a high-profile outing.
   b. The trouble appears to have started after a protester rugby-tackled a police officer

(24)   *Back-formation* (from Adams 2001)
   a. Like Chaucer, he role-plays himself.
   b. ... a 76-year-old who has lost both legs, but still parachute-jumps for charity.
   c. ... the government's idea to road-build us out of recession
   d. On [the cell door] has been chalk-marked a very poor representation of a skull and cross-bones.

Although the productivity of such examples is not controversial, we can add the following examples to underline the point.

(25)   *Conversion*
   a. Right-hand-manning in your outfit. (James, Bill. 2003. *The girl with the long back.* London: Constable, p. 203)
   b. Perlman poker-faced Scullion. (Armstrong, Campbell. 2006. *Butcher.* London: Allison & Busby, p. 83)
   c. They're probably wondering where I'm going so they can roadblock me up ahead. (Is *roadblock* a verb? It should be.) (Patterson, James & David Ellis. 2013. *Mistress.* New York: Little Brown, p. 377)

(26)   *Back-formation*
   a. On Saturday we houseclean. (Kotzwinkel, William. 1994. *The game of thirty.* Boston and New York: Houghton Mifflin, p. 183)
   b. You'd [...] axe-murder the entire crew. (Siddons, Anne Rivers. 1979. *The house next door.* London: Collins, p. 38)

However, these are not the only compound verbs in English. The *OED* gives †*blue-beat, butt-fuck, cold-call, high-tail, nibble-nip, pistol-whip* as being formed as compounds (there may be many more, but it is hard to search for them). Bauer and Renouf (2001) list several examples of compound verbs which are not obviously derived by conversion or by back-formation (although it must be said that it is not always easy to tell). Some of their examples are given in (27).

(27)   a. ... it uses a kerosene heater to **dry-burn** human excrement.
   b. ... he **thumb-strummed** zig-zag bristling, funk-rock riffs.
   c. The Woking-based company [...] will **custom-produce** other smells on request.

　　　d. He **mock-whispers** that his ideal relationship is the one between Stephen
　　　　Rea and Jaye Davidson in *The Crying Game*.

Other examples are presented in (28).

(28)　　a. Dubal dead and then **car-carved** on the warehouse floor introduced quite
　　　　bleak elements. (James, Bill. 2003. *The girl with the long back*. London:
　　　　Constable, p. 194)
　　　b. Most nights the Agincourt put on medieval banquets with wench
　　　　waitresses **breast-flashing** like Nell Gwyn. (James, Bill. 2003. *The girl
　　　　with the long back*. London: Constable, p. 208)
　　　c. I feel like Alice **tunnel-chasing** the hatter. (Reichs, Kathy. 2004. *Monday
　　　　mourning*. London: Heinemann, p. 109)
　　　d. I **air-jabbed** my fork for emphasis. (Reichs, Kathy. 2008. *Devil bones*.
　　　　Large print edition. Anstey, Leicestershire: Thorpe, p. 130)
　　　e. I **badge-flashed** my way to the scene. (Karp, Marshall. 2006. *The rabbit
　　　　factory*. San Francisco: MacAdam, p. 179)
　　　f. 'And you don't think what happened today might be because of him and' –
　　　　Waker **air-quoted** – 'his supply business?' (Stevens, Taylor. 2013. *The
　　　　doll*. New York: Crown, p. 13)

The examples in (28) may suggest that the presence of such verbs is a feature
of individual writers, but it is clear that such constructions can easily be found.
Even if we exclude instances of conversion because they have a derivational
process applied to a compound, the cases of back-formation imply that compound verbs are not considered unusual, and along with the other examples
show that verbal compounding is no longer marginal in current English.

　　Adams (2001) also discusses verbs made up of Particle + V. Established
examples are given in (29).

(29)　　by-pass, download, indent, outfit, oversew, upgrade

There is a complex relationship between noun and verb in these cases, and
with stress, as illustrated in (30).

(30)　　*verb*　　　*noun*
　　　*　　　　óutfall
　　　ínput　　　ínput
　　　óversew　　*
　　　upgráde　　úpgrade
　　　upróot　　　*

Each of the examples in (30) represents a much larger class: there are cases
with the expected noun-verb stress shift and those without, cases with no verb
and cases with no noun, cases with initial or final stress on the verb. Such

constructions surely deserve a more thorough study. Adams (2001: 73) suggests that in cases like *input* where the stress is on the first syllable in both cases, there is conversion from the noun to the verb. That seems entirely plausible.

Adams also suggests that the type is productive, albeit not greatly so. The most recent example she cites is *underride* (*OED*, dated as 1977, though the earliest citation for this in a geological sense is now 1970). The *OED* now contains *insource* (1983), *outsource* (1979), *overclock* (1989), *upcycle* (1994), *upsize* (1978), *upskill* (1983) and others, which supports Adams's comment.

The relationship between these verbs and phrasal verbs is also perplexing. To *downplay* seems to be synonymous with *play down*, but *downsize* is not the same as *size down* (*OED*: '(a) To arrange in sizes downwards; (b) to size up; to comprehend.'). It is not clear for the *downplay* case why there would be two similar forms with the same meaning if they are not transforms of each other (which the *downsize* case suggests is not true).

It is not necessarily clear whether we have compounds in all these cases, or whether some of them are instances of prefixation. The form *out-*, for example, seems to form a prefix in instances like (31) (from Bauer & Renouf 2001; for other examples see Bauer et al. 2013: 343).

(31)   And it must be said, OJ [Simpson] **outsoaped** the soaps

This judgement is based on the fact that *out-* in such formations has an evaluative sense and no physical sense of 'not within' that we might expect if *out-* were a compound element (as, perhaps, in *out-going*). This does not imply, however, that it is always clear where the borderline is to be drawn.

Finally, a different type of compound is available in expressions like *go get, go figure*, which may be serial verbs (see Section 4.8), though the *OED* relates *go get* to *go-getter* and thus makes it look like a compound by backformation. In most cases these collocations seem to be related to a version with an overt *and* or *to* linking the verbs, and many are based on a verb of motion (*come* or *go*) in the first position. The pattern seems to be very productive in American English. Some examples (all from COCA) are given in (32).

(32)   **Come build** the best, the finest castles in the world,
         Come say good-bye, boys,' he called.
         it does not give you the right to **go shoot** innocent people
         it's easier to **go buy** a battery
         there were friends who would **come finish** the job,
         why **go play** a U.S. Open course to qualify for a championship held on British links?
         Wilbur told us to **go fuck** ourselves

The construction is mentioned only briefly by Huddleston (2002a: 290, 2002b: 1225), and he does not seem to appreciate its level of productivity. In these examples with *come* and *go*, the two verbs are inseparable, share the same subject and occur preferentially in the infinitive or imperative form, although there are a few examples in COCA of these verbs agreeing with a personal subject, or showing a different tense, as in (33).

(33)   I have a rule that when **I go see** him or anyone I love, I don't touch my phone
He then **goes sit** # on a tree stump and starts rolling a cigarette.
when I **went visit** him and heard the stories that he was telling me, [. . .]

The construction is wider than is implied by these examples, though. Some instances with other verbs, again from COCA, are given in (34).

(34)   We'll **jump start** your weekend entertainment right after this.
Do you **want come** fishing?
I **want show** you my secret weapon. Follow me.
I **hope make** life a little easier for your wife.
Future studies may **wish test** the importance of SDT's other basic psychological needs, [. . .]

Other collocations such as *let go*, *let slip*, *make believe*, *make do*, if they are the same construction, do not correspond to phrases with deleted *and* or *to*, may allow an inserted pronoun between the elements (*let it go, let it slip*), do not necessarily require the same subject for both verbs (*let slip*), or allow tense inflection on the first verb more easily (*makes believe, made do*). Whether or not these are compound verbs, they seem to fit somewhere within the spectrum of di-verbal constructions, and require further study.

6.4   Plural Modifiers

Most of the Germanic languages allow linking elements between the elements of nominal compounds. While these elements are common, they are not the default. In German, for instance, it is clear that the majority of compounds have no linking elements and are created by the simple juxtaposition of stems, as in the word *Hand·buch* 'hand-book, manual'. One count puts the proportion of compounds with no linking element in German as high as 70 per cent (Neef 2009). Where there is a linking element, *-s-* is probably the most common (see Booij 2002: 180 on Dutch, Allan et al. 1995: 544–545 on Danish). The same linking element is also said to appear on the end of the embedded compound in compounds of the form [[X Y] Z], so that in Danish we find *vin·glas* 'wine glass' but *rødvin·s·glas* 'red-wine glass', in Swedish we find *boll·plan* 'ball pitch' but *fotboll·s·plan* 'football pitch' (Holmes & Hinchliffe 1994: 10) and in German we find *Werk·zeug* 'work thing = tool' but *Handwerk·s·zeug* 'hand work thing = hand tool' (Erben 1975: 59). In Faroese, though, any historical genitive marker can have the same function (Thráinsson et al. 2004: 205–207), and in any case, Bauer (2009) provides a rather more sceptical view of this rule.

There is a terminology associated with this in German, where those compounds with no linking elements are called *echt* or *eigentlich* 'genuine' and those with a linking element, a later development in German, are called *uneigentlich* 'non-genuine, false'.

Finally, on Germanic in general, it should be noted that linking elements are nearly always derived from genitive or plural inflections. Whether there is any trace of these original meanings left is controversial, and not entirely consistent from language to language. Booij (2002: 179) points out that there are some places, at least, in Dutch, where singular versus plural first elements are contrastive, though Neef (2009) is sceptical for German.

All of this of particular interest since English, another Germanic language, is not described as having linking elements at all. We have compounds by simple juxtaposition (*handbook, football, wine glass*), but linking elements are not discussed with reference to English.

This is odd, if we consider the different types of form illustrated in (35).

(35)

Boyle's law	All Hallows Eve	cracksman	arms race
cat's eye	beeswax	craftsman	careers officer
dog's body	bullseye	draughtsman	communications technology
king's-chair	coltsfoot	groundsman	companies legislation
king's-hood	hawksbill	huntsman	drugs problem
lady's maid	hogshead	marksman	examinations board
lady's man	houndstooth	oarsman	greetings card
mother's day	lambswool	salesman	jobs file
pheasant's eye	menswear	sportsman	letters column
rat's-tail	ratsbane	townsman	publications committee
snail's pace	sportswear	tradesman	textiles industry
snake's head		woodsman	
wolf's bane		yachtsman	
women's movement			

In the first column of (35) we find a number of things which we might treat as compounds, but they are written as though they have a genitive in the first element. These are unlike ordinary genitives, though, in that they take stress on the first element (like many compounds), and in that the first element does not refer, but classifies: we cannot sensibly ask which cat we are talking about when we mention *cat's eyes*, for example.

In the second column of (35) we find items which have an <s> written (and pronounced), but it is not marked specifically in the orthography as being genitive. In some of these cases it feels as though it might be genitive (*bullseye*, for instance), in others it looks as though it might be plural or genitive plural.

In the third column of (35) we have a special case where the second element of the compound is *man*, and *man* seems particularly prone to having first elements ending in -*s*, even though there are many examples where this is not the case: *boatman, ferryman, journeyman, milkman, nurseryman, seaman, signalman* and so on.

In the final column of (35) we have instances that are normally seen as having a plural first element. They are not all the same. *Arms* and *communications* are not simply plurals of *arm* and *communication*, and so the final <s> is required to keep the appropriate lexical item. But the difference between *examination board* and *examinations board* or *job file* and *jobs file* is obscure, if there even is one. Where these are discussed in the literature (e.g. Mutt 1967, Dierickx 1970), there seems to be agreement that this is an increasing trend in modern English, though I am not aware of any corpus study of the matter to indicate this.

Although we are faced with various spelling conventions here, and although some of these <s> forms seem more plural than others, given that English speakers are notoriously bad at using the apostrophe, and given that people do not know whether to write *girls school, girl's school* or *girls' school*, all we can say with any certainty here is that there is an <s>-form between the elements of the construction. Is there any reason why we should, or should not, call that element a linking element?

The first thing to notice is that these <s> forms are not necessarily fixed: there can be variability between the form with the <s> and the form without it. This has already been suggested with relation to *job(s) file*, and dictionaries list both *lineman* and *linesman* as synonymous, and both *sport coat* and *sports coat* as synonymous. On the other hand, *head man* is not synonymous with *headsman* (and probably does not have the same stress pattern). However, this is not incompatible with a linking element analysis, since there can be some variation in the use of linking elements in other Germanic languages. English does not show itself to be different on this measure.

Where linking elements are concerned, the fundamental rule seems to be that they belong to the first element of the compound (Neef 2009: 390), and that the first element is consistent in what kind of link it takes: given *Handbuch* in German, one would expect to find *Hand* used consistently with no linking element, and given *Liebe·s·brief* 'love letter' we would expect to find *Liebe* consistently using a linking -*s*. While there are exceptions, only 10 per cent of nouns allow more than one linking elements, and in most cases, the variants are either extremely old or were specifically coined to avoid homonymy (see Neef 2009: 392). In English this seems not to be true. To the extent that *man* is preceded by an -*s*, it seems to be the second element which is important in its presence. Many words have both forms with an <s> and forms without one: consider *harebell, hare's-tail; ladybird, lady's man; land girl, landsman; town house, townspeople*. The same is true if we look at second elements: *house maid, lady's maid; ox-eye, cat's eye; goose-foot, cocksfoot*.

Finally, what about the *rødvin·s·glas* effect? Just occasionally, we see something that appears similar in English. I find several hits on Google for the phrase *membership services department*, for example, and I have earlier commented on an attested difference between *[[British council] jobs] file* and *[British Council] [job file]* (Bauer 1978: 40). Not only is this too small a database to justify any solid analysis, I now think that both of these are probably due to random variation in the system rather than to systematic marking of constituency.

Perhaps the evidence is weaker than would be desirable, but it looks as if these <s> markers are not just the same as Germanic linking elements at the moment. On the other hand, the Germanic linking elements developed from genitive and plural markers, and perhaps what we are seeing is the start of a similar development in English.

All in all, it is probably best to say that at the moment a similarity of form is just a similarity in form, and there is no good evidence of these <s> links being seen as markers of compounds, as is found elsewhere in Germanic. That being the case, we have to accept that we have plural marking in the first element of some compounds. Just why that should be the case is not necessarily clear, nor what the effect of the plural marking might be. But even if the plurals were totally irregular (which I do not believe), we would have to deal with them as irregularities in a system which generally avoids inflections in the first element of compounds.

If we look at some data from COCA, we find that the most common collocation with *mice* in the first element is *mice droppings*; there are five hits for this collocation in COCA. At the same time there are twenty-two hits for *mouse droppings*. Overall there are only fifty-two hits for compounds with *mice*, while there are more than 1,500 hits for compounds with *mouse* (which are often compounds where *mouse* is a computer part or where *Mouse* is part of *Mickey Mouse*). Even this small amount of data makes two points: that plural first elements are relatively rare, even where possible, and that plural first elements are not necessarily fixed – there is variation between unmarked and plural first elements.

If we take a regular noun like *examination*, we find only four hits for *examinations* + N compounds in COCA (not including *examinations board* cited above), while there are over 800 with *examination* + N. Again the implication is that plural marking is exceptional rather than the norm, but it does not explain why there should be plural marking on these first elements.

If we consider data with *job* or *jobs* (where we do find both forms), it is clear that second element whose arguments (or pragmatically appropriate closely-linked nouns) are expressed in the first element overwhelmingly prefer the singular form. We find many examples in COCA such as *job elimination, job offering, job redefinition, job supervisor, job swap* and so on, but only a few like *jobs creators, jobs growth, jobs listings*. While such examples cover only a small part of the compounds with *job/jobs* in the first element, they start to indicate that there may be some difference.

Some idea of the increase in the use of plurals, and also some idea of the balance between singular and plurals, can be found from Google ngrams (https://books.google.com/ngrams/). Figure 6.1 provides graphs which show the relative density of singular and plural forms in texts over a century. Only where *communications* is clearly different from *communication* do we see a really relatively high use of the plural.

However, there is some sign that the final -*s* may indeed be marking a genuine plural. Although it is not entirely clear what *letter/s column* might refer to (the section of letters to the editor, a series of individual letters of the alphabet), it seems likely that there is more than one letter involved, and here Google does show rather more plural marking (Figure 6.2). Yet something like *files security* (though it is found) gets very few hits in comparison with *file security*.

So there seems to be a lexical factor involved here. *Shoes shop* is very rare (though it is found in Google books), *hats shop* is not found, *sweets shop* is slightly more common, but *sweets factory* is less common than *sweet factory* while *munitions factory* is much more common that *munition factory* after about 1935 (but vice versa before that date). Again the increase in plurals is evident, but individual modifiers and specific combinations influence the likelihood of a plural in the first element.

(a)

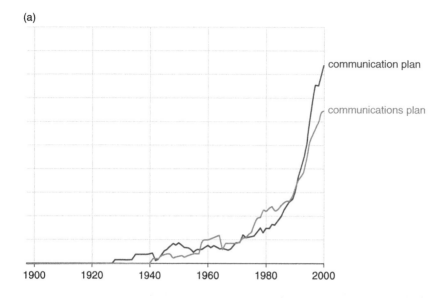

communication plan

communications plan

(b)

company legislation
companies legislation

Figure 6.1 Relative textual density of forms with unmarked or plural first elements from Google ngrams. Note that the scales differ for each comparison, since the scale in each diagram indicates relative density only for the pairs mentioned.

(c)

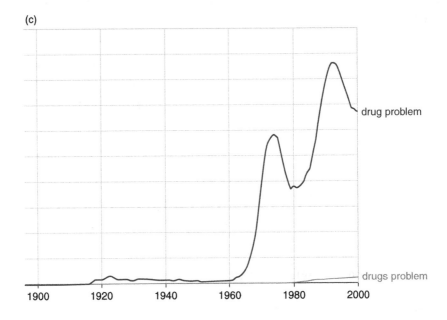

(d)

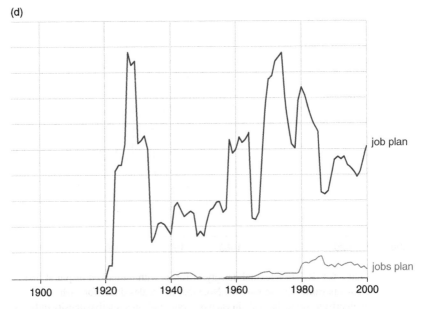

Figure 6.1 (*cont.*)

(e)

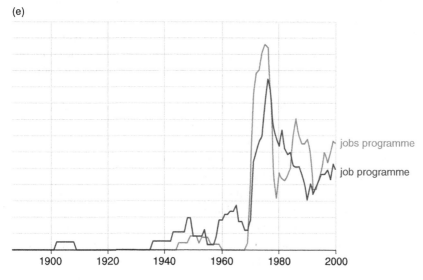

Figure 6.1 (*cont.*)

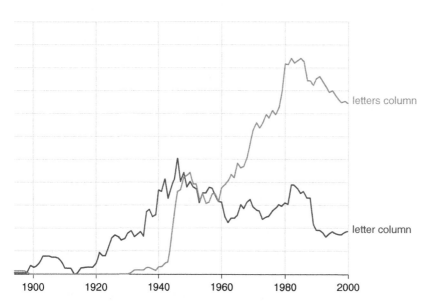

Figure 6.2 Relative textual density of *letter column* vs. *letters column* from Google ngrams

While these few examples do not represent a thorough corpus-based approach to the question, they are sufficient, I think, to show something of the complexity of the issue. Whether or not *jobs programme* is a different construction from *job programme*, it is unclear what factors lead to the selection of one form rather than the other, and number is at best one of those factors.

One interesting claim that has been made about items like *jobs programme* is that they must be made up of NP + N, not of two nouns (Pinker 1999: 185). Pinker argues that where an adjective precedes such a construction, it can only submodify the first element of the construction, forming an NP with that element. A *green spiders eater*, he claims, can only be something that eats green spiders, not something green that eats spiders. The first thing that needs to be said about this observation is that it is wrong. COCA gives us examples such as *the State Department jobs program* and *We need a massive jobs program to put black kids to work*, where the pre-modifier must go with *program* in both instances. But even if it were right, it is not particularly helpful: *job programme* and *jobs programme* appear to be synonymous, and assigning different structures to them does not explain that synonymy. Moreover, if *jobs* were an NP in *jobs programme* and *job* just an N in *job programme*, we would expect to find that *jobs* was much more freely submodifiable than *job*. So we would expect to find *a really stupidly dangerous jobs programme* but not *a really stupidly dangerous job programme*, where *a really stupidly dangerous* modifies *job/jobs* in each case. As with most compounds, my intuition is that the modifying element is not itself freely modifiable, and only limited and item-familiar modifiers are permitted. If that is true in both cases, assigning them to two different constructions is even odder.

6.5   Neoclassical Compounds

Neoclassical compounds remain something of a descriptive puzzle for the morphology of English and many other European languages. Even in English, which has several layers of borrowed vocabulary and word-formation, they are a stand-alone borrowed pattern which has become entangled with native patterns. Questions about neoclassical compounds include the following:

- Are they compounds?
- How are they to be analysed, especially where the linking elements are concerned?
- Are their forms predictable?

- How are apparently derivational endings on neoclassical compounds, in words like *philosophy* and *philosopher*, to be analysed?
- What is the implication of these analyses for forms like *socio-linguistics*, which blend neoclassical elements with elements of other types?
- How does the morphology of neoclassical compounds interface with other types of shortening and combining in English? For example, a form like *autocide* might be viewed as a neoclassical form meaning the same as *suicide*, or it might be a clipping based on *automobile suicide*, or it might mean 'the killing of cars'.

There are basically two main patterns of neoclassical compound, one, the more common one, based on Greek, the other based on Latin.

Although early Greek allowed case-marked first elements in compounds, alongside nominal stems, so many nouns had a stem vowel *-o-* that the *-o-* became viewed as a composition vowel, possibly an interfix (Palmer 1980: 258–260). The two stems are placed side-by-side, with the *-o-* perhaps increasingly viewed as a linking element, and then a final inflection is added. This gives us English words like *acropolis* 'upper city', *ichthyophagy* from Greek *ichthyophagos* 'fish eating', *monarch* from Greek *monarchos* 'alone-ruler', *physiology* from Greek *physiologos* 'nature student', *strategic* from Greek *stratēgos* 'army leader, commander-in-chief'. Other vowels are found in Ancient Greek (strictly, thematic vowels from the first element rather than linking vowels; Tribulato 2015: 23), though most of them do not make their way through to modern English, but consider *polymer* with no *-o-*. The *-o-* is usually missing when it is flanked by another vowel: *cardi·algia* 'heartburn', *gyn·andry* 'woman man = hermaphroditism'. Although most Greek compounds are right-centred, a few are not, such as *hippopotamus* 'horse-river' (Buck 1933: 356–357).

In Latin compounds two lexical stems are put together with some morphophonological changes at the junction between them. If the second element begins with a vowel, then any final short vowel of the first element is deleted ($V ⇨ Ø$ / __ + V: *fūn(i)·ambulus* 'tightrope walker'). If the second element begins with a consonant, and the first with a vowel, that vowel is replaced by a short /i/ ($V ⇨ i$ / ___ + C: *bell(u ⇨ i)·potens* 'mighty in battle'). If the second element begins with a consonant and the first element ends in a consonant, a short /i/ is inserted between the two stems ($Ø ⇨ i$ / C __ + C: *lēg·i·fer* 'law giver') (Oniga 2014: 164–165). Then a final inflection is added, appropriate to the word-class of the compound. Thus in *agricola* 'field cultivate-SUFF = farmer', the final suffix *-a* is appropriate for a noun, even though it is directly added to the verb stem *col-*. This gives us English forms such as *equinox* from

Latin *aequ·i·noct·ium* (Oniga 2014: 169) 'equal night', *magnanimous* from *magn·anim·us* 'great souled' (Oniga 2014: 170), *patricide* from Latin *patr·i·cid·ium* (*OED*).

In both Greek and Latin, compounds may be endocentric or exocentric, with bahuvrihi compounds being found in both languages, such as Latin *citi·rēm·is* 'with quick oars' (Oniga 2014: 169) and Greek *rhododactylos* 'having rosy fingers' [of the dawn] (Rau 2010: 183). Greek also has coordinative compounds, like *latro-mantis* 'physician and seer' (Buck 1933: 354). Compounding is very productive in Greek, but rather less so in Latin (Buck 1933: 354).

6.5.1   *Are Neoclassical Compounds Really Compounds?*

The argument for neoclassical compounds being compounds comes from two sources. The first is etymological: these forms are compounds in the languages from which they originate, and so they remain compounds when borrowed into English. This is not a particularly strong argument for their status in English. The second argument is based on the alternatives. If we consider words like *photo-synthesis* and *addressograph*, we might conclude that *photo-* is a prefix, and *-ograph* is a suffix. If there were no more data to consider than this, such a conclusion would seem entirely logical: *photo-* and *-ograph* are obligatorily bound morphs which are attached to a lexemic base to create new words. Even though there are obligatorily bound bases in native English morphology (in words like *disheveled, inept, unkempt*), and even more in Latin-based morphology (in words like *baptize, baptism, baptist*) the default in English is for lexemic bases to be potentially free forms, and the analysis of *photo-* and *-ograph* as affixes would be in line with this general principle of English word-formation. However, alongside words like *photo-synthesis* and *addressograph*, we find words like *photograph*. If *photo-* and *-ograph* are affixes, then *photograph* is made up of a prefix and a suffix, with no base. There are other (non-neoclassical) words which can be analysed in the same way, but they are few and far between. One of the clearest examples is *superette*, a word found in some parts of the English-speaking world to denote a small supermarket. However, *superette* itself is so odd that it seems unlikely that it was formed by the combination of prefix and suffix rather than by a clipping of *supermarket* or a blend of *supermarket* and something like *kitchenette*. In other words, the constraint against rootless words is stronger than the constraint against obligatorily bound bases in English, even though both constraints are observable. If *photo-* and *-ograph* are not affixes, the only other possible analysis would seem to be that they are obligatorily bound bases, and if that is the case, then words like *photograph* are compounds.

This analysis has certain implications, which are not necessarily welcome. The first of these is that the elements of a word like *photograph* are themselves lexemes. This problem is not restricted to such elements (which are often termed 'combining forms') but is greatly magnified by them. In principle, if word-formation is the creation of new words by (among other things) attaching affixes to existing words (lexemes) (Bauer 1998a: 25), then the bases in *inept* etc. are lexemes (or there is no affix, and such words are monomorphemic). With *inept*, it might be difficult to choose between the options, but with *bapt-* in *baptize*, *baptism*, *baptist* there seems to be little option, if you want to see all these words as being derived by suffixation.

There is an alternative analysis. That analysis sees *baptism* and *baptist* being derived from the lexeme *baptize* by affix-replacement (or replacement of an apparent affix) in some kind of paradigmatic process (see Bauer et al. 2013: ch. 23). There is much to commend such an analysis, although it introduces a new morphological element whose status is rather unclear: the sub-lexemic obligatorily bound base. If we accept the existence of such a unit, then it is not clear whether the combination of two such units is the same as a compound (usually defined as the combination of "words"; see Section 2.1) or whether it is different in some trivial or important way. Whether neoclassical compounds are 'compounds' or not depends on how these are treated. In the lack of any particular evidence that the combination of sub-lexemic obligatory bound bases leads to something which is in nature different from a compound, calling things like *photograph* 'compounds' does not seem a particularly dangerous piece of terminology. But it does depend on the idea that this lack of evidence is a solid enough foundation for the classification.

The second implication of calling combinations of combining forms 'compounds' is that the elements have their own specifiable meanings and word-classes. The meanings are unlikely to be controversial. Most analysts are happy with the notion that *neo-* means something like 'new' and that *photo-* means something like 'light'. The word-class part may be slightly more controversial. First of all, such an implication cannot hold in a model such as Distributed Morphology where word-class is determined by the syntactic tree, not by the lexical element. This implication is also at odds with the view of those who hold that bound stems do not have a word-class (e.g. Giegerich 1999: 74). But if we assume, as we have elsewhere, that words may "have", inherently, a word-class, then we still have to accept that *neo-* is an adjective by virtue of its meaning and that *-ograph* is a noun by virtue of its meaning. In the second case, we have further evidence. Words ending in *-ograph* are usually nouns. Where they are not nouns, they seem to be derived from nouns by conversion in ordinary ways: *addressograph* can be a verb meaning 'address using an Addressograph machine'. There is an assumption here that neoclassical compounds are right-centred, but that seems to be consistent with patterns in Greek and Latin as well as in English, as far as we can tell under the assumption that the combining forms carry their own meanings.

One potential problem with the notion that combining forms have their own meaning is the increase in synonyms. We have to accept that *light* and *photo-* both mean 'light' (assuming that the definition of *photo-* cannot be further refined) and so on for hundreds of such elements. This probably does not cause much more of a problem than the rate of synonymy already found in any natural language, but is included here as a potential problem for those who believe that the one meaning-one form equation is a linguistic ideal.

If we accept that items like *photograph* are compounds and contain two lexemes, then it follows that items like *photo-synthesis*, *socio-linguistics* are also compounds, because they, too, must contain two lexemes. This corollary has not been universally accepted.

Overall then, there is little evidence that it is misleading to call words like *photograph* 'compounds', though doing so forces us into certain assumptions, most of which are probably well-accepted. The question is worth raising because queries about the status of such words remain.

6.5.2   *The Forms of Neoclassical Compounds*

Latin patterns of neoclassical compounds are productive in very limited areas, such as with a final combining form in *-icide* (including *infanticide, insecticide, pesticide*). Here, the <i> which I have given as part of the combining form is, historically speaking, the Latin linking element. *Genocide* has an unexpected form, from the Latin point of view: we might have expected *genicide*.

The Greek patterns with linking <o> are much better established in English, and much more productive. There are at least two ways of analysing a word like *photograph*. Either we can analyse it as *phot + graph* with an interfix *-o-* added to mark the compound, as is the case in Greek, or we analyse it as *photo- + -ograph* with a rule of simplification removing the resultant geminate *-oo-*. The latter seems to be a good option because when these elements arise adjacent to normal English words, they take the form with the <o>, which we would have no particular reason to insert into a sequence of *phot + synthesis*. Also, geminate vowels are in general rare in English. However, that is an orthographic rule, not a surface phonological rule, since although *photo-* ends in /əʊ/, *-ograph* typically begins with /ə/. If it is a rule at some underlying level of phonology, it is not clear why we should have a form like *oolite, zoon* or *zoology* (for speakers who pronounce it /zəʊɒlədʒi/) where similar underlying forms are not simplified.

On the other hand, if the <o> is added as an interfix, it need not be added where there is already a vowel at the point of juncture, as in *laryngitis, monosemy, telephone* and the like, just as was the case in Greek. If the insertion point is defined as any juncture with a Greek element, then we might even explain the *-o-* in *photosynthesis* without extra mechanisms. However, corresponding to examples like *steroid-o-genesis* (COCA, cited in Bauer et al. 2013: 456), which support such an analysis, there are examples like (36) and (37) below which show that no such rules are followed. In any case, since the <o> is frequently pronounced /ə/, it can be respelt with other vowels in modern English, as in (38). The main difficulty with such a proposal is that implies that speakers recognise Greek elements, which seems inherently unlikely (there is already great discussion about whether native speakers of English can be expected to distinguish between native and foreign; it may be, of course, that only partly bilingual people produce new words with Greek elements, though even that seems a dangerous assumption to make).

(36)   Slider loathed buffets. Atherton said he suffered from smorgasphobia.
         (Harrod-Eagles, Cynthia. 2014. *Star fall*. Sutton, Surrey: Severn House,
         p. 64)

(37)   We – we [don't] have the smell-o-vision on this morning, but really it smells
         like Thanksgiving. (COCA)

(38)   She [. . .] pulled on another pair of disposable gloves. Gemma wondered if
         there was a proper name for a glovaphiliac. (Lord, Gabrielle. 2002. *Baby did
         a bad bad thing*. Sydney: Hodder, p. 272)

Overall, then, neither analysis is perfect, and there seem to be a handful of forms which defy analysis according to rule. This is not necessarily unexpected. Another locus of variation is what happens before <h>. Greek speakers seem not to have considered /h/ to be a consonant, whether because of its phonetic nature as a voiceless vowel or whether because it acts as a prosody in Greek (Allen 1974: 50–53), or whether because the /h/ was lost leaving a vowel early enough not to have affected the word-formation pattern, and the result is that forms before an <h> do not require a linking <o>. English treats <h> as a consonant, so that an <o>-link is required where the phonology demands something interconsonantally. *Glycemia* and *glycohemia* appear to be alternate forms of the same English word, depending on how

<h> is treated (Bauer et al. 2013: 456). Similarly there is variation between *hydraemia* and *hydrohaemia*, between *pachyaemia* and *pachyhaemia* (*OED*).

Forms like *photograph* and *allomorph* end with a Greek root and are thus fairly unambiguously compounds. There are problems even with that statement. *Photograph* (but not *allomorph*) is commonly used as a verb, and if we want to use an analysis of *photograph*$_V$ as being conversion, then we have to allow that derivation can occur outside the neoclassical compounding. Such a conclusion is not unexpected: Bauer et al. (2013: 510) show that native compounds frequently provide bases for subsequent derivation in forms like *basketballer, blockbusterish, childfirendliness, folklorist, lipstickless*. With a case like *patricide*, which can mean either 'the killing of one's father' or 'a person who kills their father' (probably from different Latin forms), it is less clear whether a conversion analysis is appropriate, but it is certainly possible.

What then with forms like *philosopher*? *Philosopher* carries a native affix, not a Greek affix, and so must be an English formation, and we appear to have a case parallel to *basketballer*, with *-er* added to a compound base, and *philosopher* being a derivative, not a compound. But what is the base in *philosopher*? *Philosoph* is not an English word, and a *philosopher* is a person who is a practitioner of *philosophy*, so that it looks as though *philosopher* should be derived as *philosophy-er*. But how is *philosophy* then derived? Is it a compound, or is it an obligatorily bound compound base with a *-y* suffix? If we take all of these as derivational suffixes, we end up with large numbers of obligatorily bound compounds; if we take all of them as combining forms, we end up with a large number of very similar combining forms, such as *-(o)sophy, -(o)sophist, -(o)sopher*, or *-(o)logy, -(o)loger, -(o)logist, -(o)logism, -(o)logize* and so on. If we choose a third option, and allow both structures, we have to have a way of determining which structure is found in which word. Bauer et al. (2013: 455) say that speakers treat *-ology* (at least) as a separate item, but that does not give a ready metric for taking decisions. It also seems likely that *-(o)logist* words are based on *-(o)logy* words and are created by some kind of paradigmatic process, replacing one sequence with another, rather than by independent suffixation. So a case could be made for taking some basic form – like *philosophy* – as a compound, and having other forms derived from it. But even *-y* is not reliably basic. We find *synonym*, for example, from which we would perceive *synonymy* to be derived, much as *synonymous* is. But although these examples might make it seem that there is a generalisation to be captured here in terms of the individual combining forms, that is not the case. The combining form *-(o)graph(y)* fits both patterns. *Geography* is fine, but there is no *geograph*, while *photography*, which presumably has the same combining form in it, does have a corresponding *photograph*. Similarly we find *ideologue* (where he <ue> is simply a foreign orthographic device to make the final /g/) to go with *ideology*, but no *psychologue* to go with *psychology*. That is, we cannot claim that the final -*y* is part of some combining forms but not of others: we have to look at the individual lexeme rather than the particular combining form if we want to determine the status of the -*y*. In general terms this would seem to suggest that the final -*y* (and the other sequences) should be treated as suffixes, whether or not the word can stand alone without them.

It may be of interest to note that in this regard English neoclassical compounds are not necessarily the same as those in other European languages: French does have a noun *philosophe* 'philosopher', German does have a noun *Photograph* 'photographer', Danish does have a noun *psykolog* 'psychologist', and so on; Russian has all of these. These have the effect of making it look as though *philosophe, Photograph* and *psykolog* are derived by a subtraction process from *philosophie, Photographie* 'photograph, photography', and *psykologi* respectively, since the greater amount of meaning ('practitioner of ~') goes with the shorter form. English has fewer instances of this particular marked structure (although it does have a few cases like *osteopath*, which give rise to the same questions) but does have other countervailing problems here.

Even that is not the end of the problems, however. A further question is how to recognise a combining form as opposed to an affix. Bauer (1983a: 214) suggests that only combining forms can combine with other combining forms, though, of course, both combine with words. However, in principle the outcome of the combination with words is not the same in the two cases: *biodegradable* is a compound (it contains two lexemes – see the discussion above), while *non-degradable* is a derivative; *Mondayitis* is a compound, *Mondayism* is a derivative. This is counter-intuitive for many linguists, because of the apparently parallel function of things like *hyper-* and *super-* in *hypermarket* (compound) and *supermarket* (derivative). However, it follows from the discussion here, and if it is not acceptable, then it has implications elsewhere.

There can still be problems in drawing a distinction between prefixes (in particular) and combining forms, though. This is particularly the case where a combining form has taken on a life of its own. For instance, *mega-* (which is a combining form by virtue of words such as *megalith, megaphone*) has become an adjective in its own right (used both attributively and predicatively), where it means 'very large and impressive'. A word like *megastar* could, therefore, be a compound with a combining form, or a native compound, with the word *mega* in the first element. *Mega-* also has a use meaning 'one million' when attached to units of measurement, as in *megawatt, megahertz, megaton*. Because the element with this meaning is added only to units of measurement, it is added only to words, so there is a possibility that *mega-* in *megawatt* is a prefix, even if it is a combining form in *megalith*. While it is clear that problems with borderlines do not of themselves indicate that the things on either side of the borderline can or should not be distinguished, such problems nevertheless make matters more difficult to analyse.

6.5.3 The Borders of Neoclassical Compounds

We have seen that there are problems at the border between neoclassical compounding and affixation, but that is not the only borderline where the extent of neoclassical compounding may not be clear. One of the reasons is that final *-o* can result from other processes as well as from neo-classical compounding.

One obvious one is clipping. *Auto* is a clipped form of *automobile*. So items with an initial *auto-* could be neoclassical compounds or could be compounds with the clipped form of *automobile*. In this particular case, the meaning should determine which is which. *Auto-suggestion* must be a compound with a combining form, while *automotive* seems to be an ordinary compound built on the 'car' meaning. In *auto-pilot* we appear to have a third meaning, another clipping, this time from *automatic*. In *autocide* we get *auto-* apparently linked to another combining form, *-cide*, but if the meaning is 'suicide by car', then it becomes clear that this is a blend (*automobile suicide*) and that the apparent neo-classical structure has arisen through some other mechanism. The problem here is basically the same as the one outlined with *mega-* above: the same form may arise by different means and with slightly or importantly different meanings/functions, and this may complicate analysis.

Not only do we have to deal with clippings, we have to deal with splinters. Splinters are abbreviated elements that arise in blends and then have the potential to be used productively. For instance, *-scape* started life in *landscape*, and then formed blends like *seascape*, and eventually becomes a morpheme in its own right. As a bound morpheme in its own right, its status is unclear: is it a combining form or an affix? It is not strictly neoclassical, but it is a rather odd suffix, if only because of its meaning, which is lexical rather than grammatical. There is some variation in the literature as to whether an element which is found only in one blend (perhaps *-on* in *tigon*) counts as a splinter or whether a splinter can only be recognised by a certain degree of productivity. In this discussion, only the second type will be of relevance.

Some splinters have a vowel at their juncture, such as *-(a/o)delic, -(a/o)holic, -(o)matic, -(o)rama* (Bauer et al. 2013: 526–527), *Euro-, tele-* (in the sense of 'television'). Such elements can create words which look like neoclassical compounds – possibly, even, should be treated as neoclassical compounds – even if that is not their origin. For instance, *telethon* looks as though it is a neoclassical compound, but is historically a blend from ~~television~~ ~~marathon~~ (an exocentric compound): it is not clear how far that matters from the analyst's point of view.

Both Bauer (1998b) and López Rúa (2004) have argued, in different terms, that categories in this part of the grammar have a tendency to merge into one another without firm boundaries between them. Certainly, there are questions of classification to be raised. For instance, Cannon (1987: 193–194), in a very informative work on the productivity of various patterns of English word-formation, classes *-oid* and *-osis* as suffixes rather than combining forms, and *self-* and *mini-* as combining forms and not prefixes. I do not wish to try to argue about whether Cannon is right or not, or why; I just wish to point out that this classification looks controversial. Bauer et al. (2013: 333) call *meta-, neo-* and *proto-* (among others) prefixes, again a decision which is surely controversial. Marchand (1969) includes *poly-, pseudo-* and *retro-* as prefixes. Other examples could no doubt be given. Even if we assume that such classifications are really a shorthand version for 'elements which are prefixed to or attached before a base' rather than literally indicating prefixes, it shows that the line between the two types is not firmly drawn and maintained.

Even if we are convinced of the necessity of having a class of neoclassical compounds, it is not a particularly stable or well-defined class. Central, canonical examples may be easily recognised, but the class shades off into things whose status is unclear or which we would normally classify as something else. When a knowledge of etymology is required in order to classify a particular example, it is a sure sign that the classification is not meeting all the requirements of a synchronic grammar; but even without such instances, we really need better criteria for what is or is not a neoclassical compound.

6.6   Blends

There is a sense in which we can argue that all word-formation is a matter of blending. A new form like *shitless* ('scared ~' can be seen as a blend of *shit + witless*, *settler participation* as a blend of *settler + student participation* (see also the discussion of Tarasova's view of compounds in Section 4.3).

However, blends are usually defined far more narrowly, as the interpenetration of two (or more) words to form a third, such that the blend contains the beginning of the first source word, the end of the last source word, but does not contain all the phonological material from all of the source words. Some examples of blends of different patterns are provided in (39).

(39)   stagflation   from   stag~~nation~~ + ~~in~~flation
        boatel   from   boat + ~~ho~~tel
        Medicare   from   medi~~cal~~ + care
        shoat   from   shee~~p~~ + ~~g~~oat
        bastitcherbator from   basta~~rd~~ + ~~b~~itch + ~~mas~~turbator
        ambisextrous   from   ambi~~dex~~trous + sex

(Examples from Cannon 1987; Beliaeva 2014)

The last example from (39) does not strictly fit within the definition that has been given but will nonetheless be included in the discussion.

There is another definition of blending that includes items like *romcom* (*romantic comedy*) and *sci-fi* (*science fiction*), where the first parts of each of the elements are concatenated. There is now sufficient evidence of various kinds that such items are compounds but are distinct from blends as illustrated in (39) to justify their exclusion from the category of blends (see e.g. Gries 2012, Beliaeva 2014). Such formations are variously termed 'clipped compounds', 'clipping compounds' and 'complex clippings' in the literature.

Blends can be classified in various ways, and some authorities exclude some sub-types from the domain of blending completely.

Medicare is headed, in that it is derived from the expression *medical care*, which is a headed structure, and in that the *Medi-* element still clearly modifies the *-care* element. *Shoat*, on the other hand, looks more like a coordinative compound in having two elements of equal status. This matter will be discussed again below. Some authorities exclude the headed blends from the set of blends (Dressler 2000: 5, who calls the headed type 'syntagmatic shortenings'; Plag 2003: 122, who calls the headed type 'abbreviated compounds'). Note that although the headed type in English has the head on the right, just like the majority of compounds, this is not a necessary correlation: in Hebrew the order of elements in a blend is not determined by the same principles as it is in compounds (Bat-El 2000: 72).

Boatel contains the entire word *boat*, but only part of the word *hotel*; *stagflation*, on the other hand, does not include the entire word *stagnation* or the entire word *inflation*. Some authorities include only the second type as blends (for some discussion with relation to Greek, see Ralli & Xydopoulos 2012).

Blends can also be classified in terms of how many words are involved and what parts of those words are retained (Beliaeva 2014). The discussion here will not require such a classification.

A large part of the discussion on blends is associated with questions such as which element comes first in a coordinative blend, the length of the material remaining in blends (and the balance of material remaining between the elements), where the cutting point in the two (or more) elements in a blend is made so that the pieces fit together into a new word, the influence of stress in the formation of blends in language where stress is a relevant parameter and so on. While it would be premature to say that these matters are resolved, it is certainly the case that a great deal more is known about what is going on than was the case in the latter part of the twentieth century (see Gries 2012 for some illuminating discussion). It is also the case that modern descriptive methods in linguistics have made it easier to see the types of constraint that may be operating in blends (see many of the papers collected in Renner et al. 2012). I have nothing further to add to such discussions and will not consider such matters here.

Neither will I discuss whether blends "are" compounds or an independent type of word-formation. They are sufficiently compound-like to fit under the general definition of compound that we started off with (see Section 2.1), although they clearly have other properties, too.

What I do want to discuss is the meanings of blends. The meanings of what I have termed 'headed blends' are derivable from the meanings of the underlying structures, though with some further degree of semantic opacity due to specialisation. *Medicare* is derived from *medical care*, but is more specialised in that it is used as a name for a particular insurance scheme dealing with medical insurance. The coordinative blends are potentially more interesting.

Consider a sample of coordinative compounds (40) and a sample of coordinative blends (41).

(40) blue-green
      comedy-thriller
      green-blue
      jazz-rock
      linguistic-philosophical
      murder-suicide
      Nelson-Marlborough
      singer-songwriter
      tractor-trailer

(41) catalo   from   cattle   +   buffalo
      compander   from   compressor   +   expander

diesohol	from	diesel	+	alcohol
gasohol	from	gasoline	+	alcohol
hebra	from	horse	+	zebra
labradoodle	from	labrador	+	poodle
liger	from	lion	+	tiger
shoat	from	sheep	+	goat
Spanglish	from	Spanish	+	English
spork	from	spoon	+	fork
tigon	from	tiger	+	lion
Yinglish	from	Yiddish	+	English
zorse	from	zebra	+	horse

There are some noticeable differences between the two lists, which seem to reflect some genuine differences between the two constructions. Coordinative compounds include adjectives and verbs, blends very rarely do. There are exceptions: *Spanglish* can be a noun or an adjective, *Californicate* (from *California + fornicate*) is a verb. Beliaeva (2014) adds some forms such as *awesmazing* (from *awesome + amazing*) and *bragplain* (from *brag + complain*), but such forms are minority ones. It is not clear to me to what extent this can be explained by the general predominance of nouns in the English vocabulary; totals would certainly be affected by what counts as a verbal coordinative compound. But my sense is that there is still a difference here.

English, as we have seen, does not have many coordinative compounds denoting places. Neither does it have many blends with this function. For some reason, there are rather more onomastic coordinative compounds in New Zealand than elsewhere, including *Bay of Plenty-Rotorua, Napier-Hastings, Nelson-Marlborough, Southland-Otago*; there are also rather more onomastic blends from the United States than from elsewhere, including *Texoma* (from *Texas + Oklahoma*, the name of a lake), *Texico* (from *Texas + New Mexico*, the name of a city),*Texarkana* (from *Texas, Arkansas* and *Louisiana*) (Bright 2013). The general rarity of onomastic formations of this type could be linked to the lack of pragmatic functioning of two places as one, that is, to a simple reflection of society. The areal distinction, if it is correct, is rather less explicable.

Multifunctional compounds like *singer-songwriter* whose elements denote two functions of the same individual are common. Such words do not appear to occur as blends.

On the other hand, cross-breeds seem to have blends as their preferred realization. While compounds denoting cross-breeds are found as well, they tend to be preferred as attributive elements: *a lion-tiger cross*. Several

examples of the blends denoting cross-breeds are given in (41), and there is a
whole joke industry based on the question 'What do you call a cross between
an X and a Y?' where the expected answer is in the form of a blend. The trope
persists even where it is manipulated: What do you call a cross between an
elephant and a rhino? Answers: (1) *Elephino* (= Hell if I know) or (2) Isn't that
a *rhelephant*? (Isn't that irrelevant?).

Some of these blends – but not, apparently, all of them – are not straight
coordinations, but are headed. The difference between a *tigon* and a *liger* is
whether the tiger is the dam (*liger*) or the sire (*tigon*). The same is true with a
zorse (zebra stallion) and a *hebra* (zebra mare). Whether this makes these
constructions right-headed or left-headed is not necessarily clear, though right-
headed seems more plausible given the general structure of English: it certainly
means that the two elements that make up the blend are not of equal status. On
the other hand, *labradoodles* appear to be so-called independent of the dam
and the sire. *Poobrador* can be found, but does not seem to be distinguished
semantically from *labradoodle*.

Something similar (but more confusing) can be found with words like
Chinglish and *Spanglish*. Consider the *OED* definitions in (42).

(42)   Chinglish: A mixture of Chinese and English; *esp.* a variety of English used
        by speakers of Chinese
        Hinglish: a mixture of Hindi and English; *esp.* a variety of English used by
        speakers of Hindi
        Japlish: A blend of Japanese and English spoken in Japan: either the Japanese
        language freely interlarded with English expressions or the English language
        spoken in an unidiomatic way by a Japanese speaker.
        Singlish$_1$: An informal variety of English spoken in Sri Lanka, incorporating
        elements of Sinhala
        Singlish$_2$: An informal variety of English spoken in Singapore
        Spanglish: A type of Spanish contaminated by English words and forms of
        expression
        Yinglish: A jocular name for a blend of English and Yiddish spoken in the
        United States; a form of English containing many Yiddishisms.

If we go beyond the *OED*, we find more variety.

(43)   Czenglish: Poor English heavily influenced by Czech. (https://
        en.wiktionary.org/wiki/Czenglish accessed 26 Jan. 2016)
        Danglish: 'The term is used in Denmark to refer to the increasingly strong
        influx of English or pseudo-English vocabulary into Danish.' (https://en
        .wikipedia.org/wiki/Danglish accessed 26 Jan. 2016)
        Dinglish is an English-relexified Dutch (http://delta.tudelft.nl/article/
        surviving-dinglish/29856 accessed 22 Jan. 2016) or a German-English mix
        spoken by a child being raised in a bilingual home (http://claireseuroamerica

.blogspot.co.nz/2009/06/we-sprechen-dinglish.html accessed 22 Jan. 2016), or corrupted German (http://diaryofacommunicator.com/2015/08/27/ditch-the-dinglish-from-your-international-content/ accessed 22 Jan. 2016), or a variety of English with Arabic admixture spoke in Dubai (http:// englishmanindubai.com/2009/10/30/ten-dubai-phrases/ accessed 22 Jan. 2016)

Swenglish: English strongly influenced by Swedish. Contrasted with *Svengelska*, Swedish heavily laced with anglicisms. (https://en.wikipedia.org/ wiki/Swenglish accessed 26 Jan. 2016)

Swinglish: Apparently English words used in Swiss German with meanings that are not transparent to the English-speaking observer. [Some of the examples given, like *handy* 'mobile phone', are not restricted to Swiss German. LB] (www.dicconbewes.com/2010/07/16/an-introduction-to-swinglish/ accessed 26 Jan. 2016)

We can summarise all this by saying that the default reading for these words ending in *-(g)lish* is that they represent a type of English and are thus right-headed. In some cases, however, they can indicate a blend without indicating which is the fundamental variety (if it is even possible to make that judgement), and in the case of *Spanglish*, the word seems to be left-headed. (Note, parenthetically, that the definition of *franglais* – a corrupt version of the French language produced by the indiscriminate introduction of words and phrases of English and American origin (*OED*) – is affected by the left-headedness of French compounds, and the same may be true of *Spanglish*, under the influence of Spanish.)

These examples are worrying on various levels. First, items which on one level look as though they are formed from coordinated elements are nonetheless headed. It becomes a matter of some interest how far this can be extended: are there also coordinative compounds which are headed, and if so, how many of them? Second, observed headedness is not regular. This is a problem for any rule-based approach to word-formation.

Consider next colour terms like *green-blue*. Böhmerová (2010: 90) reports *bleen* as a blend indicating the same transition, and *grue* is also found, though not necessarily with the same meaning ('(linguistics) Green or blue, as a translation from languages such as Welsh that do not distinguish between these hues.' https://en.wiktionary.org/wiki/grue accessed 26 Jan. 2016). *Blue-black* is not the same as *black and blue*, *blue-black* being a compromise colour and *black and blue* being the presence of both colours. *Red-blue* could be a compromise colour, but, to the extent that it is used, seems to be used for the presence of both colours. *Yellow-green* is a compromise colour, as are *orange-yellow* and *red-orange* and *blue-magenta*. *Red-white*, however, to the extent that it is used as a colour term at all, appears to mean the presence of both colours, and not to denote a shade of pink. *Grellow* is found in the *Urban Dictionary*, as is *yorange*. *Greige* (a mixture of *grey* and *beige*) seems to have become quite a fashionable term in recent years. Perhaps the relative paucity of compromise terms here, either in the form of compounds or in the form of blends, is due to the existence of so many other colour terms: *chartreuse* (green-yellow), *magenta* (red-blue), *cornsilk* and *saffron* (orange-yellow), *cyan* (blue-green) and so on. Where overt labelling is required, English speakers seem to prefer term like *greenish yellow*, *bluey-green*, where head-edness is syntactically overt and the relevant colour requires less cultural agreement than terms like *chartreuse, puce, turquoise, heliotrope* and the like.

Having discussed these categories, there is a large remnant where the difference between a coordinative compound and a coordinative blend is less clear. Note, though, examples like *fridge-freezer, tractor-trailer* where the alliteration of the compound makes the use of a blend problematic (*tractor* + *trailer* = *tractor? trailer?*). The same problem allows Kipling's *grey-green* and prevents a blend, which would have to be *green*. But in many instances we find a compound in preference to (sometimes to the exclusion of) a blend, and it is not clear whether this asymmetry is significant or explicable. Some examples are given in (44).

(44)   *murder-suicide* is preferred over *murdercide*, which is also found
       space-time is preferred over *spime* (defined by the *Urban Dictionary* as 'A real life physical object with knowledge of itself', so not the same as *space-time*, though related to both concepts)
       cough-laugh is preferred to *claugh* (found with the same meaning in the *Urban Dictionary*)
       fighter-bomber is preferred to a putative *fomber*

It may be that we simply have two distinct ways of forming words from coordinated bases, and that the two compete as do many other word-formation processes. It may be that the distinction is mainly one of style, with blends being seen as lighter-hearted, less formal, wittier formations than compounds. There is room for further research on this aspect of compounding and blending.

6.7   Form and Usage

One aspect of compounds that has been commented on by many linguists, dealing with a range of languages, is their compactness (see Bauer 1978: 14–16 for some examples). This compactness is, of course, related to their relative lack of explicitness: *windmill* is more compact that *mill powered by the wind* because it is not explicit about the semantic relationship which holds between the two elements. This might be expected to be a disadvantage for communicative purposes, but there are some places where compactness is itself a desirable goal.

The first of these is in headlines. Headlines are well-known for using short forms wherever possible, preferring *bid* to *attempt*, *chop* to *eliminate*, *mull* to *consider*, *slam* to *criticize* and even *wed* to *marry*, which saves only two letters. A headline like that in (45) therefore saves several letters by using compounds rather than the corresponding N + P + N constructions.

(45)   Paris terrorist killed in Brussels explosion 'had cocaine traces in her body'
        (www.thesun.co.uk/sol/homepage/news/ 6 Jan. 2016)

Another place where space can be at a premium is in advertising. Leech (1966: 136–141) lists a number of compound words found in advertising slogans and in print advertisements, including *slot-together assembly*, *satin-soft*, *feather-light*, *honey-coated*, *coffee-pot-fresh*, *man-appeal* and *flip-tops*.

Perhaps less obviously, compactness also has a value in bureaucratese. This was highlighted – at least in relation to German – in a news item put out by the BBC on 3 June 2013. The beginning of the news item is reproduced in (46).

(46)   **The German language has lost its longest word thanks to a change in the law to conform with EU regulations**.
        Rindfleischetikettierungsueberwachungsaufgabenuebertragungsgesetz – meaning 'law delegating beef label monitoring [tasks]' – was introduced in 1999 in the state of Mecklenburg-Western Pomerania.
        It was repealed following changes to EU regulations on the testing of cattle.

A quick scan of a single edition of the Wellington (New Zealand) broadsheet the *Dominion Post* (for 13 Jan. 2016) provides examples such as the following, most, but not all, from the New Zealand context: *District Health Board*, *New Zealand Qualifications Authority*, *off-shore detention centre*, *Trans-Pacific Partnership Agreement*, *University Entrance* (national examination at the end of secondary school), *Wellington Emergency Management Office*, *World Bank*. Compounds make good labels for official bodies and other entities of repeated official concern, and sometimes present a suitable input to an initialism or acronym (*NZQA* and *TPPA* in the examples above). Interestingly enough, what is officially, in New Zealand, *the Ministry of Education* is often called *the Education Ministry* in news reports, even in radio news, where the space-saving value of compounds is not of the same importance. It seems that compounds are viewed as having not only a function in terms of compactness, but also a function as marking the language of a particular register.

A less familiar use of the compactness of compounds is in creating cross-references. Examples are provided in (47). In each of these cases the compound creates a classification with only a single member and so guarantees reference, and it does so without the fully explicit semantic structure that was necessary in the first introduction of the referent.

(47) a. ... an agitated lady ... who told me her parrot was sick. [17 lines] I steered the sick-parrot lady into the entrance hall. (Francis, Dick. 1991. *Comeback*. London: Michael Joseph, p. 74)

      b. ... the one with the lady in the orange coat ... [22 lines] The orange coat lady, now in grey with pearls, was the driver. (Francis, Dick. 1991. *Comeback*. London: Michael Joseph, p. 103)

      c. Instead the whole place was alive with Leven Vale and Greater Birchester officers searching like so many cumbrous bumblebees. ... [17 pages] Sgt Wintercombe's bumble bee-buzzing searchers came up with nothing. (Keating, H. R. F. 2001. *A detective in love*. London: Macmillan, pp. 37, 54)

      d. I saw a woman standing in the lighted kitchen, leaning back against a counter. In her left hand was a bottle of tequila ... [101 pages] The tequila woman almost certainly lived in the house. (Layman, Richard. 2001. *Night in the lonesome October*. London: Headline, pp. 51, 152)

Other types of word-formation may also have these space-saving functions, but it is the compounds which are the focus of attention here.

One result of the compactness of compounds is often said to be their vividness (see e.g. Darmsteter 1875: 118). This is part of their value in advertising. The vividness can often be enhanced by the use of alliteration, assonance, rhyme or other parallelism. Vestergaard and Schrøder (1985: 62) cite the example of *freezer-pleezers*. We also find brands like *Longlife* (oil).

Vividness also has literary uses. In fact, compounds can have various uses in a literary context. Consider, for example, (48), where the compound structure gives rise to compactness, which means that the relevant words are collocated in such a way as to give the alliteration force. In fact, in (48) there are three instances of alliteration and one of assonance made possible in the short line by compounding.

(48) warm-laid grave of a womb-life grey; (Hopkins, Gerard Manley, *The wreck of the Deutschland*)

In other cases, the use of compounds leads to a construction in which an appropriate prosodic structure can flourish. The examples in (49) illustrate this.

(49)   a. I move along life's tomb-decked way
             And listen to the passing bell Summoning men (Hopkins, Gerard Manley,
             Nondum)
        b. Where youth grows pale, and spectre-thin and dies;
             Where but to think is to be full of sorrow
             And leaden-eyed despairs; (Keats, John, *Ode to a nightingale*)
        c. But come thou goddess fair and free,
             In Heaven yclept Euphrosyne,
             And by man, heart-easing Mirth,
             Whom lovely Venus at a birth
             With two sister Graces more
             To ivy-crownéd Bacchus bore. (Milton, John, *L'Allegro*)

In other cases, while prosodic factors may remain relevant, it is the vividness which seems to be to the fore.

(50)   a. With far-heard whisper o'er the sea
             Off shot the spectre-bark. (Coleridge, Samuel Taylor, *The rime of the
             ancient mariner*).
        b. The breezy-call of incense-breathing morn (Gray, Thomas, *Written in a
             country churchyard*)
        c. Ah, what is woman that you forsake her,
             And the hearth-fire and the home-acre
             To go to the old grey Widow-maker (Kipling, Rudyard, *Song of the Dane
             women*)
        d. in thy sight Storm-flakes were scroll-leaved flowers, lily showers – sweet
             Heaven was astrew with them (Hopkins, Gerard Manley, *The wreck of the
             Deutschland*)

In general terms, Millroy (1977: 183) comments of Hopkins's use of
compounds that

> Where it appears that the form my be interpretable in a number of different
> ways (as in *rockfire*), the effect is not so much one of uncertainty as of
> richness and suggestiveness ...

And later (p. 185):

> [C]ompounding is part of Hopkins's compression of language and elliptical
> style that so many critics have commented on.

What we see here is the form of compounds leading to particular usages. The
compactness of compounds and their inexplicit semantic structure allow for
space-saving and at the same time for vividness of expression. These factors
make compounds particularly suited to use in particular registers, where they
may become established as a part of that register.

6.8   Envoi

What I hope to have shown in this chapter is that, even with such a well-described language as English, and with such a specific area of grammar as compounding, there are matters of interest that have not been fully investigated. In some of these, the question of what is happening in English may have implications for the wider study of compounding, word-formation or indeed for grammar as a whole. While this chapter has been necessarily selective in the questions considered, there is plenty of evidence that a detailed analysis of English compounding still has much to teach us.

7 *Discussion*

7.1   Taking Stock

Compounding is a process of producing non-canonical modification of a head in a construction consisting of two constituents (see Section 3.7). A compound is a construction produced by the process of compounding, or else by some other process which mimics the output of the compounding process (see Section 4.7). Because compounds are constructions which provide a classification, and classifications of entities act as names for those entities, they are often treated as words and considered to be words, though they may not be entirely canonical words (see Chapter 2). Because some classifications are of less permanent pragmatic or cultural importance than others, some compounds seem less word-like than others. Because compounds are often somewhere between words and clauses (argumental compounds contain verbs and arguments of those verbs just like clauses), they may be best described by syntactic or by morphological rules, depending on the language involved (or possibly on the theoretical approach of the analyst). Alternatively, they can be seen as being intermediate between morphology and syntax, and sharing some aspects of each. At the same time, because they are perceived as word-like they may take on some other features of words, such as stress patterns.

Compounds may have a literal interpretation of the head or a figurative one; in the former case we speak of endocentric compounds, in the latter of exocentric compounds (see Section 4.3). The distinction between the two is not stable, and what is considered to be a figurative interpretation is subject to the theoretical stance of the analyst. Thus there may be dispute as to whether particular compounds are endocentric or exocentric. Some compounds are exocentric by virtue of having a head which is not of the word-class of the compound. In such cases, exocentricity is not controversial. In Construction Grammar, the word-class of such compounds can be viewed as being determined by the construction itself. Both exocentric and endocentric compounds have heads, but the head of the compound may not be the centre of the compound (defined as the element of the compound of which the entire compound names a hyponym; see Section 3.2.3). Exocentric compounds lack a centre, but not a head.

Coordinative compounds are not canonical compounds, because they do not show straightforward modification, and because some of them may be analysed as having multiple centres. Because of the tension between the use of compounds for classifying and the conjoined nature of the elements of coordinative compounds, the interpretation of coordinate compounds may be awkward where these two pressures conflict.

The semantic interpretation of compounds is determined by pragmatic factors valid at the point of creation of the compound. While it is possible to gloss the meaning of a literal compound in terms of the elements and the relationship which holds between them, such a gloss is not a part of the grammar of compounding per se, but is part of the pragmatics of lexicology (see Section 4.4). The fact that *cat gut* has nothing to do with cats, that a *killer whale* is not a whale has no relevance to the value of these constructions as names, and no grammatical relevance; in the same way, it is not part of grammar that a *red admiral* is not an admiral but a butterfly or that a *collation* 'light meal' is not collated, or that *exclaim* has nothing to do with claiming.

Although compounds are names which allow classification, they are not the only constructions which have that function. Languages may have several constructions with apparently similar functions in this regard, but with slightly different foci. These other constructions may be morphological or syntactic. Thus how compounds contrast with other constructions – and what constructions are available for them to contrast with – is something that needs to be specified for individual languages. This may even influence whether it is considered more appropriate to deal with compounds as morphology or as syntax: if all the competitors are syntactic, compounds may look more syntactic than they would if they were competing with morphological constructions.

7.2   Some Typological Considerations

Because there are many possible ways of creating constructions which have the same – or very similar – functions to those held by compounds, it is perfectly possible for there to be languages which exclusively employ some of the other structures to fulfil these functions. Therefore, it is possible to have languages without compounds, but in principle, the lack of compounds may be due to a number of different factors, including at least the following:

- The function of allowing non-canonical modification may be filled by a construction other than a compound structure. If this is the case, it is useful to know what structure is used and how lexical the outputs of that structure tend to be in the language concerned: are they, for instance, semantically specialised, are they paradigmatically only partly predictable, is there evidence of a historical shift towards single-word status for such constructions? We might expect such formations, like compounds, to show evidence of chain formations, that is, formations of series of constructions with a fixed element and a fixed meaning which may create a construction in its own right and may, over a longer period of time, lead to the fixed element being interpreted as an affix. If this is the case, we would expect some constructions to be more widely used in these ways than others: markers of possessive structures will be more usual than the use of correlative adjectives, for instance.
- It may be that there is no such thing as non-canonical modification in a given language. Many Polynesian languages, for example, have been analysed as having far looser connections between individual forms and specific word-classes than is the case for most Indo-European languages. While the lack of fixed word-class for individual forms does not necessarily imply that no compounds will be formed (Maori provides an example of a language which does have compounds), this is a very different basis for not having compounds than the first one considered above.
- Non-canonical modification may be obtained by some other morphological means (for instance, a specific affix for creating attributive forms from forms of other word-classes), or non-canonical modification may not match with the semantic function of classification. While compound-like constructions might arise that are not classificatory or that involve only canonical modification, such constructions might be better viewed as some type of quasi-compound. It is not clear to me what implications this might have.

Where languages do have compounds, they may, of course, be similar or differ in the types of compound that they show. Compound nouns are often thought to be the compounds most widely used across languages, but languages may have only compound nouns or only compound verbs. Because of the relative markedness of a category of adjectives, we would be surprised to find a language which had compound adjectives but no other compounds. Similarly, it would seem odd to have a language which has both adjectives and adverbs having compound adverbs but not compound adjectives. And because we expect compounds to have a semantics based on classification, it would seem odd to have compound prepositions to the exclusion of other types.

Although it seems that the distinction between subordinative and coordinative compounds is not as clear-cut as might be thought, it would not be surprising to find a language which uses one to the exclusion of the other, or uses one to the exclusion of the other in a particular word-class. The classes of coordinative compound are numerous, and it is often difficult to distinguish them; accordingly, it would be surprising to find all coordinative compounds in a given language belonged to just one of these classes.

It would, however, be surprising to find a language which uses endocentric subordinative compounds to the exclusion of exocentrics. This is because, as we have seen (Section 4.3), some compounds are exocentric by virtue of having a metaphorical interpretation (and perhaps all of them are exocentric by virtue of a figurative interpretation). Since all languages contain metaphors and other figures of speech, and speakers do not seem to be able to identify figures consistently, it would be surprising if it were possible to have a set of endocentric subordinative compounds without some of them becoming exocentric by these routes. This would account for the perception that endocentric compounds are unmarked in relation to exocentric compounds (Dressler 2006). On the other hand, some compounds are exocentric by virtue of their grammatical form. If there are languages which have exocentric compounds to the exclusion of endocentric ones, it would be expected that they have patterns of exocentricity which are exocentric by virtue of their grammar.

If compounds are defined by their non-canonical patterns of modification, we would expect verbal modification of nouns and nominal modification of verbs to be more common compounding patterns than adjectival modification of nouns or adverbial modification of verbs. Nominal modification of nouns and verbal modification of verbs should both be common, but verbal modification of verbs is frequently treated as a syntactic pattern separate from compounding.

Because nouns are generally more numerous in languages than verbs, we would expect compound nouns to be more usual than compound verbs. This effect may be exaggerated to the extent that verb compounds are viewed as some other construction. In particular, because many verbal compounds with nominal modifiers are treated as incorporation, compound verbs appear to be less frequent than they might justifiably be considered to be. While incorporation is clearly a special kind of compounding, with its own problems of description (see Section 3.6), it nevertheless fits in the overall definition of compounding given here.

7.3   Where Next?

This book has raised a host of problems, and if it has suggested solutions in many instances, it would be irresponsible to presume that it has solved the problems. There are alternate views on virtually everything that has been said, and this book has provided no more than a relatively consistent viewpoint around which further discussion can take place.

The questions that have been asked here range from the absolutely fundamental one of how we recognise a compound, through extremely polarising, but not necessarily so fundamental, of whether compounding is morphology, syntax, both or neither, to extremely minor questions concerning the predictability of headedness in blends. Many of the questions raised are tied together at some point. The consistency of headedness in coordinative blends depends upon the possibility of seeing coordinated constructions as headed at all, on the idea that headedness is a valuable notion in morphology as well as in syntax, on the idea that blends can be headed, on the notion that headedness is a feature we need to recognise in grammars. When we look at the meaning links between the elements in N + N compounds, it is sometimes useful to be able to specify specific meaning links, and sometimes helpful to be able to leave the link unspecified. Either we have to give up one of the options (specific links exist or do not), or we have to agree on a suitable demarcation of duty between the two. Where the solution proposed here is not approved of by other scholars (for whatever reason), there may still be multiple solutions to choose between, and we need good arguments for going one way or the other. It may be that the arguments I have presented here for my opinion are not strong enough. That does not mean that the diametrically opposing view is necessarily correct.

In the light of the material canvassed in Section 7.2, I would suggest that one of the benefits of the proposals made here is that they open the doors to rather different typological studies than have previously been considered. It remains to be seen, of course, how valuable such studies turn out to be. Some small beginnings have been made, for example, by Nagano (2016), who considers relational adjectives across languages of different language families. Such work shows that similar functions are not necessarily performed by similar grammatical process in different languages. If we add to that the notion that even where similar functions can be performed by similar processes, the distribution of the processes among the forms may differ, we are heading into a rather more nuanced kind of typology than has often been applied.

More radical conclusions could also be entertained. Although Giegerich (2015) does not overtly say this, it seems to me that one of the conclusions that could be drawn from his research, and possibly also from this book, is that the label 'compound' is not a helpful one at all; rather there is a series of construction types which share some features, but not enough to say that there is an overarching type. In this book I have tended to argue for a position lumping constructions together rather than splitting them into more specific constructions, but the splitting solution also has some advantages. The most obvious is that the differences between the various sub-types of compound are then expected, rather than things that demand an explanation. The biggest disadvantage of the splitting proposal is that the commonalities have to be explained, perhaps by reference to more general processing constraints. If these two positions, splitting and lumping, exist, then there must also be intermediate positions, allowing a certain degree of lumping. An alternative radical position is that the sub-types of compound arise through the variability of application of some kind of canonical ideal. This would be a conclusion based on exemplar theory (see e.g. Pierrehumbert 2001, 2003). Again, I think this would be compatible with much that has been said here, but I have not argued specifically for such an approach, except with reference to stress. As a third radical proposal, consider the possibility that lexical/non-lexical and word/syntax are not related concepts, but orthogonally distinct scales. This is, I think, implicit in some of the material considered here, and in Giegerich (2015), and so is perhaps less radical a proposal than the other two. Nevertheless, it contradicts the general presupposition that lexical and morphological are fundamentally identical concepts. I have also suggested that endocentric/ exocentric and subordinative/coordinative might not be such distinct categories as has previously been supposed. I do not try to elaborate on any of these proposals here, but merely add them to show that the debate is not closed, and that there are several avenues for further developments in the study of compounding.

I am painfully aware that my view of what a compound is and how it operates is restricted by my Indo-European bias, even though I have read descriptions of compounding in a range of languages. I do not have expertise in the kind of range of languages outlined by Spencer (2011). A wider evaluation of my conclusions here, based on a wider range of languages, is clearly required. I hope that despite this, the position I have outlined here will not only shed light on compounding in English and Germanic, but also act as a spur to such further discussion and provide a useful starting position for scholars who wish to explore compounds and compounding in more detail.

Appendix: Lexical One

The question of *one* has been dealt with by a number of authors in recent times, with different outcomes. Payne and Huddleston (2002) overtly set up *one* as a test of the syntactic or lexical nature of N + N constructions. Giegerich (2015) questions the extent to which the real distinction is lexical versus syntactic rather than a matter of parallel transparent semantic structures. For Payne and Huddleston, the non-acceptability of (a) is because *railway* is a lexical item; for Giegerich it arises because the link between *rail* and *way* is not parallel to the link between *motor* and *way* (rails constitute the way, but motors do not constitute the way, rather motor vehicles drive on it). The fact that the relationship between *motor* and *way* is not particularly transparent (is *motor* a noun or a verb, if a noun is it a clipping from *motor car* or not?) may be an extra factor leading to the non-acceptability as far as Giegerich is concerned.

(a)   Does that line on the map show a railway or a motor one? [i.e. a motorway]

For Giegerich, the use of *one* is easier where there is ascriptive attribution rather than associative attribution. If that is right, (b) ought to be more easily accepted than (c). Part of the difficulty with such items is that they are, in any case, extremely rare, and intuitions about them are not firm.

(b)   Are the boy scouts on the camping site tonight or the girl ones?
(c)   Is he a lion-tamer or a tiger one?

In order to gain some data on whether *one* could be used to refer within a word, I asked my English language-teaching colleagues at Victoria University to fill out a short questionnaire, saying whether various uses of *one* were or were not acceptable. I argued that practical language teachers were used to making judgements about acceptability, but were unlikely to be deeply involved in the theoretical controversies surrounding such usage. I should like to thank all those teachers who responded to my questionnaire. The questionnaire and the numbers of responses are presented below.

Table A *Results of the questionnaire*

Sentence	OK	?	NOT OK
A wooden bridge is not as strong as a steel one.	12		
Windmills are just as picturesque as water ones.	2	1	9
Red squirrels are much prettier than grey ones.	12		
Calves are much softer than adult ones like cows and bulls.	1		11
A pseudoscorpion is not as dangerous as a real one.	5	3	4
Spiderlings are not as scary as big ones.	2		10
Piglets are much cuter than adult ones.	2		10
A non-book is one without real content, but just pictures.*	3	2	6
At the zoo they have a black bear and a polar one.	1	4	7
I'd rather look at a rural landscape than at an industrial one.	11	1	
A miniskirt displays a lot more leg than a full-length one.	5	4	3
Intercity trains travel much faster than those that run within one.			12
A semiquaver is half the length of a full one.	3		9
A toadlet is just as ugly as an adult one.	1		11
It makes no difference to you whether you're hit by a bomblet or a full-sized one.		1	11
Neo-beatniks can look just as odd as old-fashioned ones.	2	2	8
A meta-rule can tell you more than a basic-level one.	5	4	3

* One respondent changed the sentence in a way which made it irrelevant

Some of the examples can be taken as checks on reliability: the first example, for instance, is typically cited as a place where *one* can be used. The question is whether, or to what extent, *one* can be used to refer back to a part of a word. In general, there was reluctance to use *one* in this way, even where the referent was presumably transparent (as with *spiderling*, for instance). Familiarity of the derivative did not seem to make a difference: references by *one* to the *pig* and the *toad* in *piglet* and *toadlet* are both deemed unacceptable. But where *one* refers to a lexical head, there is a lot of variation. It is not clear to me why the use of *one* in the *non-book* example should have been so much less acceptable that the use of *one* in the *mini-skirt* or *meta-rule* examples. However, since only a quarter of my respondents, who are likely to be fairly conservative judgers of acceptability, found the *mini-skirt* and *meta-rule* examples unacceptable, I feel justified in claiming that for at least some speakers *one* can be used to refer to elements of words.

There are several problems with this mini-experiment. The respondents do not all speak the same variety of English, and differences between British,

North American and New Zealand usages could have been masked; I did not ask for gender or age, although this is an area where conservatism in language use might have a role to play; the numbers are low; some of the examples turned out to be unhelpful: some speakers pronounce *black bear* with fore-stress, others with end-stress, and that could have made a difference, for instance.

Finally, note that the *red squirrel* example is problematic. Both *red squirrel* and *grey squirrel* must be lexical constructions in that the colour is not gradable but classificatory, and they are names of species, yet they clearly accept *one*.

References

Adams, Valerie. 1973. *An introduction to modern English word formation*. London: Longman.

2001. *Complex words in English*. Harlow: Pearson.

Aikhenvald, Alexandra Y. 2003. *A grammar of Tariana*. Cambridge: Cambridge University Press.

Allan, Robin, Philip Holmes & Tom Lundskær-Nielsen. 1995. *Danish: a comprehensive grammar*. London: Routledge.

Allen, Margaret Rees. 1978. *Morphological investigations*. Unpublished PhD dissertation, University of Connecticut.

Allen, W. Sidney. 1974. *Vox graeca: the pronunciation of Classical Greek*. 2nd edition. Cambridge: Cambridge University Press.

Amaya, Maria Trillos. 1999. *Damana*. Munich: LINCOM Europa.

Arnaud, Pierre J. L. & Vincent Renner. 2014. English and French [NN]$_N$ units: a categorical, morphological and semantic comparison. *Word Structure* 7: 1–28.

Arndt-Lappe, Sabine. 2011. Towards an exemplar-based model of stress in English noun-noun compounds. *Journal of Linguistics* 47: 549–585.

Aronoff, Mark. 1976. *Word formation in generative grammar*. Cambridge, MA: MIT Press.

Ayto, John. 1990. *The Longman register of new words, volume 2*. Harlow: Longman.

Baker, Mark C. & Carlos A. Fasola. 2009. Arucanian: Mapudungun. In Rochelle Lieber & Pavol Štekauer (eds.), *The Oxford handbook of compounding*, 594–608. Oxford: Oxford University Press.

Ballier, Nicolas. 2015. "Phrasal compounds" and the discourse/lexicology interface: "conglomeration" within the French tradition of English lexicology. *SKASE Journal of Theoretical Linguistics* 12/3 (*A Festschrift for Pavol Štekauer*): 115–141.

Bally, Charles. 1950 [1932]. *Linguistique générale et linguistique française*. 3rd edition. Berne: Franke.

Barcelona, Antonio. 2008. The interaction of metonymy and metaphor in the meaning and form of 'bahuvrihi' compounds. *Annual Review of Cognitive Linguistics* 6: 208–281.

Bat-El, Outi. 2000. The grammaticality of "extragrammatical" morphology. In Ursula Doleschal & Anna M. Thornton (eds.), *Extragrammatical and marginal morphology*, 61–81. Munich: LINCOM Europa.

Bauer, Laurie. 1978. *The grammar of nominal compounding*. Odense: Odense University Press.

1980. Deux problèmes au sujet des noms composés comprenant un premier élément verbal en français moderne. *Le français moderne* 48: 219–224.

1983a. *English word-formation*. Cambridge: Cambridge University Press.

1983b. Stress in compounds: a rejoinder. *English Studies* 64: 47–53.

1990. Be-heading the word. *Journal of Linguistics* 26: 1–31.

1998a. *Vocabulary*. London: Routledge.

1998b. Is there a class of neoclassical compounds, and if so is it productive? *Linguistics* 36: 403–422.

2000. Word. In Geert Booij, Christian Lehmann & Joachim Mugdan (eds.), *Morphology: an international handbook of inflection and word-formation*, 247–257. Berlin: de Gruyter.

2001. *Morphological productivity*. Cambridge: Cambridge University Press.

2003. *Introducing linguistic morphology*. 2nd edition. Edinburgh: Edinburgh University Press.

2004a. *A glossary of morphology*. Edinburgh: Edinburgh University Press.

2004b. Adjectives, compounds and words. *Nordic Journal of English Studies* 3/1 (= *Worlds of Words: A tribute to Arne Zettersten*): 7–22.

2008a. Dvandva. *Word Structure* 1: 1–20.

2008b. Exocentric compounds. *Morphology* 18: 51–74.

2009. IE, Germanic: Danish. In Rochelle Lieber & Pavol Štekauer (eds.), *The Oxford handbook of compounding*, 400–416. Oxford: Oxford University Press.

2010a. Co-compounds in Germanic. *Journal of Germanic Linguistics* 22: 201–219.

2010b. The typology of exocentric compounding. In Sergio Scalise & Irene Vogel (eds.), *Cross-disciplinary issues in compounding*, 167–175. Amsterdam: Benjamins.

2014. Grammaticality, acceptability, possible words and large corpora. *Morphology* 24: 83–103.

2015a. Expletive insertion. *American Speech* 90: 122–127.

2015b. Regularities in irregularities in English inflection. *Te Reo* 56–57: 3–12.

2015c. Stressing about the news. Paper presented at the New Zealand Linguistic Society meeting, Dunedin, December 2015.

2016. Re-evaluating exocentricity in word-formation. In Daniel Siddiqi & Heidi Harley (eds.), *Morphological metatheory*. Amsterdam: Benjamins.

In press. Compounds. In Bas Aarts, Jill Bowie & Gergana Popova (eds.), *The Oxford handbook of English grammar*. Oxford: Oxford University Press.

Bauer, Laurie & Rodney Huddleston. 2002. Lexical word formation. In Rodney Huddleston & Geoffrey K. Pullum (eds.), *The Cambridge grammar of the English language*, 1621–1721. Cambridge: Cambridge University Press.

Bauer, Laurie, Rochelle Lieber & Ingo Plag. 2013. *The Oxford reference guide to English morphology*. Oxford: Oxford University Press.

Bauer, Laurie & Antoinette Renouf. 2001. A corpus-based study of compounding in English. *Journal of English Linguistics* 29: 101–123.

Bauer, Laurie & Elizaveta Tarasova. 2013. The meaning link in nominal compounds. *SKASE Journal of Theoretical Linguistics* 10: 1–18.

Bauer, Winifred. 1997. *The Reed reference grammar of Māori*. Auckland: Reed.
Beard, Robert. 1981. *The Indo-European lexicon*. Amsterdam: North-Holland.
    1982. The plural as a lexical derivation. *Glossa* 16: 133–148.
Beliaeva, Natalia. 2014. *Unpacking contemporary English blends: morphological structure, meaning, processing*. Unpublished PhD thesis, Victoria University of Wellington.
Bell, Melanie. 2011. At the boundary of morphology and syntax: Noun noun constructions in English. In Alexandra Galani, Glynn Hicks & George Tsoulos (eds.), *Morphology and its interfaces*, 137–168. Amsterdam: Benjamins.
    2014. The English noun-noun construct: a morphological and syntactic object. In Angela Ralli, Geert Booij, Sergio Scalise and Athanasios Karasimos (eds.), *Morphology and the architecture of grammar*, 59–91. https://geertbooij .files.wordpress.com/2014/02/mmm8_proceedings.pdf.
Bell, Melanie & Ingo Plag. 2012. Informativeness is a determinant of compound stress in English. *Journal of Linguistics* 48: 485–520.
Bell, Melanie & Martin Schäfer. 2016. Modelling semantic transparency. *Morphology* 26: 157–199.
Benczes, Réka. 2014. Repetitions which are not repetitions: the non-redundant nature of tautological compounds. *English Language and Linguistics* 18: 431–447.
Berman, Ruth. 2009. Children's acquisition of compound constructions. In Rochelle Lieber & Pavol Štekauer (eds.), *The Oxford handbook of compounding*, 298–322. Oxford: Oxford University Press.
Bisetto, Antonietta. 2010. Recursiveness and Italian compounds. *SKASE Journal of Theoretical Linguistics* 7: 14–35.
Bisetto, Antonietta & Sergio Scalise. 2005. The classification of compounds. *Lingue e Linguaggio* 4: 319–332.
    2007. Selection is a head property. *Acta Linguistica Hungarica* 54: 361–380.
Bloomfield, Leonard. 1935. *Language*. London: Allen & Unwin.
Bogoras, Waldemar. 1922. Chukchee. In Franz Boas (ed.), *Handbook of American Indian languages Part 2*, 639–903. Washington, DC: Government Printing Office.
Böhmerová, Ada. 2010. *Blending as lexical amalgamation and its onomasiological and lexicographical status in English and Slovak*. Bratislava: ŠEVT.
Booij, Geert. 2002. *The morphology of Dutch*. Oxford: Oxford University Press.
    2007. *The Grammar of Words*. 2nd edition. Oxford: Oxford University Press.
    2009. Compounding and construction morphology. In Rochelle Lieber & Pavol Štekauer (eds.), *The Oxford handbook of compounding*, 201–216. Oxford: Oxford University Press.
    2010. *Construction morphology*. Oxford: Oxford University Press.
Borer, Hagit. 1988. On the morphological parallels between compounds and constructs. *Yearbook of Morphology* 1988: 45–65.
    2009. Afro-Asiatic, Semitic: Hebrew. In Rochelle Lieber & Pavol Štekauer (eds.), *The Oxford handbook of compounding*, 491–511. Oxford: Oxford University Press.
Breindl, Eva & Maria Thurmair. 1992. Der Fürstbischof im Hosenrock. Eine Studie zu den nominalen Kopulativkomposita des Deutschen. *Deutsche Sprache* 20: 32–61.

Brekle, Herbert E. 1970. *Generative Satzsemantik und transformationelle Syntax im System der englischen Nominalkomposition*. Munich: Fink.

1973. *Zur Stellung der Wortbildung in der Grammatik*. Trier: LAUT.

1978. Reflections on the conditions for the coining, use and understanding of nominal compounds. In Wolfgang U. Dressler & Wolfgang Meid (eds.), *Proceedings of the Twelfth International Congress of Linguists, Vienna, August 28– September 2, 1977*, 68–77. Innsbruck: Institut für Sprachwissenschaft.

Bresnan, Joan & Sam A. Mchombo. 1995. The Lexical Integrity Principle: evidence from Bantu. *Natural Language & Linguistic Theory* 13: 181–254.

Bright, William. 2013. *Native American placenames of the Southwest*. Norman: University of Oklahoma Press.

Brugmann, Karl. 1900. Das Wesen der sogenannten Wortzusammensetzung. Berichte über die Verhandlungen der Königl.-Sächsischen Gesellschaft der Wissenschaften zu Leipzig, *Philologisch-Historische Klasse* 52: 359–401.

Buck, Carl Darling. 1933. *Comparative grammar of Greek and Latin*. Chicago: University of Chicago Press.

Burrows, T. 1973. *The Sanskrit language*. 3rd edition. London: Faber and Faber.

Cannon, Garland. 1987. *Historical change and English word-formation*. New York: Lang.

Carr, Charles T. 1939. *Nominal compounds in Germanic*. London: Oxford University Press.

Carstairs-McCarthy, Andrew. 2002. *An introduction to English morphology*. Edinburgh: Edinburgh University Press.

2005. Phrases inside compounds: a puzzle for lexicon-free morphology. *SKASE Journal of Theoretical Linguistics* 2/3: 34–42.

Chao, Yuen Ren. 1968. *A grammar of spoken Chinese*. Berkeley: University of California Press.

Chomsky, Noam. 1970. Remarks on nominalization. In Roderick A. Jacobs and Peter S. Rosenbaum (eds.), *Readings in English transformational grammar*, 184–221. Waltham, MA: Ginn.

Chomsky, Noam & Morris Halle. 1968. *The sound pattern of English*. New York: Harper and Row.

Corbett, Greville G. 2007. Canonical typology, suppletion and possible words. *Language* 83: 8–42.

Corbin, Danielle. 1991. Introduction. *La formation des mots: structures et interprétations*. *Lexique* 10: 7–30.

Coseriu, Eugene. 1977. Inhaltliche Wortbildungslehre (am Beispiel des Typs *coupe-papier*). In Herbert E. Brekle & Dieter Kastovsky (eds.), *Perspektiven der Wortbildungsforschung*, 46–61. Bonn: Grundmann.

Creissels, Denis. 2004. Bambara. In Pierre J. L. Arnaud (ed.), *Le nom composé: données sur seize langues*, 21–46. Lyon: Presses Universitaires de Lyon.

Cruse, Alan. 1986. *Lexical semantics*. Cambridge: Cambridge University Press.

Crystal, David. 2008. *A dictionary of linguistics and phonetics*. 6th edition. Malden, MA: Blackwell.

Cubberley, Paul. 2002. *Russian: a linguistic introduction*. Cambridge: Cambridge University Press.

Dansk Sprognævn. 2015. Retskriviningsregler §19. www.dsn.dk/retskrivning/retskriv ningsregler/ (accessed 17 June 2015)

Darmsteter, Arsène. 1875. *Formation des mots composés en français*. Paris.

Davies, Mark. 2004. *BYU-BNC*. (Based on the British National Corpus from Oxford University Press). Available online at http://corpus.byu.edu/bnc/.

2008. *The Corpus of Contemporary American English (COCA)*: 450+ million words, 1990–present. www.americancorpus.org/.

Davies, William. 1986. *Choctaw verb agreement and Universal Grammar*. Dordrecht: Reidel.

Derbyshire, Desmond C. 1979. *Hixkaryana*. Amsterdam: North-Holland.

Detmold, Gaye Çinkılıç & Helmut Weiß. 2012. Kopulativkomposita. *Linguistische Berichte* 232: 417–435.

Dierickx, Jean. 1970. Why are plural attributives becoming more frequent? In Jean Dierickx & Yvan Lebrun (eds.), *Linguistique contemporaine: hommage à Eric Buyssens*, 39–46. Brussels: Editions de l'institut de sociologie de l'université libre.

Di Sciullo, Anna Maria & Edwin Williams. 1987. *On the definition of word*. Cambridge, MA: MIT Press.

Dixon, R. M. W. 1982. *Where have all the adjectives gone?* Berlin: Mouton.

Dixon, R. M. W. & Alexandra Y. Aikhenvald. 2002. Word: a typological framework. In R. M. W. Dixon & Alexandra Y. Aikhenvald (eds.), *Word: a cross-linguistic typology*, 1–41. Cambridge: Cambridge University Press.

Don, Jan. 2009. IE, Germanic: Dutch. In Rochelle Lieber & Pavol Štekauer (eds.), *The Oxford handbook of compounding*, 370–385. Oxford: Oxford University Press.

Douloureux, P. R. N. Tic. 1971. A note on one's privates. In Arnold M. Zwicky, Peter H. Salus, Robert I. Binnick, Anthony L. Vanek (eds.), *Studies out in left field: defamatory essays presented to James D. McCawley on the occasion of his 33rd or 34th birthday*, 45–53. Reprinted in 1992. Amsterdam: Benjamins.

Downing, Pamela. 1977. On the creation and use of English compound nouns. *Language* 77: 810–42.

Dressler, Wolfgang U. 2000. Extragrammatical vs. marginal morphology. In Ursula Doleschal & Anna M. Thornton (eds.), *Extragrammatical and marginal morphology*, 1–10. Munich: LINCOM Europa.

2006. Compound types. In Gary Libben & Gonia Jarema (eds.), *The representation and processing of compound words*, 23–44. Oxford: Oxford University Press.

Einarsson, Stefán. 1949. *Icelandic*. Baltimore: Johns Hopkins University Press.

Eisenberg, Peter. 2006. *Grundriß der deutschen Grammatik: Das Wort*. Stuttgart: Metzler.

England, Nora C. 1983. *A grammar of Mam, a Mayan language*. Austin: University of Texas Press.

Erben, Johannes. 1975. *Einführung in die deutsche Wortbildungslehre*. Berlin: Schmidt.

Evans, Nicholas & Hans-Jürgen Sasse. 2002. *Problems of polysynthesis*. Berlin: Akademie.

Fabb, Nigel. 1998. Compounding. In Andrew Spencer & Arnold M. Zwicky (eds.), *The handbook of morphology*, 66–83. Oxford: Blackwell.

Fábregas, Antonio & Sergio Scalise. 2012. *Morphology: from data to theories.* Edinburgh: Edinburgh University Press.

Fleischer, Wolfgang & Irmhild Barz. 2007. *Wortbildung der deutschen Gegenwartssprache.* Tübingen: Niemeyer.

Fortescue, M[ichael]. 1994. Morphology, polysynthetic. In R. E. Asher (ed.), *The encyclopedia of language and linguistics*, 2600–2602. Oxford: Pergamon.

Fradin, Bernard. 2009. IE, Romance: French. In Rochelle Lieber & Pavol Štekauer (eds.), *The Oxford handbook of compounding*, 417–435. Oxford: Oxford University Press.

Fudge, Erik. 1984. *English word-stress.* London: Allen and Unwin.

Gagné, Christina L. 2009. Psycholinguistic perspectives. In Rochelle Lieber & Pavol Štekauer (eds.), *The Oxford handbook of compounding*, 255–271. Oxford: Oxford University Press.

Gagné, Christina L. & Edward J. Shoben. 1997. The influence of thematic relations on the comprehension of non-predicating conceptual combinations. *Journal of Experimental Psychology: Learning, Memory, and Cognition* 23: 71–87.

Geerdts, Donna B. 1998. Incorporation. In Andrew Spencer & Arnold M. Zwicky (eds.), *The handbook of morphology*, 84–100. Oxford: Blackwell.

Giegerich, Heinz J. 1999. *Lexical strata in English.* Cambridge: Cambridge University Press.

    2004. Compound or phrase? English noun-plus-noun constructions and the stress criterion. *English Language and Linguistics* 8: 1–24.

    2005. Associative adjectives in English and the lexicon–syntax interface. *Journal of Linguistics* 41: 571–591.

    2009. The English compound stress myth. *Word Structure* 2: 1–17.

    2015. *Lexical structures: compounding and the modules of grammar.* Edinburgh: Edinburgh University Press.

Gijn, Rik van & Fernando Zúñiga. 2014. Word and the Americanist perspective. *Morphology* 24: 135–160.

Gove, Philip B. (ed.) 1966. *Webster's third new international dictionary of the English language.* Springfield, MA: Merriam.

Gries, Stefan Th. 2012. Quantitative corpus data of blend formation: psycho- and cognitive-linguistic perspectives. In Renner et al. (eds.), 145–167.

Grzega, Joachim. 2009. Compounding from an onomasiological perspective. In Rochelle Lieber & Pavol Štekauer (eds.), *The Oxford handbook of compounding*, 217–232. Oxford: Oxford University Press.

Haas, Wim de & Mieke Trommelen. 1993. *Morfologisch handboek van het Nederlands.* 's-Gravenhage: SDU.

Hacken, Pius ten. 2013. Semiproductivity and the place of word formation in grammar. In Pius ten Hacken & Claire Thomas (eds.), *The semantics of word formation and lexicalization*, 28–44. Edinburgh: Edinburgh University Press.

Hall, Christopher. 1992. *Modern German pronunciation.* Manchester: Manchester University Press.

Harris, Alice C. 2000. Where in the word is the Udi clitic? *Language* 76: 593–616.

    2006. Revisiting anaphoric islands. *Language* 82: 114–130.

Haspelmath, Martin. 1993. *A grammar of Lezgian*. Berlin: Mouton de Gruyter.

2002. *Understanding morphology*. London: Arnold.

2016. The serial verb construction: comparative concept and cross-linguistic generalizations. *Language and Linguistics* 17: 291–319.

Hatcher, Anna Granville. 1960. An introduction to the analysis of English noun compounds. *Word* 16: 356–373.

Heusinger, Klaus von & Christoph Schwarze. 2013. Italian V+N compounds, inflectional features and conceptual structure. *Morphology* 23: 325–350.

Hippisley, Andrew. 2015. The word as a universal category. In John R. Taylor (ed.), *The Oxford handbook of the word*, 246–269. Oxford: Oxford University Press.

Hoeksema, Jack. n.d. Elative compounds in Dutch: properties and developments. www.let.rug.nl/~hoeksema/elative.pdf

Hoffmann, Carl. 1963. *A grammar of the Margi language*. London: Oxford University Press.

Holmes, Philip & Ian Hinchliffe. 1994. *Swedish: a comprehensive grammar*. London: Routledge.

Hualde, José Ignacio & Jon Ortiz de Urbina. 2003. *A grammar of Basque*. Berlin: Mouton de Gruyter.

Huddleston, Rodney. 2002a. The clause: complements. In Rodney Huddleston & Geoffrey K. Pullum (eds.), *The Cambridge grammar of the English language*, 213–321. Cambridge: Cambridge University Press.

2002b. Non-finite and verbless clauses. In Rodney Huddleston & Geoffrey K. Pullum (eds.), *The Cambridge grammar of the English language*, 1171–1271. Cambridge: Cambridge University Press.

Hudson, Richard A. 1987. Zwicky on heads. *Journal of Linguistics* 23: 109–132.

1993. Do we have heads in our minds? In Greville G. Corbett, Norman M. Fraser & Scott McGlashan (eds.), *Heads in grammatical theory*, 266–291. Cambridge: Cambridge University Press.

Itô, Junko & Ralf Armin Mester. 2005 [1986]. The phonology of voicing in Japanese. *Linguistic Inquiry* 17: 49–73, reprinted in Natsuko Tsujimura (ed.), *Japanese linguistics*, 38–64. London: Routledge.

Iwasaki, Soichi & Preeya Ingkaphirom. 2005. *A reference grammar of Thai*. Cambridge: Cambridge University Press.

Jackendoff, Ray. 1977. *X-bar syntax*. Cambridge, MA: MIT Press.

2016. English noun-noun compounds in Conceptual Semantics. In Pius ten Hacken (ed.), *The semantics of compounding*, 15–37. Cambridge: Cambridge University Press.

Jespersen, Otto. 1927. *A modern English grammar on historical principles. Part III: syntax, second volume*. London: Allen and Unwin and Copenhagen: Munksgaard.

1942. *A modern English grammar on historical principles. Part VI: morphology*. London: Allen and Unwin and Copenhagen: Munksgaard.

Johnston, Michael & Frederica Busa. 1999. Qualia structure and the compositional interpretation of compounds. In E. Viegas (ed.), *Breadth and depth of semantic lexicons*, 167–187. Dordrecht: Springer.

Julien, M[arit]. 2006. Word. In Keith Brown (ed.), *Encyclopedia of language and linguistics*, 2nd edition, vol. 13, 617–624. Oxford: Elsevier.

Karlsson, Fred. 1983. *Finnish grammar*. Porvoo: Söderström.

2006. Finnish as an agglutinating language. In Keith Brown (ed.), *Encyclopedia of language and linguistics*, 2nd edition, vol. 4, 476–480. Oxford: Elsevier.

Kageyama, Taro. 2009. Isolate: Japanese. In Rochelle Lieber & Pavol Štekauer (eds.), *The Oxford handbook of compounding*, 512–526. Oxford: Oxford University Press.

Kasar, Sündüz Öztürk. 2004. Turc. In Pierre J. L. Arnaud (ed.), *Le nom composé: données sur seize langues*, 269–285. Lyon: Presses Universitaires de Lyon.

Katamba, Francis & John Stonham. 1986. *Morphology*. 2nd edition. London: Macmillan.

Kenesei, István. 2014. On a multifunctional derivational affix. *Word Structure* 7: 214–239.

Kiefer, Ferenc. 2009. Uralic, Finno-Ugric: Hungarian. In Rochelle Lieber & Pavol Štekauer (eds.), *The Oxford handbook of compounding*, 527–541. Oxford: Oxford University Press.

Killingley, Siew-Yue & Dermot Killingley. 1995. *Sanskrit*. Munich: LINCOM Europa.

Kingdon, Roger. 1958. *The groundwork of English stress*. London: Longman.

Klinge, Alex. 2005. *The structure of English nominals*. Doctoral dissertation, Copenhagen Business School.

Kornfilt, Jaklin. 1997. *Turkish*. London: Routledge.

KorpusDK. 1990–2002. København: Det Danske Sprog- og Litteraturselskab. http://ordnet.dk/korpusdk

Körtvélyessy, Lívia, Pavol Štekauer & Július Zimmermann. 2015. Word-formation strategies: semantic transparency vs. formal economy. In Laurie Bauer, Lívia Körtvélyessy & Pavol Štekauer (eds.), *Semantics of complex words*, 85–113. Cham: Springer.

Koshiishi, Tetsuya. 2002. Collateral adjectives, Latinate vocabulary, and English morphology. *Studia Anglica Posnaniensia* 37: 49–88.

Kövecses, Zoltan & Günter Radden. 1998. Metonymy: developing a cognitive linguistic point of view. *Cognitive Linguistics* 9: 37–77.

Kunter, Gero. 2011. *Compound stress in English*. Berlin: De Gruyter.

Leech, Geoffrey N. 1966. *English in advertising*. London: Longmans.

Lees, Robert B. 1960. *The grammar of English nominalizations*. Bloomington: Indiana University Press.

1970. Problems in the grammatical analysis of English nominal compounds. In Manfred Bierwisch & Karl Erich Heidolph (eds.), *Progress in linguistics*, 174–186. The Hague: Mouton.

Levi, Judith. 1978. *The syntax and semantics of complex nominals*. New York: Academic.

Levin, Beth & Malka Rappaport Hovav. 1995. *Unaccusativity at the syntax-lexical semantics interface*. Cambridge, MA: MIT Press.

Li, Charles & Sandra A. Thompson. 1981. *Mandarin Chinese*. Berkeley: University of California Press.

Libben, Gary. 2010. Semantic transparency in processing compounds. Consequences for representation, processing, and impairment. *Linguistische Berichte Sonderheft* 17: 1–14.

Libben, Gary, Monika Boniecki, Marlies Martha, Karin Mittermann, Katharina Korecky-Kröll & Wolfgang U. Dressler. 2009. Interfixation in German compounds: what factors govern acceptability judgements. *Rivista di Linguistica* 21: 149–180.

Lichtenberk, Frantisek. 2008. *A grammar of Toqabaqita*. Berlin: Mouton de Guyter.

Lieber, Rochelle. 1992. *Deconstructing morphology*. Chicago: University of Chicago Press.

   1994. Root compounds and synthetic compounds. In R. E. Asher (ed.), *Encyclopedia of language and linguistics*, vol. 7, 3607–3610. Oxford: Pergamon.

   2016. Compounding in the lexical semantic framework. In Pius ten Hacken (ed.), *The semantics of compounding*, 38–53. Cambridge: Cambridge University Press.

Lombard, Alf. 1930. *Les constructions nominales dans le français modern*. Uppsala: Almqvist & Wiksells.

López Rúa, Paula. 2004. The categorial continuum of English blends. *English Studies* 85: 63–76.

Lowe, John J. 2015. The syntax of Sanskrit compounds. *Language* 91: e71–e115.

Luo, Yongxian. 2008. Zhuang. In Anthony V. N. Diller, Jerold A. Edmundson & Yongxian Luo (eds.), *The Tai-Kadai languages*, 317–377. London: Routledge.

Luschützky, Hans Christian & Franz Rainer. 2013. Instrument and place nouns: a typological and diachronic perspective. *Linguistics* 51: 1301–1359.

Lyons, John. 1968. *Introduction to theoretical linguistics*. Cambridge: Cambridge University Press.

   1977. *Semantics*. Cambridge: Cambridge University Press.

Macdonell, A[rthur] A[nthony]. 1926. *A Sanskrit grammar for students*. 3rd edition. New Delhi: Oxford University Press. Reprinted in 1997, New Delhi: D. K. Printworld.

Marchand, Hans. 1969. *The categories and types of present-day English word-formation*. 2nd edition. Munich: Beck.

Matthews, Stephen & Virginia Yip. 1994. *Cantonese: a comprehensive grammar*. London: Routledge.

Meibauer, Jörg. 2007. How marginal are phrasal compounds? Generalized insertion, expressivity, and I/Q-interaction. *Morphology* 17: 233–259.

Ménová, Martina. 2012. *Phrasal compounds in contemporary British newspapers*. Unpublished thesis, Charles University of Prague.

Millroy, James. 1977. *The language of Gerard Manley Hopkins*. London: Deutsch.

Mithun, Marianne. 2000. Incorporation. In Geert Booij, Christian Lehmann & Joachim Mugdan (eds.), *Morphology: an international handbook of inflection and word-formation*, 916–928. Berlin: de Gruyter.

Mukai, Makiko. 2008. Recursive compounds. *Word Structure* 1: 178–198.

Mutt, O. 1967. Some recent developments in the use of nouns as pre-modifiers in English. *Zeitschrift für Anglistik und Amerikanistik* 15: 401–408.

Nagano, Akiko. 2011. The right-headedness of morphology and the status and development of category-determining prefixes in English. *English Language and Linguistics* 15: 61–83.

2016. Are relational adjectives possible cross-linguistically? The case of Japanese. *Word Structure* 9: 42–71.

Neef, Martin. 2009. IE, Germanic: German. In Rochelle Lieber & Pavol Štekauer (eds.), *The Oxford handbook of compounding*, 386–399. Oxford: Oxford University Press.

2015. The status of so-called linking elements in German: arguments in favour of a non-functional analysis. *Word Structure* 8: 29–52.

Nichols, Johanna. 1986. Head-marking and dependent-marking grammar. *Language* 62: 56–119.

Nielsen, Sten Hedegård. 1998. Adstantiver: en ny ordklasse i dansk? *Mål og Mæle* 21/1: 23–25.

Nikolaeva Irina & Andrew Spencer. 2012. Possession and modification – a perspective from canonical typology. In Dunstan Brown, Marina Chumakina & Greville G. Corbett (eds.), *Canonical morphology and syntax*, 207–238. Oxford: Oxford University Press.

Nikolaeva, Irina & Maria Tolskaya. 2001. *A grammar of Udihe*. Berlin: Mouton de Gruyter.

OED. OED [*The Oxford English Dictionary*] Online. Oxford University Press. www.oed.com/. Consulted between June 2015 and November 2016.

Olsen, Susan. 2001. Copulative compounds: a closer look at the distinction between morphology and syntax. *Yearbook of Morphology 2000*, 279–320.

Oniga, Renato. 2014. Trans. Norma Schifano. *Latin: a linguistic introduction*. Oxford: Oxford University Press.

Osborne, C. R. 1974. *The Tiwi language*. Canberra: Australian Institute of Aboriginal Studies.

Packard, Jerome L. 2000. *The morphology of Chinese*. Cambridge: Cambridge University Press.

Palmer, Frank. 1987. *The English verb*. 2nd edition. London: Longman.

Palmer, Leonard R. 1980. *The Greek language*. London: Faber and Faber.

Panfilov, Valerij S. 2004. *Vietnamesisch (Viet-Muong)*. In Geert Booij, Christian Lehmann, Joachim Mugdan & Stavros Skopetas (eds.), Morphologie 2. Halbband/Morphology volume 2, 1545–1554. Berlin: de Gruyter.

Payne, John. 1993. The headedness of noun phrases: slaying the nominal hydra. In Greville G. Corbett, Norman M. Fraser & Scott McGlashan (eds.), *Heads in grammatical theory*, 114–139. Cambridge: Cambridge University Press.

Payne, John & Rodney Huddleston. 2002. Nouns and noun phrases. In Rodney Huddleston & Geoffrey K. Pullum (eds.), *The Cambridge grammar of the English language*, 323–524. Cambridge: Cambridge University Press.

Pierrehumbert Janet B. 2001. Exemplar dynamics: word frequency, lenition and contrast. In Joan Bybee & Paul Hopper (eds.), *Frequency and the emergence of linguistic structure*. 137–157. Amsterdam: Benjamins.

2003. Phonetic diversity, statistical learning, and acquisition of phonology. *Language and Speech* 46: 115–154.

Pinker, Steven. 1999. *Words and rules*. London: Weidenfeld & Nicolson.

Plag, Ingo. 2003. *Word-formation in English*. Cambridge: Cambridge University Press.

2006. The variability of compound stress in English: structural, semantic and analogical factors. *English Language and Linguistics* 10: 143–172.

Plag, Ingo, Gero Kunter, Sabine Lappe & Maria Braun. 2008. The role of semantics, argument structure, and lexicalization in compound stress assignment in English. *Language* 84: 760–794.

Pöll, Bernhard. 2015. Restricted recursion in N-N compounding: some thoughts on possible reasons. *Linguistische Berichte* 242: 141–163.

Pullum, Geoffrey K. & Rodney Huddleston. 2002. Adjectives and adverbs. In Rodney Huddleston & Geoffrey K. Pullum (eds.), *The Cambridge grammar of the English language*, 525–595. Cambridge: Cambridge University Press.

Quintero, Carolyn. 2004. *Osage grammar*. Lincoln: University of Nebraska Press.

Quirk, Randolph, Sidney Greenbaum, Geoffrey Leech & Jan Svartvik. 1985. *A comprehensive grammar of the English language*. London: Longman.

Radford, Andrew. 1993. Head-hunting: on the trail of the nominal Janus. In Greville G. Corbett, Norman M. Fraser & Scott McGlashan (eds.), *Heads in grammatical theory*, 73–113. Cambridge: Cambridge University Press.

Radimský, Jan. 2015. *Noun + noun compounds in Italian*. Česke Budějovice: Jihočeska Univerzita.

Rae, Megan Elizabeth. 2010. *Ordering restrictions of modifiers in complex nominals*. Unpublished doctoral thesis, Università Ca' Foscari Venezia.

Rainer, Franz. 2013. Can relational adjectives really express any relation? An onomasiological approach. *SKASE Journal of Theoretical Linguistics* 10: 12–40.

Ralli, Angela. 2009. IE, Hellenic: Modern Greek. In Rochelle Lieber & Pavol Štekauer (eds.), *The Oxford handbook of compounding*, 453–463. Oxford: Oxford University Press.

Ralli, Angela & George J. Xydpoulos. 2012. Blend formation in Modern Greek. In Renner et al. (eds.), 35–50.

Rau, Jeremy. 2010. Greek and Proto-Indo-European. In Egbert J. Bakker (ed.), *A companion to the ancient Greek language*, 171–188. Malden, MA: Wiley-Blackwell.

Renner, Vincent. 2008. On the semantics of English coordinate compounds. *English Studies* 899: 606–613.

Renner, Vincent, François Maniez & Pierre J. L. Arnaud. (eds.) 2012. *Cross-disciplinary perspectives on lexical blending*. Berlin: De Gruyter Mouton.

Roeper, Thomas & Muffy E. A. Siegel. 1978. A lexical transformation for verbal compounds. *Linguistic Inquiry* 9: 199–260.

Rosenbach, Anette. 2006. Descriptive genitives in English: a case study on constructional gradience. *English Language and Linguistics* 10: 77–118.

Ryder, Mary Ellen. 1994. *Ordered chaos: the interpretation of English noun-noun compounds*. Berkeley: University of California Press.

Sadock, Jerrold M. 1986. Some notes on noun incorporation. *Language* 62: 19–31.

Scalise, Sergio & Antonietta Bisetto. 2009. The classification of compounds. In Rochelle Lieber & Pavol Štekauer (eds.), *The Oxford handbook of compounding*, 34–53. Oxford: Oxford University Press.

Scalise, Sergio & Antonio Fábregas. 2010. The head in compounding. In Sergio Scalise & Irene Vogel (eds.), *Cross-disciplinary issues in compounding*, 109–125. Amsterdam: Benjamins.

Scalise, Sergio & Irene Vogel. 2010. Why compounding? In Sergio Scalise & Irene Vogel (eds.), *Cross-disciplinary issues in compounding*, 1–18. Amsterdam: Benjamins.

Schäfer, Martin. 2015. Semantic transparency and anaphoric islands. In Pius ten Hacken & Claire Thomas (eds.), *The semantics of word formation and lexicalization*, 140–160. Edinburgh: Edinburgh University Press.

Seegmiller, Steve. 1996. *Karachay*. Munich: LINCOM Europa.

Simpson, Jane. 2009. Pama-Nyungan: Warlpiri. In Rochelle Lieber & Pavol Štekauer (eds.), *The Oxford handbook of compounding*, 609–622. Oxford: Oxford University Press.

Sinclair, John (ed.). 2005. *The Collins COBUILD English grammar*. 2nd edition. Glasgow: HarperCollins.

Sohn, Ho-Min. 1999. *The Korean language*. Cambridge: Cambridge University Press.

Spencer, Andrew. 1991. *Morphological theory*. Oxford: Blackwell.

2011. What is a compound? *Journal of Linguistics* 47: 481–507.

Sridhar, S. N. 1990. *Kannada*. London: Routledge.

Štekauer, Pavol, Salvador Valera & Lívia Körtvélyessy. 2012. *Word-formation in the world's languages*. Cambridge: Cambridge University Press.

Strang, Barbara M. H. 1968. *Modern English structure*. 2nd edition. London: Edward Arnold.

Sulkala, Helena & Merja Karjalainen. 1992. *Finnish*. London: Routledge.

Suomi, Kari. 1985. On detecting words and word boundaries in Finnish. *Nordic Journal of Linguistics* 8: 211–231.

Szubert, Andrej. 2012. *Zur internen Semantik der substantivischen Komposita im Dänischen*. Poznań: Wydanictwo Naukowe.

Szymanek, Bogdan. 2009. IE, Slavonic: Polish. In Rochelle Lieber & Pavol Štekauer (eds.), *The Oxford handbook of compounding*, 464–477. Oxford: Oxford University Press.

Tarasova, Elizaveta. 2013. *Some new insights into the semantics of English N+N compounds*. Unpublished PhD thesis, Victoria University of Wellington.

Thompson, Laurence. 1965. *A Vietnamese grammar*. Seattle: University of Washington Press.

Thráinsson, Höskuldur, Hjalmar P. Petersen, Jógvan í Lon Jacobsen & Zakaris Svabo Hansen. 2004. *Faroese*. Tórshavn: Føroya Frøðskarpafelag.

Tribulato, Olga. 2015. *Ancient Greek verb-initial compounds*. Berlin: de Gruyter.

Urban Dictionary. www.urbandictionary.com

Verhoeven, Ben. 2012. *A computational semantic analysis of noun compounds in Dutch*. Unpublished doctoral thesis, Antwerpen.

Vestergaard, Torben & Kim Schrøder. 1985. *The language of advertising*. Oxford: Blackwell.

Villoing, Florence. 2009. Les mot composés VN. In Bernard Fradin, Françoise Kerleroux & Marc Plénat (eds.), *Aperçus de morphologie du français*, 175–197. Paris: Presses Universitaires de Vincennes.

Wälchli, Bernard. 2005. *Co-compounds and natural coordination*. Oxford: Oxford University Press.

Wandruszka, Ulrich. 1972. *Französische Nominalsyntagmen*. Munich: Fink.

Ward, Denis. 1965. *The Russian language today*. London: Hutchinson.

Ward, Gregory, Richard Sproat & Gail McKoon. 1991. A pragmatic analysis of so-called anaphoric islands. *Language* 67: 439–474.

Watters, David E. 2002. *A grammar of Kham*. Cambridge: Cambridge University Press.

Wells J[ohn] C. 2008. *Longman pronunciation dictionary*. 3rd edition. Harlow: Pearson.

Whitney, William Dwight. 1889. *Sanskrit grammar*. 2nd edition. Cambridge, MA: Harvard University Press and London: Oxford University Press.

Wiese, Richard. 1996. *The phonology of German*. Oxford: Oxford University Press.

Williams, Edwin. 1981. On the notions 'lexically related' and 'head of a word'. *Linguistic Inquiry* 12: 245–274.

Williams, Marianne Mithun. 1974. *A grammar of Tuscarora*. Unpublished PhD dissertation, Yale University.

Wisniewski, Edward J. and Jing Wu. 2012. Emergency!!!! Challenges to a compositional understanding of noun–noun combinations. In Wolfram Hinzen, Edouard Machery, & Markus Werning (eds.), *The Oxford handbook of compositionality*, 403–417. Oxford: Oxford University Press.

Wray, Alison. 2015. Why are we so sure we know what a word is? In John R. Taylor (ed.), *The Oxford handbook of the word*, 725–750. Oxford: Oxford University Press.

Zwicky, Arnold M. 1985. Heads. *Journal of Linguistics* 21: 1–29.

    1993. Heads, bases and functors. In Greville G. Corbett, Norman M. Fraser & Scott McGlashan (eds.), *Heads in grammatical theory*, 292–315. Cambridge: Cambridge University Press.

Þorsteinn G. Indriðason. 2000. Morfologi møter syntax: Om genitivsammensatte ord i islandsk. *Nordica Bergensia* 22: 174–200.

Language Index

General Index